LET'S TAX CARBON

AND OTHER IDEAS FOR A BETTER AUSTRALIA

ROSS GARNAUT

LA TROBE
UNIVERSITY PRESS

IN CONJUNCTION WITH BLACK INC.

Published by La Trobe University Press in conjunction with Black Inc.
Wurundjeri Country
22–24 Northumberland Street
Collingwood VIC 3066, Australia
enquiries@blackincbooks.com
www.blackincbooks.com
www.latrobeuniversitypress.com.au

La Trobe University plays an integral role in Australia's public intellectual life, and is recognised globally for its research excellence and commitment to ideas and debate. La Trobe University Press publishes books of high intellectual quality, aimed at general readers. Titles range across the humanities and sciences, and are written by distinguished and innovative scholars. La Trobe University Press books are produced in conjunction with Black Inc., an independent Australian publishing house. The members of the LTUP Editorial Board are Vice-Chancellor's Fellows Emeritus Professor Robert Manne and Dr Elizabeth Finkel, and Morry Schwartz and Chris Feik of Black Inc.

9781760645335 (paperback)
9781743823842 (ebook)

 A catalogue record for this book is available from the National Library of Australia

Cover design by Beau Lowenstern
Text design by Dennis Grauel and Marilyn de Castro
Typesetting by Marilyn de Castro

Printed in Australia by McPherson's Printing Group.

CONTENTS

INTRODUCTION

Australia would be richer and safer from climate change if only the Australian parliament, or a majority in opinion polls, could amend the laws of physics and economics.

Alas, they can't. The laws of economics insist that the living standards of ordinary citizens sometimes stagnate or fall unless decisions are taken that confront powerful private interests in the public interest.

Living standards stagnate or fall unless laws are made and enforced that require businesses to desist from actions that damage others, or to compensate society for the damage they cause, or to pay taxes that enhance general wellbeing. Living standards of citizens can stagnate if officials make mistakes in policy because they have not understood changes in the structure of the economy.

The political order and the living standards that depend on it could fall apart if the climate changes enough in certain ways, even if governments are elected democratically on statements that the relevant laws of physics do not apply. And democracy itself is challenged by a sustained fall in the standard of living.

Reality crashes on, oblivious to our beliefs and hopes and fears. Avoiding big decisions because they are difficult or impossible in current political circumstances does not mean their consequences go away. Reality crashes on, oblivious to opinion polls and general elections.

I was reminded of one dimension of that reality in Brisbane in December 2023. I was with Ros Morauta on the third anniversary of the death of her late husband and my close friend of five and a half decades, Mekere. I had dedicated the book *Reset* to Mekere. He was the best of men and a great leader of Papua New Guinea's economic policy and then the nation in earlier days. Ros had come from organising the rebuilding on higher ground of their family house in the Papuan village of Kukipi after a high tide superimposed on a rising sea had claimed it. Villagers who could not afford rebuilding had moved into the less damaged houses of relatives. The continuing migration from the Kukipi area and other deteriorating rural regions to Port Moresby, increases the pressures on a city that in January 2024 erupted into riots from deepening poverty and despair. The Kukipi villagers are among more than a million on the island of New Guinea who will be displaced by rising seas and intensifying extreme weather events if we fail to stop human-induced climate change.

Reality now places us at the beginning of a reset of Australian thinking, policy and political culture. That reset is necessary if the living standards of ordinary Australians are to rise again after a rare, probably unprecedented, decade of stagnation. Reality places us part of the way towards Australia using its opportunity to contribute disproportionately to the global climate change solution by exporting zero-carbon goods to a world that is taking effective action against climate change. Reality will exact a painful cost if we fail to complete the reset journey.

This book describes where we are at in the reset and where we could go next. The concluding chapter spells out the path ahead. Taxing carbon emissions is on that path. We will get to that later.

The reset quintet

Let's Tax Carbon is the last in a quintet of books since Australia turned away from nearly a quarter-century of exceptional prosperity eleven years ago. All five books discuss the links between policy decisions and the living standards of most Australians. All five explore the links between the zero-carbon transition and Australian economic performance. The links between the transition and living standards have come to be understood better over time as we have made our way through these eleven years.

In 2013, *Dog Days: Australia After the Boom* placed before Australians some fateful decisions. We had spent too much of the beneficence of the China resources boom of 2002–12 as it arrived, before we knew how much of it was with us to stay. We would be wise to live frugally for a while. How we used the incomes and wealth that remained with us would determine whether the years ahead would lay the foundations of future prosperity or see us sink into continuing underperformance, stagnation of living standards, and national vulnerability to future threats of many kinds.

Dog Days foreshadowed a period of stagnation of incomes and community unhappiness unless we accepted large changes in policy. Such change would only be possible with a strengthening of the independent centre of the polity against the rising influence of vested business interests in the policymaking process. The years between the global financial crisis of 2008–09 and the COVID-19 pandemic were hard for the general run of citizens in all developed countries. In the United States they followed several decades of stagnation of real wages and living standards of ordinary citizens, and in the United Kingdom almost as long. Unhappiness at income stagnation eventually accumulated into populist rebellion against the established political systems and the election of Donald Trump as president of the United States and the vote for Brexit in the United Kingdom. Australians started from a better place after the productivity and China resources booms but fared worse than most people in other developed countries from 2013 until the pandemic. Growth in output per person fell to the lower ranks of the developed world (Garnaut 2021, Chart 1.1). The decade from 2013 delivered what was probably the largest ever fall in average Australian real wages over a comparable period.

On climate change, *Dog Days* followed my two then-recent reviews for Australian governments (Garnaut 2008, 2011). It was strongly in Australia's national interest to do its fair share in the global climate change mitigation effort. But there would be short-term costs – incomes would fall by a couple of percentage points by the middle of the twenty-first century. We should still do our fair share in the global effort, because later costs of failure would be much larger and would increase over time and continue indefinitely.

Carbon pricing ended on 30 June 2014, the day before the Australian emissions trading scheme was due to be integrated into the European one. The laws of economics and physics continued to grind out their awful consequences. Disparate interventions and uncertainty over climate and energy contributed to a decline in productivity and output growth. Political contests over climate and energy policy contributed unnecessarily to weak economic performance. There was one brighter spot: investment increased in solar and wind power generation. There, once investors understood that the Abbott government did not have the numbers in the Senate to remove the Renewable Energy Target (RET), investment lifted and remained high until early in the 2020s. Renewable generation investment has slumped under the Albanese government as the RET has approached the legislated end of its life.

Australia was a significant drag on the global mitigation effort during these years. After the United Nations conference in Paris in 2015 until Glasgow in 2021, Australia was the only developed country not to commit to zero net emissions by 2050 or earlier. When Australia eventually joined the developed world with net zero commitments at Glasgow in 2021, it announced uniquely weak interim targets for reducing emissions by 2030. Australia declined to join the leaders of most of the developed democratic countries in agreements on methane and coal power generation. Australia's position as a laggard was curious, as the developed country likely to be damaged most by a failure of mitigation, and the country standing to gain more than any other economically from success.

Through the Dog Days, it gradually became clear that full participation in the world's movement to net zero emissions need not be a drag on and could be a large contributor to economic growth, even in the early years. In 2019, *Superpower: Australia's Low-Carbon Opportunity* laid out the evidence.

Australia had five large advantages that together added up to great opportunity to be a major supplier of zero-carbon goods to the world. It had unequalled renewable energy resources relative to its economic size. It had exceptional resources for sustainably growing the biomass that would have high value as an input into zero-carbon chemical manufactures and transport fuels. Australia was the world's largest source of minerals that required large amounts of energy for conversion to metals, led by iron and aluminium. It had unusually large endowments of the energy transition minerals for which there would be disproportionately rapid growth in demand. And the old mining, metals processing, agricultural and forestry industries left a legacy of knowledge, management capacity, labour skills, industrial culture and infrastructure that would have high value in the emerging zero-carbon world economy.

Reset: Restoring Australia After the Pandemic Recession, published in 2021, was based on lectures delivered remotely from the central west of Queensland in the depths of pandemic recession in June and July 2020. The book discussed how we could recover from the economic damage from the lockdowns and the collapse of global economic activity and trade while laying the foundations for a long new period of Australian prosperity.

Reset told the story of Australia's remarkable three decades of continuous economic growth, from the recession we didn't have to have in 1990–91 to the pandemic recession of 2020. No developed country, including Australia in earlier times, had ever before experienced growth unbroken by recession for so many years.

Three different periods through the three decades of continuous growth had very different origins and effects on Australians' standards of living. The first decade to about 2002 was the productivity boom. Australia experienced rapid productivity growth at the top of the developed world, following far-reaching economic reforms in the 1980s and early 1990s. Strongly rising productivity supported large and sustainable increases in real household incomes. The second decade to about 2012 was the China resources boom, in which Australia experienced productivity growth in the middle of the developed countries' range. Real incomes growth was even more rapid, supported by high export prices and mining investment. The third period, as discussed, was the Dog Days leading up to the pandemic recession in 2020.

At the beginning of 2013, US unemployment was much higher than Australia's. On the eve of the pandemic in 2019 it was much lower. US unemployment fell by more than half while Australia's stood still. Meanwhile Australian underemployment increased by large amounts. The United States had experienced unemployment of 4 per cent or lower for several years before the pandemic and around 3.5 per cent in the year before, without inflationary pressures from the labour market. I asked: why couldn't Australia do as well?

The Superpower Transformation: Building the Zero-Carbon Australian Economy in 2022 described how the Superpower could underpin a long period of full employment with rising incomes for a growing Australian population. Australia's achievement of net zero would reduce global greenhouse gas emissions by about 1.25 per cent. Its export of zero-carbon goods to countries that would find it difficult to supply themselves would reduce global emissions directly by around 7 per cent. Australia's exports of zero-carbon goods would make it possible for the rest of the world to achieve net zero carbon emissions.

The Superpower Transformation was completed in the weeks after the election of May 2022. The Australian Labor Party won a narrow absolute majority and formed a government. Prime Minister Anthony Albanese in his acceptance speech on election night said that Australia would be a renewable energy Superpower. The new government quickly brought Australia into the international mainstream on climate targets and participation in the aspirational sectoral agreements. On the detail of how to reach targets, it had mostly promised to continue Coalition approaches and to make them work better. That meant myriad interventions rather than economy-wide incentives. The promise mostly to continue Coalition approaches was a serious constraint on progress towards announced targets and agreements. On wider economic policy, too, the Labor government had mostly promised to make only small changes. The government explained that more fundamental policy reform would be achieved in later parliaments.

Success on the economy and building the Superpower are closely related. We will not succeed in one without succeeding in the other. Without a strong economy, we will not be competitive in supply of zero-carbon goods to others, nor have the economic resources to manage a major restructuring of the economy to build the Superpower. Without the benefits of a strong economy being broadly distributed across the community, we will not have the political support and coherence necessary for far-reaching reform. Without the Superpower, the absence of opportunities for expansion of productive export industries will hold back economic growth.

Reset identified the need for major reforms in many areas if the pandemic were to be followed by restoration of prosperity rather than post-pandemic Dog Days. Five reforms were particularly important: changes to macroeconomic policy to achieve full employment with low inflation and the right amount of debt; reforms to increase growth in productivity and output per person; reforms to secure more equitable income distribution; embrace of Australia's opportunity to be a renewable energy Superpower of the zero-carbon world economy; and changes in political culture and policy coordination to secure restored prosperity.

This last member of the quintet, *Let's Tax Carbon*, tells the story of Australia's partial reset as it happened during the first two years of the Albanese Labor government. It reproduces a dozen public lectures, speeches and journal articles. A concluding chapter discusses what needs to be done to complete and build the Superpower.

Chapter 2 was first delivered as the after-dinner speech to the Economic Summit hosted by the prime minister, in the first few months of the new government. In it, I refer to Australia's two episodes of far-reaching economic reform that were followed by long periods of broadly based prosperity: postwar reconstruction initiated by the Curtin government in 1945; and the Hawke government's reform era starting in 1983. I conclude with words from Brutus in Shakespeare's *Julius Caesar*. On the night of the speech, the prime minister repeated those words to me: 'On that full sea we are now afloat.'

Chapter 3 was originally a lecture in honour of Professor Fred Gruen, in which I reflected on the very different roles that emigrants from German-speaking Europe between and after the two world wars played in the development of economic ideas in Australia and in the United States. Here, they expanded and enriched an established social democratic tradition. In the United States, they challenged postwar Keynesian approaches with ideas rooted in the pre-democratic political economy of Franz Joseph's Austro-Hungary. The Austro-Hungarian ideas were highly influential and contributed to the decline in economic performance of the North Atlantic English-speaking countries from about 1980. Australia did better from the influence of Gruen, Heinz Arndt and Max Corden.

Chapter 4 began as the Manning Clark lecture. In it, I place the challenge of reset into Clark's interpretation of history as a contest between enlargers and straighteners. I recall John Maynard Keynes' *The Economic Consequences of Mr Churchill* in 1925. By naming the chapter 'The Economic Consequences of Mr Lowe' I invite comparison between the formulaic application of the gold standard then and the rigid application of inflation targeting in 2022.

Chapter 5, 'The Economic Consequences of Mr Trump and Mr Biden', honours my longtime friend and colleague Max Corden, in a lecture delivered ten days before his death after a long illness. The chapter demonstrates the continuing relevance of the ideas on international trade and macroeconomics for which Corden was the economic profession's great teacher. Mr Trump followed by Mr Biden made large budget deficits and protection central pillars of economic policy. They were bound to fail in their stated objectives, and to damage the economic welfare of

Americans in the process. Mr Biden's approach at least would deliver a large contribution to American decarbonisation, even if it raised some obstacles for the rest of the world along the way.

Chapter 6, written with Peter Dawkins, was first published for the sixtieth anniversary of the Melbourne Institute: Applied Economic & Social Research in 2022. It shows that full employment is centrally important to productivity growth, labour force participation and equitable distribution of income. That makes it the central objective of economic policy now, as it was in earlier times of economic success.

Chapter 7, written with David Vines, was first presented to the Melbourne Economic Forum in early 2023. It examines the contribution of errors in monetary policy to unnecessarily low economic growth and high underemployment and unemployment during the Dog Days. Sound monetary policy requires observation of the economy as it is evolving over time, not rigid application of formulae drawn from analysis of the past. Good outcomes depend on judicious coordination of monetary, fiscal and prudential policies.

Chapter 8 was delivered to the 132nd annual dinner of the Henry George Society (now Prosper Australia) in Melbourne's Kelvin Club. A bicycle accident that day had broken my leg, but I did not know that on the night. I had a sore leg, and when I could not navigate on crutches the grand staircase at the club, I was carried into the dinner by two gallant young Georgists. The *Australian Financial Review* next day gave greater prominence to the standing ovation for my entrance than to the wisdom of my address. I noted that free trade and efficient taxation of economic rents are crucially important now, as they were in earlier periods of Australian history.

In introducing me to the dinner that evening, the chair referred generously to the influence of my work with Anthony Clunies-Ross on mineral taxation. In response, I said that I had initially thought the statement of our influence was excessive, until I recalled the tax case between Esso and the American Internal Revenue Service (IRS) in the US Tax Court in

Washington, IRS v. Esso, 1998. The amount of money in dispute was larger than in any previous case before the court. The case settled out of court for a large sum. I was the main witness for the IRS. Both sides were referring to our book *Taxation of Mineral Rents* (Garnaut and Clunies-Ross 1983). Esso had engaged large numbers of barristers from London and New York. The IRS had advised me that many of the defendant's barristers would cross-examine me and that I should expect a week before the Court. About an hour into the first cross-examination, the defendant asked for an adjournment. The Esso lawyers, returned after half an hour. 'Your Honour,' their spokesman said, 'we have no further questions of this witness.' I asked the IRS legal team what had happened. 'They worked out,' I was told, 'that their prospects were better the less time the judge spent listening to you.'

Chapter 9, the 2023 Bannerman Competition Lecture, expands on the discussion of rents. The role of economic rent in the Australian economy has grown in recent decades. That will be damaging to output growth and equitable income distribution unless it is countered by the combination of free trade, competition policy, regulatory reform and rent taxation that is appropriate in each sector.

Chapter 10 discusses the crucial role that China plays in the global decarbonisation effort. It is overwhelmingly the world's largest and lowest-cost supplier of most of the capital goods required in the zero-carbon economy. Its comparative disadvantage in zero-carbon goods is as strong as its advantage in equipment. Global decarbonisation needs equipment from China. Australian prosperity and global climate change mitigation depend on reconciling strategic imperatives with open international trade.

Chapter 11 was a speech delivered in Tokyo on Anzac Day 2024. It places the opportunities for trade in zero-carbon goods into historical perspective. Japan has overwhelming comparative disadvantage in zero-carbon energy and goods – just as it had in coal, oil and gas in the old, carbon-based economy. The building of knowledge and trust between governments and businesspeople in Australia and Japan underwrote an immense traditional resources trade. Those same qualities can underwrite even greater interdependence in trade in the zero-carbon economy.

Chapter 12 is formed from presentations by Rod Sims, chairman of the Superpower Institute, and me to the National Press Club in February 2022. We discuss the policies required for Australia to be a renewable energy Superpower. Success requires heavy reliance on markets. It depends on current market failures being corrected systematically by a tax on carbon emissions, and fiscal support for the knowledge and other benefits that innovators in the zero-carbon economy confer on others.

Chapter 13, with David Vines, was the keynote address to the 2023 Australian Economic Society's Conference of Economists in Brisbane. It discusses the economic ideas in Australia of the past century and their relevance today. It emphasises the importance of sound economic ideas as the foundation of policy (the composer and her 'score'), and of effective coordination (the 'conductor') across many areas of policy (the 'orchestra').

The five major reform tasks
Full employment and the right amount of debt

I attribute the persistent unemployment and rising underemployment after 2013 to monetary policy being tighter here than in other developed countries when our economy was no stronger. The deficiency in demand from relatively high interest rates could have been countered by more expansionary fiscal policy. Indeed, this was suggested by the governor of the Reserve Bank of Australia later in the period. However, larger budget deficits would have led to a stronger real exchange rate and higher rates of public debt. These were inappropriate in Australia's circumstances.

Immigration affects the real wage at which full employment is possible. Immigration relative to population size was twice as large in the Dog Days as in the productivity boom. Worse for lower-income Australians, a higher proportion of migrants now lacked skills with high value in the labour market. Worse still, a lower proportion of migrants were on a path to Australian citizenship, with the protections that provides against exploitation by employers. *Reset* suggested lower immigration levels and greater concentration on valuable skills. An appendix in *Reset* showed that full employment with the right amount of debt could be achieved with higher real wages with higher taxes on economic rent. Chapter 2 in this book sketches the relationships involved.

The pandemic shocked Australia and all developed countries into recession. The fiscal and monetary authorities responded with massive expansion of money supply and public expenditure. The fiscal and monetary expansion greatly increased demand for goods, services and labour. Unemployment fell to the lowest it had been in half a century, and labour force participation rose to the highest ever. Unemployment fell below 4 per cent in early 2022 and to around 3.5 per cent later in the year. It stayed around that level for a year and a half without inflationary pressures from the labour market.

Josh Frydenberg was the first treasurer in half a century to preside over an economy approaching close to full employment. He was the first treasurer in several decades to talk about full employment as a central objective of economic policy. For the first time in more than a generation, the RBA spoke regularly about the second element of its dual mandate: full employment.

Chapters 2, 6, 7 and 13 discuss the labour market after the recession. Being close to full employment brought all the benefits expected of it. Unemployable Australians at the margins of the labour force entered jobs, and held them. More people in jobs meant that budget deficits fell far more rapidly than anticipated. The budget went into surplus in 2022–23 for the first time since the global financial crisis in 2007–08 and repeated the achievement a year later. Pressures on agencies responsible for care of the indebted, the poor and the destitute reported reduced stress.

Reality had delivered a welcome (and, to those who had not absorbed *Reset*, surprising) demonstration that the rate of unemployment that could be sustained without accelerating inflation was much lower than officials had presumed. Nevertheless, there was an impulse during the early recovery to go back to the policies and attitudes of the pre-pandemic years, on full employment and other things. 'Wrong way', I said in *Reset*. 'Don't go back.' I noted that the fiscal and monetary expansion in the world as a whole, and in Australia, in response to the pandemic recession may turn out to be inflationary. The greatest risk was from inflation imported from the United States. That possibility became reality in the recovery from the pandemic recession. It was exacerbated by the sharp rise in global coal, gas and oil prices that followed the Russian invasion of Ukraine.

Chapter 7 in particular, and chapters 2, 4 and 13, discuss responses to the inflation that was coming to Australia from abroad from 2022. Chapters 7 and 13 note that tightening money earlier in line with the Federal Reserve in the US could have kept out imported inflation. Simultaneous expansion of expenditure would have avoided unemployment while keeping inflation low – ideally from payments to reduce the impacts of the Russian war in Ukraine on energy prices. These chapters recognise the risks and costs if unemployment falls below levels consistent with low and stable inflation. The questions are about the rate of unemployment at which pressures in the labour market cause inflation to accelerate. These chapters show that the non-accelerating inflation rate of unemployment (NAIRU) is no higher than about 3.5 per cent in contemporary circumstances.

Some commentators from the financial media, financial market economists and academic economists deeply steeped in the orthodoxy returned instinctively to the perspectives that had kept unemployment unnecessarily high before the pandemic. In the tenacious established view that had shaped policy in the Dog Days, there could be no reduction of inflation without pain from increased unemployment. It did not matter that there was no evidence of excess demand in the labour market raising real wages and lifting prices.

My mind went to the Aztec rituals of human sacrifice. The sun god was waging never-ending war against darkness. If the darkness won, the world would end. To keep the sun moving across the sky and rising in the morning, the sun god had to be fed blood and beating human hearts. And it worked, because the sun rose in the morning and moved across the sky. The role of the superior echelons of the political order in preserving creation was confirmed by their success.

Overall, the full employment objective was taken more seriously than before the pandemic. Following the review of the RBA, Treasurer Jim Chalmers confirmed that the law would continue to require the RBA to give similar weight to full employment and currency stability. Statements from the governor after board meetings now emphasised the importance of keeping unemployment as low as possible while inflation returned sustainably to its target range. In September 2023, *Working Future: The Australian Government's White Paper on Jobs and Opportunities* defined full employment more completely than before, taking into account underemployment, and making employment available for all who wanted it with a reasonable amount of search.

Productivity and per capita output growth

For real incomes to rise sustainably with full employment, economic reform is required to lift productivity growth. Reforms to business taxation, immigration and competition could all contribute.

Business tax reform could help by shifting the fiscal burden away from productivity-raising investment and towards economic rent. This had been an aspiration of the Henry Tax Review under the Rudd Labor government of 2008–10. Conversion of aspiration into law was defeated by companies in the mining industry that stood to lose. The aspiration then disappeared without trace.

In *Reset*, I proposed introduction of business taxation based on cash flow, which would have its main incidence on economic rent. That would increase business investment, innovation and productivity growth, without weakening the fiscal position by reducing revenue. It would also contribute to more equitable distribution of higher national income across the community. The rationale for reform along these lines is discussed in Chapters 8 and 9.

Immigration reform would raise productivity growth. In Chapter 2,

I suggest restricting employer-sponsored immigrants to jobs attracting earnings above the average.

Greater competition would lead to more efficient use of resources. Where the characteristics of an industry made competition inefficient or impossible, more effective taxation of rents would reduce damage from monopoly and oligopoly. Chapters 8 and 9 take up the issue.

Equity

Equitable distribution of income is crucial to sustain political support for economic reform which brings inevitable structural changes.

In *Reset*, I proposed integration of personal income taxation and social security within an Australian Income Security system – a form of universal basic income. This would raise incomes of lower-income people. It would also increase production per person, in two ways. The support of workers on low wages through tax and social security reform made it unnecessary on equity grounds to raise wages by regulation. And by lowering effective marginal taxation rates, it would promote labour force participation. Chapter 6 updates the discussion, suggesting in part that the stage 3 tax cuts could be altered to raise incomes in a way that increases participation in work. A variation on this suggestion was eventually introduced by the government. Chapter 6 also emphasises that early childhood education has immense benefits for equity as well as economic output – including through allowing parents to do more paid work.

The Superpower

Australia must embrace its zero-carbon opportunity if it is to return sustainably to full employment with rising incomes. This eventually requires carbon pricing linked to international carbon markets. If carbon pricing is politically blocked for the time being, we should seek now to build support for its introduction at some date far enough in the future to be outside contemporary political contests. *Reset* suggested 2035. In the meantime, we could reintroduce a green premium to maintain incentives for investment in renewable energy by strengthening the Renewable Energy Target and extending its life from 2030 until the date slated for carbon pricing. Chapter 12 discusses carbon pricing and chapters 3 and 5 the role of the RET. Chapter 5 discusses how interaction of Australia's incomparably rich solar and wind resources and incentives from the RET made Australia the country and South Australia the region with the highest intermittent energy proportions in the world.

The publication of *Superpower* in 2019 and *The Superpower Transformation* in 2021 was followed by announcements from all state governments, and after the 2022 election the Commonwealth, that they intended to make their regions part of the Australian renewable energy Superpower.

Chapter 12, with Rod Sims, discusses the policies that are necessary to build the Superpower. First comes a strong budget and open trade. This and Chapter 5 show why the US approach to supporting rapid decarbonisation would be unsuitable for Australia. It raises questions about whether the protection and budget deficits embodied in America's *Inflation Reduction Act* are suitable even for the United States.

Chapter 12 puts carbon pricing back on the Australian policy agenda as the best way to correct the market imperfection associated with greenhouse gas emissions. It suggests a carbon solutions levy (CSL) on all oil, coal and gas produced in or imported into Australia. This would greatly strengthen Australia's budget, while correcting the market failure otherwise associated with carbon emissions. Countries that already penalised use of carbon and provided a green premium for exports of zero-carbon goods from Australia would be exempt. There would be exceptions for exports to the European Union and other European countries now, and hopefully to other trading partners later. Those who innovate with broader benefit would be supported by a Superpower Industries Innovation Scheme.

Chapter 12 anticipates immediate rejection of the CSL proposal by the major political parties. Discussion of the relative merits of the CSL and alternative approaches to achieving climate and economic development will reveal its political as well as economic and environmental policy advantages. This general approach to innovation is supported by the Treasury's Future Made in Australia National Interest Framework, released with the budget papers in 2024.

The Superpower requires access to markets for zero-carbon goods in countries with poor resources for making them themselves. The largest potential markets in the decades immediately ahead are the densely populated industrial economies of Europe and Northeast Asia. Chapters 10 and 11 discuss China and Japan. Southeast and South Asia will be important markets in later decades.

Climate and energy policy through the first Albanese government have been deeply affected by the higher energy prices from the war in Ukraine. Chapters 3, 4 and 5 discuss the advantages for the domestic economy of driving a wedge between international prices and costs to users of energy. Such measures would not directly help decarbonisation – although they would remove one erroneous but influential criticism of renewable energy. The 2024 budget's subsidy to power users adopts this approach.

Policymaking and political culture

These reforms require changes in economic policy ideas, political culture and leadership. They require capacity and willingness to enforce policy reform in the public interest in the face of fierce opposition from vested business interests. They also require more effective coordination of policy.

In earlier, successful periods of Australian economic reform, success was built on high levels of economic analysis and knowledge shared with the wider community. Different areas of policy were coordinated effectively when they interacted with each other in important ways. Leaders were willing to push through with reforms in the public interest against opposition from vested interests that would be damaged by change. Leaders appealed to the wider community over the heads of sectional interests. Public education was supported in the reform era by newspapers willing and able to invest in understanding and explaining complicated policy choices to broad readerships.

Changes in media technologies and political culture have raised the degree of difficulty for reform. The Dog Days brought a downgrading of knowledge and analysis in discussion of public policy. Vested interests came to dominate policymaking. The fragmentation of information caused by reliance on social media and narrowcasting through the internet created barriers to the sharing of knowledge and building support for difficult change.

The political campaigns by vested interests in 2013 to repeal the carbon pricing and mineral rent taxation laws were a watershed. Australian living standards have stagnated ever since. Close analysis showed that neither campaign had been effective in persuading majority opinion in the electorate. But the collective memory is that the campaigns were decisive in forcing a change of government. That false memory deterred future governments from standing up to vested interests when making policy.

Beyond these political and information technology developments, Australia faces many other headwinds. The accumulation of debt from fiscal expansion in the pandemic is one. Government sees the international security environment as requiring much greater expenditure on defence. We can pretend that it will be paid for out of thin air. In truth, it will divert resources from other activities and lower growth in productivity and incomes. The increasing damage from climate change is another headwind, reflected in rising infrastructure and insurance costs and more costly damage from extreme weather events. Other countries' commitments to reducing greenhouse gas emissions mean that our second- and third-largest export industries, coal and gas, will decline. For productivity and average output to grow, we need expansion of exports that use Australia's advantages in the zero-carbon world economy.

The degree of difficulty is higher now. But so are the stakes for the Australian community.

Chapter 13 develops the metaphor of economic policymaking as an orchestra. In the first weeks of the Hawke government, advertisements appeared in the newspapers featuring two orchestras. One was emitting discordant sounds as the players of the various instruments each belted out their own tune. The other had the players and their instruments coordinated by a conductor to produce harmonious music. In the latter case, the conductor was the Accord between the government and the trade union movement.

The score for today's reset has to be a set of policies that serve the Australian public interest. Conceptions of the public interest and policies to secure them are contested. Outcomes and judgements about them at elections determine whether a favoured score attracts broadly based support and thrives, or disappears into history.

Let's Tax Carbon presents a set of policies that in my view can deliver full employment with rising incomes for a growing Australian population, while contributing disproportionately to the global effort to defeat climate change. Some of the suggestions have been taken on board by Commonwealth and state governments. Others are subject to ongoing debate. The score will emerge over time.

The orchestra needs the right instruments, well tuned. We have some good instruments, and as yet lack others. Sound preparation for a successful performance will make sure that the gaps are filled.

A good performance needs a talented conductor. Conductors can occupy various positions in relation to the players, just as long as they are in their line of sight and are followed.

Chapter 13 discusses how the score, the instruments and the conductor combined in productive ways at earlier times in our history. In my conclusion, Chapter 14, I suggest a set of policies that can complete Australia's reset for prosperity and building the Superpower. They include eventual readoption of a general tax on carbon emissions.

Unfortunately, that tax has been said to be 'impossible'. But it's less impossible than Australians being comfortable about the alternatives. These lead to stagnant and declining living standards and failure to make what could be decisive contributions to humanity's contest with climate change. That's impossible.

2

RESHAPING AUSTRALIAN PROSPERITY*

An economic summit at the beginning of a new government isn't the place or time to agree on a comprehensive approach to our problems and opportunities. But it can be the occasion when we stop kidding ourselves about the extent of the problems and share new thoughts about the best way forward.

We are kidding ourselves about how well our economy is perform-ing absolutely, and relative to other developed countries. True, for nearly three decades from 1991 we experienced the longest economic expan-sion unbroken by recession of any developed country ever. That ended in the first half of 2020. In late 2020 and early 2021, our economy bounced back more quickly from pandemic recession than that of most developed countries, because our fiscal expansion was bigger and faster. Since then, we have looked ordinary in a troubled developed world.

Our twenty-eight years of economic expansion were not uniformly good. Through the first decade, we had the strongest productivity growth in the developed world. For the next decade, through the China resources boom, we experienced large increases in average incomes despite lower productivity growth. In the Dog Days from 2013 to the COVID-19

---

* This chapter was first presented as the after-dinner speech at the Jobs and Skills Summit, Parliament House, Canberra, on 1 September 2022.

pandemic, productivity, wages and median incomes grew less than in other developed democracies. Unemployment moved from being well below to well above that of the United States.

We can't turn the economy back to before the pandemic. Even if we could, pre-pandemic conditions – high unemployment, underemployment and stagnant living standards – are not good enough.

The problems from the Dog Days and the pandemic have been compounded by the Russian invasion of Ukraine in February 2022 and its disruption of global energy markets. Unlike Western Europe and Northeast Asia, Australia has higher terms of trade when gas and coal prices rise. The value of goods and services produced in Australia increases. But under current policies, average Australians are poorer.

We are kidding ourselves if we think no deep wounds will be left in our polity from high coal and gas and therefore electricity prices bringing record profits for companies and substantially lower living standards to most Australians.

We must stop kidding ourselves about the budget. We need unquestionably strong public finances to have low cost of capital, private and public, for our Superpower transformation, and to shield us from a disturbed international economy and geopolity. Yet we have emerged from the pandemic with historically large budget deficits in the Commonwealth and most states and much higher levels of public debt. We have large budget deficits when our high terms of trade should be driving surpluses. Interest rates are rising on the eyewatering Commonwealth debt. We talk about the most difficult geostrategic environment since the 1940s requiring much higher defence expenditure, but not about higher taxes to pay for it. We say we are underproviding for care and underpaying nurses, and underproviding for education and failing to adequately reward our teachers. The most recent Treasury intergenerational report update tells us that the ratio of people over sixty-five to the conventionally working-age population will rise by half over the next four decades, bringing higher costs and fewer workers to carry them.

In the face of these immense budget challenges, total federal and state taxation revenue as a share of GDP is 5.7 percentage points lower than the developed country average.

Let's stop kidding ourselves.

The Pre-election Economic and Fiscal Outlook was released on 20 April 2022, to inform the discussion of economic policy during the election campaign. It said that average real wages would decline by 3 per cent in the two years to June 2023. By the time of the treasurer's statement three months later, the expected decline had increased to 7 per cent.

We should see the statement not as a forecast of the future, but as a warning of dangers to be avoided.

The facts have changed, and we should be ready to change our minds.

Two earlier crises with effective responses

When we stop kidding ourselves, we will recognise the need for policies that we now think impossible.

Australians accepted change that had been impossible on two earlier occasions when we faced deep problems and responded with policy reforms that set us up for long periods of prosperity, national confidence and achievement.

Postwar reconstruction in the 1940s was followed by a quarter-century of full employment and rising incomes. The reform era from 1983 until the end of the twentieth century set us up for a decade of extraordinarily strong productivity growth in the 1990s and the longest period of economic expansion unbroken by recession ever in any developed country.

The Curtin and Chifley governments were determined that Australians would not return to the high unemployment and economic insecurity of the interwar years. As a young economist, I learnt about this directly from the leading economists who had been in the rooms where it happened.

The 1945 White Paper on Full Employment was premised on the radical idea that governments should accept responsibility for stimulating spending on goods and services to the extent necessary to sustain full employment. Jobs would not be made for jobs' sake but would emerge from the flexible use of modern methods of production. This would achieve the highest possible standards of living for ordinary Australians. The white paper broke comprehensively with prewar monetary orthodoxy. The necessary capacity to control credit was eventually achieved through establishing the Reserve Bank of Australia, with full employment the first of its statutory responsibilities.

Success was based on using economic analysis and information to develop policies in the public interest; on seeing equitable distribution of the benefits of growth as a central objective; and on sharing knowledge through the community about economic policy choices. This built support for policies that challenged old prejudices and vested interests. Personal and corporate taxation rates were much higher than before the war. Full employment and a wider social safety net supported structural change and much larger and more diverse immigration. The real burden of what was at first an overwhelming war debt was reduced by a burst of high inflation early in the Menzies government, and then by steady, moderate growth in output and prices. Menzies' political success was built on full employment – helped by Menzies insulating policy from the influence of political donations to an extent that is shocking today.

The postwar economic success ended abruptly with the global energy shocks and recession during the Whitlam government. It was followed by nearly a decade of persistently high unemployment and inflation, slower productivity and incomes growth and fierce conflict over income distribution.

The malaise ended with the election of the Hawke government in 1983 and the beginning of a reform era extending until the end of the century. Australia experienced much higher growth in output, employment and for a while productivity and incomes relative to the rest of the developed world than ever before in our national story. The reform era defeated deeply entrenched business and trade union interests that stood against the national interest. Among much else, it delivered wage restraint, in the context of expansion of health, education and other public services and of superannuation; reductions in preferential taxation treatment of capital income, while lowering marginal rates of taxation; and removal of most industry protection.

The essential ingredients of success had much in common with postwar reconstruction: the prime role of economic analysis and public education; resistance to pressures on the policymaking process from sectional and vested interests; focus on equitable distribution of the benefits of growth. In both successful reform eras, comprehensive change across many activities, with large effects on performance of the economy as a whole, was easier than a succession of smaller changes. A reform affecting only one part of the economy would excite opposition from affected parties without attracting the interest and support of the wider polity.

Both reform eras made effective use of a professional public service. The 1945 white paper and an ambitious development program were drafted by able young officers of the Department of Post-War Reconstruction who later led other agencies. As reform momentum developed under the Hawke government, the public service secretariats of the Economic Policy Advisory Council, and after the 1984 election the Cabinet Committee on Long-Term Economic Growth, for a while became clearing houses for reform ideas and public education about them. Then and later, the public service more broadly was harnessed to the reform agenda.

Prime Minister Bob Hawke was able to change his mind when the facts changed. When he invited me to work as his economic adviser a couple of days after he was elected, he asked if I was comfortable with the new government's announced economic policies – and hastened to assure me that trade liberalisation would be possible once the community was confident that employment was growing. I expressed concern about the promised fiscal stimulus, coming on top of massive expansion in the Fraser government's dying days. That wouldn't be a problem either, the prime minister said. He had been briefed by the Treasury and the outlook was much more difficult than disclosed before the election. Policy would be adjusted to the realities.

The centrality of full employment

I grew up in a Menzies world of full employment. Workers could leave jobs that didn't suit them and quickly find others – often moving from lower- to higher-productivity firms. Employers put large efforts into training and retaining workers. Labour income was secure and could support a loan to buy a house. Labour was scarce and valuable and not to be wasted on unproductive tasks. Businesses that could not afford rising wages closed and released their workers into more productive employment. Steadily rising real wages encouraged economisation on labour, which lifted productivity.

The 1945 white paper discussed risks of inflation from full employment. The average unemployment rate went lower than the authors had anticipated, to below 2 per cent for two decades, without high or accelerating inflation.

As Peter Martin observed in 2023 in *The Conversation*, low unemployment creates opportunities for people whose long unemployment make them unattractive as employees. Employment makes them employable.

Through the Whitlam and Fraser years, wage regulation and the exercise of power by strong unions generated the 'real wage overhang' which the Accord set out to remove in 1983. The real wage overhang increased the minimum unemployment rate that could be achieved without inflation.

The lowest unemployment rate that can be achieved without inflation – in economists' jargon, the NAIRU – is not an output from an econometric model. It is an observable reality.

How low can unemployment go without accelerating inflation? Through the Dog Days, the Australian authorities spoke and acted as if it was 5 per cent or more. In 2019, Reserve Bank executives speculated that it might be as low as 4.5 per cent. In the following year, during the pandemic, the governor surmised that it might have risen back over 5 per cent again.

I discussed these matters in *Reset*. I said that it was possible that Australian unemployment could fall to 3.5 per cent without generating accelerating inflation – the rate in the United States on the eve of the pandemic. Its lowest rate without accelerating inflation may be lower – or higher. There was no need to guess. We will know when unemployment is so low that labour market pressures are causing inflation to accelerate.

Full employment disappeared from the Reserve Bank's discussion of monetary policy through the decade of persistent unemployment that preceded the pandemic recession.

Full employment has the large benefits for productivity that I have already discussed. It also has immense social benefits. It provides the best social security for people who can work. The current JobSeeker benefit may be adequate if its role is to provide sustenance briefly while recipients are looking for their first jobs, or moving quickly from one job to another. It is too low to support people for longer periods.

Full employment encourages and increases the value of high labour force participation. Employers seek out potential workers among people who had been unemployable. This encourages participation of parents who have spent long periods out of the labour force; the infirm and old; the poorly educated; and those with little established engagement with the wage economy.

Full employment is hard work for employers. Many prefer unemployment, with easy recruitment at lower wages. Yet full employment has advantages for many employers. It brings larger and more stable demand for consumer goods and services for businesses selling into the Australian market. And for employers who identify as Australians, it brings enjoyment of a more cohesive and successful society.

If we had had full employment through the Dog Days and the higher participation that comes with it, economic activity and government revenue would have been much higher. Lower unemployment and higher participation from the fiscal and monetary expansion since early in the pandemic recession have increased output and revenue. There is more to be won as we move to full employment.

I was heartened by the return of full employment in the governor's statements after RBA board meetings for a while from October 2019. The references to full employment were followed by a fundamental change in policy as the pandemic hit the economy in the first half of 2020. Together with the cessation of immigration and the radical fiscal expansion, this allowed unemployment to fall to 3.4 per cent in July 2022 – the lowest since 1974.

Commentators on the economy are asking: with employment so low, why aren't real wages rising?

There is no conundrum. We do not yet have full employment. The Reserve Bank abandoned its pursuit of full employment before we knew how low the rate of unemployment could go without becoming the source of accelerating inflation.

Will we see larger nominal wage increases if global energy and other prices continue to rise strongly? Probably. Would that tell us we have achieved full employment? Probably not. If nominal wages rise more rapidly, but more slowly than average prices, they are not the source of accelerating inflation. The spectre of a virulent wage-price spiral comes from our memories and not from current conditions.

Economics is less amenable than physics to definitive mathematical analysis because it is about people, whose responses to similar phenomena change over time. We build models in our minds or computers that fit observed reality at one point in time, and reality changes. Then we have to think harder about what is going on.

We should think hard about the implications of two big changes.

One is the tendency now for global private intentions on savings to exceed intentions on investment even at zero or negative real interest rates. That keeps global real long-term interest rates low, and ours with them. They may be negative even at full employment.

Some participants in the monetary policy discussion say that we should raise cash rates to their 'neutral' level. That doesn't remove the need for hard thinking. 'Neutral' is the rate which keeps the economy growing steadily at full employment with acceptably low inflation. What might that be? Maybe higher and maybe lower than the cash rate now. Neither is the neutral rate of interest an output from a model. It is an observable reality.

We would expect abundance of capital and declining natural increase in the labour force to raise productivity and real wages once we achieve full employment. But other factors can intervene.

One is immigration. Immigration affects the link between productivity and real wages. It is much more likely to raise rather than lower average real wages if it is focused on permanent migration of people with genuinely scarce and valuable skills that are bottlenecks to valuable Australian production and cannot be provided by training Australians. What is genuinely scarce and valuable? In *Reset*, I suggested a market test: admitting skilled migrants when they earn wages higher than the Australian average.

Ignoring the links between migration and wages can have unwelcome consequences. Western Australia's premier, Mark McGowan, gave me permission to tell a story about one unwelcome surprise. At the same time our prime minister was in Fiji talking about recruiting nurses, the premier was trying to recruit nurses in Ireland. The premier sought a meeting with the Irish minister for health – unsuccessfully, because that minister was in Perth recruiting nurses. Low wages made Australia a promising recruiting ground. Australian nurses would be great for Ireland. But replacing Australian with Fijian nurses may not be best for Australia or Fiji.

A second unwelcome surprise is oligopoly. We must think about the increasing role of economic rents in our economy. Productivity is reduced and the profit share of income increased by monopoly and oligopoly. A former chairman of the ACCC, Rod Sims, has drawn attention to the increasing role of oligopoly in the Australian economy, and the competition policy reforms that would reduce it. In some parts of the economy, competition is not possible, or would not lead to efficient use of resources. Here we must rely on taxation of economic rent or regulation of investment and prices to secure the public interest. A significant part of the increase in the profit share in recent years is in mining, where wages are high relative to other sectors. The appropriate public policy response is mineral rent taxation and not pressures for higher wages.

It matters how we get the jobs that take us to full employment. Increased employment comes from both domestic and trade-exposed industries. Employment in domestic industries is expanded by higher government expenditure, lower taxes and lower interest rates. Employment in trade-exposed industries is driven by competitiveness – by currency exchange rates, and Australian relative to international productivity and wages.

Too much domestic demand and too little export growth can lead to full employment with unsustainable levels of debt. There has to be a judicious balance between domestic and trade-exposed industries.

Strong growth in the export industries depends on access to international markets for goods and services, as well as on competitiveness. Here we face barriers from the breakdown of the multilateral trading system and our relationship with our biggest trading partner, China; and the coming climate change-induced decline of coal and gas.

Fortunately, Australia's potential as the energy Superpower of the zero-carbon world economy can allow us to bypass these blockages.

Australia's zero-carbon Superpower opportunity

Australia has a powerful national interest in the success of the international community in holding human-induced temperatures to 1.5°C above pre-industrial levels. That will require steady progress in reducing global emissions to net zero by 2050.

Some countries are much better endowed than others with natural and human resources to do well in the zero-emissions world. Australia is better placed than any other country.

We have five crucial advantages:

1. The best combinations of solar and wind resources in the developed world. Solar and wind power and storage to balance their intermittency are highly capital-intensive, so costs are much lower in developed countries than developing. With good policy and management, we will have the lowest energy costs in the post-carbon world.
2. Our position as by far the world's main exporter of mineral ores requiring large amounts of energy for processing into metals and other industrial inputs.
3. An abundance of the critical minerals required globally to build the machines and infrastructure of the zero-carbon world.
4. The largest endowments per person of land suitable and available for sustainable production of biomass as a zero-carbon industrial input and for sequestering carbon in plants and soils.
5. The human skills and infrastructure from the established mining, minerals processing, forestry and agricultural industries, which have high value in zero-emissions industries and processes.

Australia moving from an extreme laggard to one of the leading developed democracies would significantly strengthen the global effort, through its contribution to global policy diplomacy.

We can make an even larger contribution to the global effort by using our comparative advantage in zero-emissions production. We can lower the cost of other countries' timely achievement of net zero by exporting zero emissions processed metals and other materials, renewable electricity and hydrogen, critical minerals and carbon credits. *The Superpower Transformation* discusses how Australian export of zero emissions goods and services could reduce global emissions directly by about 7 per cent.

This would cover much of the hardest and costliest decarbonisation in the rest of the world. This is in addition to the 1.25 per cent of global emissions removed by Australia itself going to net zero.

Australian industry gets little competitive advantage from Australia being richly endowed with gas and coal. With the exception of Western Australian gas, these are made available to domestic industry at close to international prices.

Our low-cost renewable energy is different. Australian renewable electricity and green hydrogen will be at least twice as expensive in importing countries as in Australia. It will not make economic sense to use Australian electricity and hydrogen to process Australian materials in other countries.

Making good use of the Superpower opportunity would make immense demands on Australian capital, labour skills and administrative capacity. Capital expenditure of about 5.5 per cent of GDP in zero-carbon energy and industry would be required from now until the 2050s. That is big. But it is within the range of capital expenditure allocated to mining developments during the China resources boom.

Mobilisation of capital and labour to utilise the low-carbon opportunity requires all levels of government to plan for provision of new and complex skills and new forms of public infrastructure. It requires processes for environmental and planning approvals on an unprecedented scale. It requires systematic effort to remove bottlenecks in hugely expanded supply chains. It requires removing oligopolistic elements of supply chains that have raised Australian costs above international levels.

Productivity growth doesn't always involve improvements in individual industries and firms. It can come from stronger specialisation in activities in which Australia has comparative advantage: putting a higher proportion of our labour and capital into activities where we have exceptional strengths relative to the rest of the world. A long period of steady expansion of the zero-carbon industries will see costs falling and Australia's comparative advantage strengthening in these activities.

The restructuring of the economy to focus more strongly on these can be the source of sustained productivity and incomes growth.

The cost of capital sits alongside the quality of natural and human resources as determinants of competitiveness in the zero-carbon economy. Capital costs will be competitive if our public finances are unquestionably strong, and if we avoid large fluctuations in the real exchange rate. That, in turn, is supported by steady expansion of capital expenditure. Ensuring steady growth in capital expenditure is a responsibility of government as the regulator of new projects. This can underpin stable growth with full employment.

Most of the new development would be in rural and regional Australia. Much of the solar, wind and storage developments would require Indigenous support and in some cases leadership.

Thinking the unthinkable

> *There is a tide in the affairs of men*
> *Which, taken at the flood, leads on to fortune;*
> *Omitted, all the voyage of their life*
> *Is bound in shallows and in miseries.*
>
> William Shakespeare, *Julius Caesar*

The realities facing Australia are much more dangerous than revealed to the electorate at the 2022 election. But the zero-carbon opportunities are much richer. Policy will need to change more than we thought necessary, and more than we think possible. But if we stop kidding ourselves, make the necessary impossible changes in policy, prepare thoroughly to build the zero-emissions Superpower, we can have full employment with rising incomes and the right amount of debt for a long period ahead.

In this successful Australia, rising standards of living will rely less on regulated wages and more on fiscal transfers than in the past.

We have to raise much more revenue while increasing labour force participation and investment. I suggest for consideration two reforms from my book *Reset*. On taxation of personal income, an Australian Income Security (AIS) scheme, based on guaranteed minimum payments and lower marginal effective taxation rates, would supplement low wages while encouraging participation. On taxation of business income, using cash flow rather than accounting income as the tax base increases incentives for business innovation and investment without reducing total revenue. It shifts the burden from normal income in competitive parts of the economy to economic rent. These two reforms would increase the budget deficit in the short term, which fitted perfectly the fiscal expansion required during the pandemic recession. That opportunity has passed, but the longer-term case for the changes is stronger than ever. After a while, increased labour force participation would claw back part, but not all, of the initial revenue loss from AIS. Sooner rather than later, the efficiency gains from the new business tax base would return all of and then more than the lost revenue. Australia's high levels of public debt require us to be careful about reforms that reduce government revenue. We should be prepared to identify ways of raising public revenue to compensate for the losses. There are many opportunities for raising additional revenue in Australia while enhancing equity and improving or at least not damaging economic efficiency. The mineral rent taxation to which I have referred is one of them.

Following introduction of the AIS, increasing wages would carry less of the load of maintaining and enhancing workers' living standards. This would reduce the risk of unintentionally increasing the lowest sustainable unemployment rate.

The shift to cash-flow business taxation would encourage investment and innovation. If comprehensive corporate taxation reform were judged for the moment to be too hard, there would be large gains from applying the cash-flow tax as a trial in zero-emissions activities on an opt-in basis.

Prime Minister, I was delighted to hear you say at the National Press Club on Monday that you are ready to have a crack.

Prime Minister and Treasurer, the challenges are bigger than the public official forecasts told you to expect. And the opportunities are greater.

Some of your predecessors faced challenges of similar dimension, and left our country vulnerable by avoiding them. Others stood up to the challenges and set the country up for long periods of success. Prime Minister Curtin and his treasurer, Chifley, followed by Menzies, faced and overcame the challenges. So did Prime Minister Hawke and his treasurer, Keating, followed for the first few years by Howard.

You have become prime minister and treasurer at a critical time in our history. You have been elected with a parliament that is strongly aligned with the economic, climate and integrity reforms that can secure the next era of national prosperity and achievement.

On that full sea we are now afloat. Australians now will join you in taking the current when it serves, or lose our ventures.

3

SOCIAL DEMOCRATIC VERSUS AUSTRO-HUNGARIAN ECONOMICS APPLIED TO ENERGY*

Fred Gruen signed up as professor of economics in the ANU's Research School of Social Sciences in 1972, at the same time that I joined the Research School of Pacific and Asian Studies as a research fellow. Fred spent the next few years as a consultant to Prime Minister Gough Whitlam. My work was initially based at the ANU's New Guinea Research Unit in Port Moresby. Two years later, I was seconded from the ANU by PNG's first Papua New Guinean Secretary for Treasury and Finance, Mekere Morauta, to help him build the economic policies and institutions for independence.

From Port Moresby I kept in close contact with the economists in the institute at the ANU, presenting a number of seminars on issues I was thinking through in Port Moresby. I recall John Crawford chairing one public seminar adapting the Swan model of internal and external balance to an economy with a predominant subsistence or non-market sector, and another presenting Anthony Clunies-Ross's and my paper on the resource rent tax. Fred was present and engaged on these occasions. So was Fred's wife, Ann Gruen. She had a strong interest in Papua New Guinean development.

---

* This chapter was first presented as the F.H. Gruen Lecture at the Australian National University, Canberra, in June 2022. It was first published as: Ross Garnaut, 2023, 'Economic Ideas and Policy Outcomes: Applications to Climate and Energy', *Asia-Pacific Economic Literature*, 37, pp. 121–33.

I learnt much later that Fred's first visit to Papua New Guinea provided his first scholarly contact with Austro-Hungarian economics and also with the top echelons of wartime (and subsequently postwar) Australian social democratic economic thought – the two intellectual traditions that I discuss in this chapter.

Fred had arrived in Australia from Vienna via England as a refugee from an enemy country, and was detained on the Hay Plains. After release from detention, he joined the Australian army. He was passing north through Brisbane to Papua New Guinea at the end of the war and sought a copy of Frederick Hayek's *Road to Serfdom*. The helpful librarian said that she did not have it but her cousin was reading it and she would see what she could arrange. So Fred was introduced to Ann and Austro-Hungarian economics at the same time. Travelling on to Lae in Papua New Guinea, now occupied by inactive Australian forces, Fred provided lectures to servicemen. Nugget Coombs, visiting as secretary of the Department of Post-War Reconstruction, attended one.

The ANU was built from the work of the Curtin and Chifley governments' Department of Post-War Reconstruction. Stuart Macintyre's compelling history tells how a group of young men, believing that knowledge can guide economic policy to better outcomes for ordinary people, shaped Australian policies and institutions through the second half of the twentieth century (Macintyre 2015). Curtin and Chifley, and Minister for Post-War Reconstruction John Dedman, were committed to building a different Australia after the war, free of high unemployment and poverty. Coombs led thought about postwar reconstruction and had the administrative skills to make good new ideas work in practice. His director of research was John Crawford, who was recruited from the NSW government's agriculture department and the Rural Bank of New South Wales.

The ANU was established to provide knowledge for building sound economic and independent foreign policy. The new university would have global standing in research, and reverse the brain drain to the United Kingdom and United States. The three most influential figures in shaping the early approach to policy-related economic analysis at the new ANU were deeply steeped in an Australian version of the established North Atlantic liberal social democratic tradition. Long after the foundation of the ANU, Coombs was chancellor with an active interest in the university's work for eight years and an active visiting fellow in the Centre for Resource and Environmental Studies for twenty-one years. Crawford was inaugural director and professor of economics in the Research School of Pacific and Asian Studies and then vice chancellor, chancellor and visiting fellow in the economics department from 1960 until his death in 1984. The third, Trevor Swan, had been recruited into Coombs' Department of Post-War Reconstruction by John Crawford and joined the ANU as the foundation professor of economics in the Research School of Social Sciences in 1952.

Swan and the department made brilliant contributions over the next half dozen years or so, but then lost dynamism and impact. Fred Gruen took over in late 1975, and social sciences economics again became an important contributor to Australian economic policy discussion.

In a poignant coda to this story, Gruen and Coombs died on the same day in 1998.

Ludwig von Mises was the father of Austro-Hungarian thought in the North Atlantic. Hayek, his student, was the most influential of several émigrés from Germanic Central Europe who reshaped UK and US ideas about economic policy in the second half of the twentieth century. Von Mises, Hayek and Friedman were all major figures in the establishment and influence of the Mont Pelerin Society, which elevated the influence of the Austro-Hungarian model of untrammelled free markets, and minimal government intervention in the economy except to forcefully uphold private contracts and property rights. Friedman, born in the United States to migrant parents recently from Austro-Hungary, was intellectually close to but not altogether at one with the older professors.

Joseph Schumpeter shared some approaches to economic thought with his Austro-Hungarian confreres and differed in others. He was at the University of Vienna with von Mises and Hayek after World War I. He spent a brief time as finance minister in the postwar socialist government, struggling with the legacy of debt from war and reparations. He spent more time close to owners of substantial financial businesses in Vienna. Schumpeter contributed profound insights into capitalist development. He favoured a capitalist market system with minimal intervention by government – to the point of opposing regulatory measures to increase competition and, after publication of Keynes' general theory (Keynes 1936), to opposing any countercyclical fiscal policy in response to depression. He was pessimistic about the survival of his preferred form of capitalism in a democracy.

Austro-Hungarian thought became immensely influential in Anglo-American thinking and policy in the 1980s. Its influence reached its zenith in the Reagan presidency (1980–88) and has remained important. Martin Wolf from the *Financial Times* has noted that the brilliantly successful liberal social democratic approach to economic policy of 1946–70, with sustained strong growth in productivity, output and living standards, low unemployment and moderate inflation, was easily pushed aside in the 1970s when it ran into what now seem small problems. Brad De Long's economic history of the long twentieth century makes similar points (De Long 2022). On the other hand, the successor to liberal social democratic economics, the Austro-Hungarian approach, has shown great tenacity through the stagnation of living standards of ordinary US and UK citizens and recurring financial crises. Wolf's explanation of the paradox is that the successful mid-century consensus in mainstream economics, while favourable for business in aggregate, challenged and damaged vested interests on important matters. The Austro-Hungarian approach in practice was unambiguously supportive of vested business interests.

Austro-Hungarian economic thought always contained doubts about democracy, back to its origins under Emperor Franz Joseph. Democratic pressures are likely to lead to interventions that affect the operations of a market economy. Hayek, in particular, saw value at times in suspension of democracy, and reset of institutions with new rules to constrain interventions in economic transactions. Such was Hayek's rationalisation of and Friedman's explanation of his association with the Pinochet military dictatorship in Chile. The concern about contradictions between capitalism and democracy and support for constraints on democratic interventions in the economy has appeared in critiques of contemporary US political economy close to Donald Trump. The need to suspend parliamentary democracy when it was leading to policy decisions at odds with some prominent people's understanding of the national interest was a theme of early twentieth-century German political theorist Carl Schmitt.

Alerted by a News Corp columnist's sympathetic reference to Schmitt's political philosophy, I took time over Christmas 2021 to reread his *The Crisis of Parliamentary Democracy* (1922). In Schmitt's view, representative democracy was useful in its place. But there were times when resetting power and constitutional arrangements by a strong leader was necessary for government to work effectively. Schmitt was appreciated by Nazi leaders and he reciprocated, but withdrew his appreciation when Nazi rule had led to national ruin.

Austro-Hungarian thought makes valid points. If democratic government reduces too much the role of market exchange, large problems of economic efficiency arise. Its big positive contribution to North Atlantic economic thought was as antidote to uncritical support for central planning in the Soviet style during and immediately after World War II. The Austro-Hungarians were not concerned that untrammelled market exchange leaves behind those who, out of bad luck, or low ambition or effort, or poor genetic or cultural or financial inheritance, do badly in market competition. If poverty and inequality cause policy interventions that challenge property rights and associated resource allocation, the interventions must be stopped, if necessary by illiberal means.

These Austro-Hungarian positions on inequality had parallels in nineteenth-century British thought. In the English-speaking countries, this tendency in thought had gradually been leavened by acceptance of the advantages of democracy, including in releasing pressure for revolutionary change.

Austro-Hungarian thought was blind to the observed reality that sustained strong economic growth is more likely with effective government provision of public goods and correction for market failure.

Mainstream Anglo-American thought was in a very different place to these Austro-Hungarian positions through the middle decades of the twentieth century. It recognised the immense advantages of market exchange in goods and services in areas of economic activity in which competition could be effective. But where there were external positive or negative effects from private economic decisions, or where supply conditions for services suggested that they were 'public goods', or where sustained underemployment was caused by persistent tendencies for private savings to exceed private investment intentions, it supported fiscal, monetary or regulatory corrections. It also supported fiscal and regulatory interventions to correct undesirably large inequalities in income distribution or the presence of unacceptably high levels of poverty. It held that economic growth was strongest in practice in an optimality zone, with neither untrammelled free markets nor indiscriminate state intervention. Knowledge and analysis could inform policy about the location of the optimality zone.

Fred was part of the generation of leaders in economic thought in ANU's Institute of Advanced Studies that succeeded the group from postwar reconstruction. Over the decade or so before his retirement in 1986 he was one of three refugees from Germanic Central Europe who were influential in extending and strengthening the liberal social democratic tradition of economics at the ANU. Far from challenging and overthrowing the successful intellectual tradition into which they were welcomed, they refreshed it. The contrast with the Central European émigrés to the North Atlantic is sharp.

Fred was from Vienna, the glittering artistic and intellectual capital of central and eastern Europe, and maybe of the world. Heinz Arndt and Max Corden both were children in the culturally and then nationally

German city of Breslau, now part of Poland. Different refugee experiences took them through England to Australia and the young ANU. Max saw Fred as having the poise and confidence of a citizen of Vienna.

The three were sometimes of similar mind on particular issues and sometimes opposed. Heinz was an active supporter of Chifley and Coombs's proposals to nationalise the private commercial banks in 1949, and then the most prolific author explaining how the establishment of a central bank with Coombs as governor served the same purpose well enough. He moved across the Australian political divide over his lifetime, without moving beyond the boundaries of liberal democracy. Max remained a committed liberal social democrat from a well-anchored centrist position, at some times supporting and at others opposing current fashions in political economic thought. Fred became more actively engaged in directly advising Labor governments, and a steady defender of centrist balance against challenge from the simplicity of both market fundamentalism and neo-Marxism. All three were defenders and valuable contributors to the successful Australian liberal social democratic tradition that began with the Chifley and Curtin governments, was maintained by Menzies, survived through Whitlam and Fraser and reached its apotheosis with the Hawke and Keating governments.

Fred attended lectures by Hayek and Friedman in his graduate coursework at Chicago. We know from Fred's life's work that he was able to pick out the grain in Hayek and his Austro-Hungarian colleagues and leave the chaff. He argued the case for markets against neo-Marxist challenge at Monash University in the late 1960s and early 1970s. He was a participant in the correction of the Curtin/Chifley/Menzies underutilisation of international markets – most importantly in advocacy before and after the event of the Whitlam government's tariff cut in 1973. He wrote about Aboriginal disadvantage in 1966, favouring equal pay as a right, and increased education and training as a means of making it work. He contributed to the Hawke government's enhancement of equity in social security in the mid-1980s. He promoted informed discussion of policy and a large role for knowledge and analysis in the policymaking process. He cautioned against oversimplification of complex issues, which lends itself to extreme solutions. He helped to maintain liberal social democratic traditions in Australia when they were giving way to Austro-Hungarian simplicity in our great and powerful English-speaking friends.

Liberal social democratic traditions have come under stress in Australia in the twenty-first century. The recession of 1990–91, an economic policy mistake, provided opportunity for criticism of the Hawke reforms, as if they were echoes of developments in the United States and the United Kingdom. The Australian Labor Party in Opposition chose not to own the reforms for a critical decade or so. This allowed other traditions to claim credit for the remarkable period of broadly based economic prosperity that followed, in the longest period of economic growth unbroken by recession in any developed country ever. Misunderstanding of the success supported neglect of judicious public investment in public goods, correction of market imperfections and measures to secure equitable distribution of incomes and services.

Australia has moved too far in an Austro-Hungarian direction so far in the twenty-first century. We sought to introduce market exchange into supply of public goods. We confused doing what business wants with supporting a large role for competitive markets in the economy. We downgraded the role of knowledge and analysis in policymaking and elevated that of vested interests. Productivity growth collapsed, from the highest in the developed world in the 1990s to well below average from 2013. We entered the Dog Days that I anticipated in 2013.

Nowhere was the change towards Austro-Hungarian approaches to policy more consequential than in climate and energy policy for nearly a decade from 2013. The remainder of this lecture focuses on challenges in the climate and energy transition to net zero carbon emissions.

Australia's climate and energy policy story intersects with Fred's early life in Australia. Fred had arrived in Australia with other refugees on the ship *Dunera* in 1940. Survivors and some descendants of refugees on the

Dunera had a seventieth anniversary reunion on the Hay Plains in 2010. Nick Stern, professor at the London School of Economics and president of the Royal Society, author of the *Stern Review on the Economics of Climate Change* (2007) and member of the House of Lords, was passing through Canberra on his way to remembering his dad's experience as a refugee in our country. The two independent members of the House of Representatives, Tony Windsor and Rob Oakeshott, were in the process of deciding whether Tony Abbott or Julia Gillard should be the prime minister of Australia. They wanted the new government to take action to reduce damage from climate change. I had spent some time with them, and Nick was able to join us on one occasion. The independent members decided to support a Gillard Labor government. Nearly all the institutions and policies that took Australia forward on the climate and energy transition from 2010 to 2022 were established in that parliamentary term.

The Albanese government's energy crisis

The timing of the election of the Albanese government in May 2022 has haunting parallels with that of the Scullin Labor government in 1929. James Scullin won an overwhelming majority in elections on 12 October. The cabinet was sworn in on 22 October. On 24 October the Black Thursday sell-off on the New York stock exchange heralded the start of the Great Depression.

The energy crisis that hit the Albanese government in its first days and weeks has the potential to disrupt the economic welfare of most Australians severely. This comes on top of the stagnation in real wages and living standards through the Dog Days of 2013–19 (Garnaut 2013a, 2021) and subsequently. Poor understanding of and reaction to the crisis could knock Australian decarbonisation off course and undermine the new government.

Large increases in Australian electricity and gas prices are at the centre of the crisis. They have their immediate origins in the higher global gas and coal prices that followed the Russian invasion of Ukraine. Higher international prices found their ways into Australian domestic prices. If the high international prices persist and price-forming institutional and fiscal arrangements are left exactly as they were when the government was elected, several per cent of Australian household income would be transferred to producers of gas and coal over the three years 2022–25. The inflationary effects of the fossil energy price increases contribute to forces driving Reserve Bank increases in interest rates. Falling household real incomes and higher interest rates reduce real wages and household living standards and introduce risks of rising unemployment and underemployment.

The general election was on 21 May 2022. The minister for energy and climate change, Chris Bowen, and most of the cabinet were sworn in on 1 June. In succeeding weeks, wholesale gas prices were at times thousands of per cent higher than on average in the preceding year. Together with high coal prices, these lifted wholesale electricity prices far higher than ever before.

On 30 May, the Queensland cumulated gas price threshold over seven days (23–30 May) exceeded the extremely high levels that triggered a price cap of $40 per gigajoule (GJ) under the market rules. On 7 June, the price cap on gas was extended throughout eastern Australia.

Wholesale electricity prices through the National Electricity Market (NEM) in mid-2022 were several hundred per cent higher than on average through any of the immediately preceding years. On 12 June, the cumulated electricity price threshold in Queensland over seven days (5–12 June) exceeded the extremely high level that triggers a $300 per megawatt hour (MWh) price cap under the NEM rules. Two days later, price caps were imposed throughout the NEM.

At the capped gas and high coal prices, many generators could not operate profitably at the regulated maximum electricity price. The rules provided for generators to be compensated for losses in these circumstances. There was uncertainty about how the compensation would work. Generators began withdrawing from the market. Anxieties developed about shortfalls leading to blackouts. The Australian Energy Market Operator (AEMO) began directing generators to supply the market. Direction attracted more certain compensation and was favoured. More generators withdrew from the market, awaiting direction from AEMO. On 15 June AEMO declared the market 'impossible to operate' and for the first time since the establishment of the NEM in 1998 suspended trade. Normal operation of the market was tentatively restored on 23 June without the wholesale electricity price cap and confirmed on 24 June. Average prices remained far above any previous experience.

Commentators referred to a 'perfect storm' driving the crisis of autumn 2022. The perfect storm abated and the problems remained. The unusual weather gave way to the usual cold in late June. The rate of breakdowns returned to usual expectations from an ageing fleet. Mines ceased to be affected by floods. Extraordinarily high electricity prices remained.

The full pass-through of international into Australian power and gas prices will take at least two years, as households and businesses come off old and enter new contracts, and regulatory agencies take account of these lags in their pricing decisions. If electricity prices hold for the next two years at the forward prices set by the market for the next year, then by July 2024 household electricity bills will double. Price increases for gas and electricity will pass through to business users more quickly.

Average household usage of grid-sourced electricity in New South Wales is about 5.5 MWh per annum. The increase in wholesale prices from $60 to the June forward price of about $250 alone would increase average NSW household electricity bills by about $1000 per annum by 2025. The increase would be several hundred dollars more with normal mark-ups. Wholesale gas prices have gone up proportionately more than electricity. The average Australian household spends a bit more than a third as much on gas as on electricity. Wholesale prices represent a higher proportion of household costs for gas than for electricity. The increase in average household expenditure on gas and electricity would be around $2000. The effects of higher electricity, coal and gas prices on business costs that are passed on to consumers are on top of that. The total increase in the average household's costs might be around $3000. That is 3 per cent of mean annual household income of a bit over $100,000 or 5 per cent of disposable income of around $60,000. The proportions are higher for people on lower incomes. Direct and indirect increases in prices from higher petrol and diesel costs from the Ukraine war are on top of that. So are price increases for other goods in these inflationary times. We are Austro-Hungarian if we think that such changes do not warrant a search for a low-cost policy response.

How electricity prices are set

What is happening is incomprehensible without knowledge of how electricity prices are determined in the NEM. There are five regions, corresponding to all states except Western Australia, and with the Australian Capital Territory part of New South Wales. Interconnection allows movement of power in response to price differentials. But there is insufficient transmission capacity to equalise prices across the regions, so large price disparities persist.

Retailers and users of power in each state offer to purchase quantities of power at specified prices for each five-minute interval. The price is set so that the sum of offers to buy at or above that price equals the sum of offers to sell at or below that price. Where markets are competitive, generators offer power at the marginal cost of production.

I will now tell a stylised story of how prices are set through the interaction of supply of power from different technologies with total demand. I sacrifice some complexity for clarity.

There are three types of power generation. One is variable renewables – solar and wind. Most of the cost of these is borne at the beginning. Once the plant is in place, costs are no higher if the generator is delivering power to the network than if it is not. Indeed, total costs can be lower if power is delivered. So solar and wind generators bid into the market at a price near or below zero.

Coal power has substantial operating as well as capital costs. The main operating cost is buying or producing coal. If the coal is unsuitable for export, production costs and domestic competition or its absence determine the price. If exportable, the international price determines the cost to domestic generators.

Gas power under contemporary conditions in eastern Australia has lower capital and higher operating costs than coal generation. It has higher marginal costs than coal.

If there is enough solar and wind to meet demand, wholesale power prices are near or below zero. This now happens frequently in the regions with largest renewable energy capacity, especially South Australia.

If there is not enough solar and wind generation to meet demand in a region in some period, price is set by the source of power with the next lowest marginal cost. This is usually coal. In Victoria, the lift in global coal prices has no effect on electricity costs because it is not exportable. New South Wales and Queensland coal is exportable. The marginal cost of coal power has lifted sharply since the Russian war but remains below that of gas.

If supply of renewables and coal generation together is insufficient to meet demand, gas generation fills the gap. Prices are then higher again.

Increasing the renewables share of power supply expands the proportion of the time in which renewables meet the whole of demand and prices are very low. It expands the proportion of the time when renewables and coal together meet demand and prices are at intermediate levels. It reduces average prices.

A contraction of coal supply increases the proportion of time when some gas generation is required and reduces the proportion of time when renewables plus coal set the price. That increases average prices.

The withdrawal of large amounts of coal power generation increases the proportion of time when high-cost gas generation is required. This increases the average price of power. We saw that with the closure of the Northern power station in South Australia in 2016 and Hazelwood in

Victoria in 2017. Since those closures, the supply of renewable energy has increased by large amounts in South Australia and Victoria. This increased the proportion of the time when renewables set the price near or below zero, and reduced the proportion of the time during which gas set the price at high levels. These developments have shifted average SA prices from well above to well below Queensland and New South Wales over recent years.

The result is a saw-tooth pattern of price changes over time. Expanding renewable supplies (including from rooftops) tends to reduce power prices. At some time, this leads to the closure of a coal generator. Prices then jump to higher levels, and then resume their downward slide. The profile is of a saw-tooth blade with a downward slope.

The dynamic is disrupted if international coal and gas prices increase. This raises the level of the saw while leaving in place the downward slope and the profile of the saw teeth.

Eastern Australian electricity prices are vulnerable to increases in international gas and coal prices for as long as internationally tradable coal and gas are important. They are vulnerable to closure of coal-fired generators until the last one is closed. When renewables supply almost all requirements, average power prices are relatively low and insulated from direct international energy market pressures.

Three time horizons

There is a short-term crisis of high prices to users of power. There is a medium-term challenge of maintaining reliability of power with the lowest possible prices while we remove carbon from our electricity system. And there is a long-term opportunity for Australia as an immense supplier of zero-emissions goods and carbon credits in the emerging zero-emissions world economy.

The challenge is to respond effectively to the short-term crisis without damaging our medium- and long-term prospects. We have to start work on all three horizons, making sure that steps taken towards one do not create problems for the others.

Short-term horizon: the Russian war price crisis

Two kinds of response are available: driving a wedge between international and domestic prices to hold the latter to pre-war levels; and taxing temporary profits from the coal and gas industries directly or indirectly to fund compensatory payments to users of power. Each type of response could be implemented at state or Commonwealth level.

Measures can be designed that automatically phase out as prices return to pre-war levels. How long will that be? We do not know how long military action will continue, nor how long restrictions on Russian exports will remain after military action ceases. Disruption and higher prices are likely to remain for several years.

There are at least two ways of driving a wedge between domestic and international prices: restricting quantities of exports so that the domestic market clears at a low price; or taxing exports to provide incentives to sell into the domestic market below the international price.

Western Australia reserves a substantial proportion of gas production for domestic use. This could be done in eastern Australia. Commonwealth legislation enacted by the Turnbull government is a possible instrument for reserving gas for domestic use. To be effective in returning domestic gas prices to pre-Russian war levels, the Turnbull legislation would need to be amended. Alternatively, companies may choose to expand supplies to the domestic market by enough to push prices back to pre-war levels, to avert regulatory action by government. The three liquefied natural gas (LNG) producers operating in Gladstone would be wise to offer to expand domestic sales to reduce prices. The exporters have referred to constraints associated with contractual commitments. Small proportions of output provided to domestic markets would have large leverage over domestic prices, so substantial price reductions could be secured without disturbing contracted arrangements established before now.

A similar domestic reservation measure could be designed for coal, although the larger number of mines would complicate administration.

Whether mandated or implemented voluntarily, expansion of supply to eastern Australian markets at pre-war prices would leave the LNG and coal producers with prodigiously high profits from the large majority of their production that would be sold at wartime prices.

Alternatively, a levy could be applied to exports of coal and gas at a rate that reduced after-tax receipts from exports to average levels before the Russian war. The lower receipts from exports would hold domestic prices down to pre-war levels. Old contracts at pre-war prices would not attract a levy, so would not affect the integrity of sales contracts. The structure of the levy would see it phasing out automatically as prices fell to pre-war levels. The revenue collected would be small at first, when most exports were being sold at prices contracted before the war. Spot sales and new contracts would attract the levy. Revenue would rise over time while international prices remain high.

What would be done with the revenue from a Russian war price normalisation levy? There would not be a compelling case for compensatory payments to households, as prices for gas and electricity would return to pre-war levels. The revenue could be returned to producers, so long as amounts were not related to current export revenues – for example, in proportions equal to gas and coal companies' shares of export revenue in the year before the Russian war. It could be used to fund support for electricity infrastructure. Or it could be used to pay off Commonwealth debt.

The 11 per cent of Australians resident in Western Australia do not have an energy crisis. Gas is available at about one tenth of the eastern Australian price and in adequate supply. Electricity prices have been increasing at a rate that is similar to or lower than the consumer price index. Western Australia would be excluded from national arrangements.

Under the Australian constitution, the states own mineral resources except in offshore areas and the territories. This makes it easier for the states to implement special supply, pricing or taxation arrangements. Requirements on domestic supply, or price-related levies with rebates for domestic sales, could be introduced as conditions of mining.

Queensland's new coal royalties announced in June 2022 collect 40 per cent of revenue from high prices, which is much more than would be required to compensate domestic users of coal for increases in prices from the Russian war. There is no rebate for domestic sales, so compensation to residents would have to be provided through mechanisms other than lower prices. The royalty automatically phases down as prices fall.

New South Wales has the power to do something similar to Queensland on coal.

Victoria is not an exporter of coal or gas. Its gas producers receive much higher domestic prices as a result of the Russian war. Its coal generators' costs are not affected by higher international prices. They are handsome beneficiaries, however, of higher electricity prices driven by high gas prices and high electricity prices established by arbitrage through the NEM. Victorian users of power are heavily exposed to the Russian war prices through these mechanisms. It is open to the Victorian government to raise coal royalties to provide indirect compensation to residents paying extraordinarily high prices for gas and electricity.

Tasmania's renewable energy supply roughly matches local use. Domestic prices have risen largely through the Basslink submarine connection to Victoria and arbitrage through the NEM. This has increased profits of the state-owned electricity companies. Increased dividends to the state could support substantial direct or indirect compensatory payments.

The Commonwealth itself has powers in relation to export volumes and taxes, income-related taxes and royalties for offshore gas production. The Commonwealth petroleum resource rent tax (PRRT) operated successfully for many years for offshore projects, but its value was damaged by amendments under the Howard government to allow deductions for processing costs to denude resource rent revenue. Now is a good time to correct those anomalies. A Commonwealth role in onshore gas and coal taxation would be more difficult, as it would have to be worked out with Queensland and New South Wales and have value for them.

Rationalisation with state royalties and other measures would be necessary for good outcomes.

The highly varied circumstances across the Federation necessitate cooperation and close consultation among governments. The different histories of eastern states coal and gas warrant different responses.

Medium-term horizon: reliability and new investment
Increased investment in renewables is necessary for lower electricity prices and to reach Australian carbon emission reduction targets. That must be supported by measures to secure reliability – balancing supply and demand for power at all times. The prime minister and energy minister correctly frame the reliability challenge as one of buying insurance. What is the cheapest and best insurance?

The Energy Security Board (ESB) in its *Consultation Paper on the High-Level Design of a Capacity System* in June 2022 suggested a reliability mechanism that would significantly affect the operations of the energy market. The energy market is the one success story in the introduction of the NEM and associated privatisations and corporatisations of generation, transmission, distribution and retail businesses over the past quarter-century. The competitive energy market has facilitated large investments in new and old technologies while adjusting to huge variations in economic and policy circumstances. Until the current crisis, it delivered reasonably low wholesale power prices. The ESB's proposed capacity market would change radically the one part of the NEM that was working well before the current crisis.

Prices will be lower sooner if there is more rapid transition to zero net emissions from electricity generation. How short can the transition period be? Demands on the energy reserve described in Appendix 1.1 of *The Superpower Transformation* would be heavy during the period of retirement of coal generators and ease after that. Private markets for arbitrage will become more sophisticated and absorb more of the balancing load. Decentralised storage in home batteries and especially in electric motor vehicles will add immense depth to private storage. The growth of the Superpower economy (Garnaut 2019, 2021, 2022) with large-scale electrolysis to produce hydrogen for industry and export will greatly expand the size of the system and the proportion of demand absorbed into flexible uses. The Superpower economy will expand interregional interconnection, allowing diversification of solar and wind resources and the absorption of regional shocks over a larger market.

Long-term horizon: reliable low-cost supply of energy
in a zero-carbon economy
A generally applied carbon price would greatly assist and probably be essential to completion of transition to zero carbon emissions in some sectors and activities. That will be crucial in the later stages, after 2035. Carbon prices will be much higher than any previously contemplated in Australia and provide powerful incentives for Australians to capture and store carbon in plants and soils. A carbon price at that time would not affect the cost of electricity or have much effect on transport, which will be close to zero emissions by 2035.

Introduction of broadly based carbon pricing for the time being is ruled out politically in Australia by the legacy of disputation over policy since 2009 (Garnaut 2022). The Australian secretary-general of the OECD, former finance minister Matthias Cormann, is leading OECD efforts to establish a carbon pricing system across developed countries. The G-7 on 28 June 2022 agreed to form a club of countries committed to strong action on climate change and imposing restrictions on imports from countries thought to be doing less than their fair shares. We should join that work and participate in a scheme that emerges. I suggest that we anchor our work now with an expectation that Australia will have a new Australian emissions trading scheme with deep international links by about 2035.

In the meantime, we get on with what is possible. Measures within the new government's election policies can support reasonable progress over the next few years.

The building of Australia's opportunity economically to export large quantities of zero-emissions goods in the low carbon world economy requires international acceptance of Australia as a full participant as a developed country in the global effort to defeat climate change. Intense diplomatic activity in the first month of the Albanese government demonstrated that Australia had moved on from its destructive role in the Glasgow United Nations Framework Convention on Climate Change (UNFCCC) conference in November 2021. That early progress was consolidated at the conference in Egypt in November 2022 by confirmation of the 43 per cent commitment for 2030 and acceptance of the global methane pledge.

Minister for Energy and Climate Change Chris Bowen said on 24 June 2022 that the best way to reduce electricity prices is to accelerate the growth of renewable energy supply. He is right. The government's stated objective of 82 per cent of electricity from renewables by 2030 would make a decisive difference in reducing prices. Achieving that goal is much easier said than done. Investment in renewables has been declining in recent years, as the incentives provided by the Renewable Energy Target (RET) approach their legislated end date and increased supplies of wind and especially solar electricity depress prices at the times when their output is highest.

Removing bottlenecks from renewable energy zones to major load centres through the government's Rewiring the Nation program or other measures is a necessary condition for success. It will add momentum to important state initiatives. It is not a sufficient condition.

High electricity prices themselves provide stronger incentives for investment in renewable energy. But only for renewables investment if prices are high when the sun is shining and the wind blowing strongly, and if they are expected to persist for long enough to support the recovery of capital with an acceptable return. Investors anticipate return to old patterns of pricing at some time after the end of dislocation from the Russian war.

Wholesale power prices before the war – and from time to time since – have been negative for extensive periods in South Australia and lesser but significant periods in Victoria, when the sun is shining and the wind blowing. Negative prices lower the average cost of power. That is good. They reduce returns for generators that sell at those times. That removes the incentive to continue investment in the renewable energy that is necessary to keep average prices on a downward path. In the absence of changes in the incentive structure, renewable energy investment will not deliver anything like the government's 82 per cent renewables by 2030.

A general carbon price would have provided the required incentive. In its absence, achievement of the government's renewable objective and putting average power prices on a downward path requires other incentives. One effective approach, and the simplest, would be extension of the life of the current RET out from 2030 to 2035, and its strengthening to ensure that the objective of 82 per cent of renewables by 2030 is achieved.

Liberal social democratic and Austro-Hungarian approaches to the energy crisis

Let us return to the Fred Gruen story, and to liberal social democratic and Austro-Hungarian economic thought.

It would be Austro-Hungarian and consistent with dominant approaches to economic policy in the early twenty-first century to let high gas and coal prices from the Russian invasion of Ukraine pass through without policy modification. It would be consistent with established approaches to policy for this to lead to record-breaking profits for companies mining and exporting Australian gas and coal resources, and record-breaking declines in real wages and living standards of ordinary Australians.

That would, however, contradict the liberal social democratic approaches to policy applied in postwar reconstruction, extended and expanded by Gruen and colleagues at the Australian National University, and reaching their apogee in the Australian reform era of the late twentieth century.

Within the Australian liberal social democratic policy tradition, achieving the right balance between raw market exchange and interventions to secure greater equity in distribution of incomes is centrally important. Among other things, it is essential to the health of democracy itself.

Knowledge and analysis are required to define that judicious balance. That was the foundation of policymaking in earlier times when economic policy has worked for our community, in the immediate postwar period and the reform era late last century. Knowledge and analysis can define interventions that secure greater equity while avoiding major damage to growth in total incomes – and often in the longer term to enhancing greater total output as well as distributional equity.

Judicious interventions in the interests of equity may disappoint the expectations of business vested interests at a time when they have become accustomed to disappointment being something endured only by others in society. But wise business leaders will recognise their interests in Australian democracy working for its citizens.

Finding policies that strike the right balance between continuity in established arrangements, enhanced equity and economic efficiency is intellectually demanding. Implementing policies that deliver that right balance demands political leadership of high quality. The Australian liberal social democratic traditions provide a sound foundation from which to face the challenge.

Those traditions require knowledge and analysis to define conditions in which free operation of markets works effectively, and others in which government intervention is necessary for more equitable distribution or correction of market failures. Introducing enough renewable electricity soon enough to provide low electricity prices and climate change imperatives has to draw on the power of the competitive market, modified by fiscal or regulatory intervention to align private and public goals. That is a market with a carbon price.

Fred Gruen would agree on this approach. Actually, on a carbon price to internalise the external damage from greenhouse gas emissions, so would Milton Friedman. The Morrison and Abbott governments' slogans 'technology not taxes' and 'technological neutrality' are lonely in economic thought. Fortunately, they are now also lonely in the Australian parliament.

4

THE ECONOMIC CONSEQUENCES
OF MR LOWE*

Canberra and the ANU were young and small when I got to know Manning Clark. I was a seventeen-year-old lad from Western Australia and could handle a footy. He was what one might call a Blues tragic. Like his contemporaries Bob Menzies and Bob Santamaria, with whom he shared a great Australian faith and solemn ritual occasions, he had formed his allegiance with Carlton from the University of Melbourne. The ANU football team, like Carlton, was the Blues, so he could pretend that watching the ball bounce off the hard clay near Sullivan's Creek was something like the action in the old paddock in Jolimont. Manning would delight us at footy club dinners, with speeches that shocked with invocations of the basest Australian spirits, and stories that stirred young men's hopes and fears.

This would have been a painful week for Manning, before the football finals, with Carlton knocked out in the last minute of the game last Saturday, after a battle for the ages with Collingwood. An epic, heroic, old Australian failure, like the ANZACs, Ned Kelly and Gough Whitlam. But he would have found solace in the memory of coming from well behind in the third quarter to beat Collingwood on the last Saturday

---

*   This chapter was the 2022 Manning Clark lecture for the Australian National University, 30 August 2022, delivered on Zoom. The full transcript, including the Q&A, is available from: www.manningclark.org.au/manningclarklectures

in September in 1970. As he said in a long front-page article in *The Age* on the morning of the last September Saturday in 1981, the morning of another grand final against Collingwood:

> It is possible that scores will be level as the game enters the time on period in the last quarter. Then none of the wisdom of the ages will help. Saying to myself, *Be still my soul. It will only be for a moment*, does not help. Nothing helps, except the siren – and that seems like an eternity away.

Volume I of the big history had come out not long before I first met Manning. A buzz of excitement would run through my friends with each new volume. If the sun was shining when Manning and I bumped into each other walking down University Avenue, I would raise some question about it, and we would chat. Later on we both spoke over the open grave of a mutual friend, Alan Manning, as the historian plucked a eucalypt twig from an adjacent tree and placed it on the coffin in the ground.

Manning Clark is our Homer, our Genesis and our Shakespeare. None was the final word on fact, but all told their tribes what it was to be their sort of human. When I want to be there when they come to know what it had all been for, I can't be sure whether I am remembering Dostoyevsky, or Manning Clark's rendition of the thought.

Manning loved the enlarger who stood by his vision and in the end could not quite overcome the hopelessness of the human condition. Old white Australia's story, he thought, was bound to failure by the harshness of nature on this ancient continent. On the *7.30 Report* with Paul Lyneham and Bill Gammage for the seventy-fifth anniversary of the landing at Gallipoli, he tied that idea to our idealisation of the ANZAC story. Defeat would be the outcome. By being true to ourselves and our mates, the tragedy could be borne.

In a short essay in *Making History* in 1985, he expressed 'regret that in presenting a tragic vision of life that I unwittingly muted that voice hoping for better things for humanity. Writing in the tragic vein you have to be very careful not to be counselling resignation and acceptance'.

I think Manning did counsel resignation more than our true chances warrant. If the straightener is motivated by the enlarger's vision, the straightener's calculations of the odds can avoid heroic failure and win success. Whitlam and Hawke came after Volume VI, so we can't be sure what he would have written about them as history. But Manning loved Whitlam's heroic vision and his tragic end. In Manning's eye of pity, Hawke's success in enlarging ordinary life for ordinary Australians may, I suspect, have been evidence that he had compromised the vision.

Manning was certainly right when he said that every individual life fails but humanity can succeed. That is the truth. No-one achieves all the good for humanity for which they hope, or even what they might actually have achieved. But by doing the best they can, many people make things better for those who follow. For all the tragedy of Ethiopia, Somalia, Ukraine, the decaying governance of our Southwest Pacific neighbourhood, of Xinjiang, of Trump's Supreme Court and continuing insurrection, most humans now live better lives than eighty, 800 or 8000 years ago. And that is because enlargers taught and died on the cross, planned against the odds to defeat the might of great states, and persuaded democratic electorates to take a risk with something good. And it's also because straighteners calculated and played the odds.

What greater enlarger has there been in modern times than Abraham Lincoln? But he respected the odds and played them with careful calculation. When advised that early proclamation of freedom from slavery would bring God on the side of the union, he calculated the odds and the consequences of losing the border slave states that had stayed with the nation.

'I hope to have God,' he said, 'but I must have Kentucky.'

In this chapter, I discuss Australian leaders seeking to make life better for the mass of their compatriots in hard times. In Volume VI, Manning told the story of the new Scullin Labor government elected as the Great

Depression descended upon our country. Of the government's destruction by inability to respond cohesively to overwhelming force. He loved James Scullin, the man of generous faith who abjured apostasy. Manning wrote of Ted Theodore, deputy prime minister and treasurer, as a compromised figure, with his interests in personal wealth before (and, beyond Volume VI, after) public office. Theodore stood down at an early and critical time, in response to unproven allegations of corruption that were later rejected at law. He returned to the diminishing Labor fold, and developed the response with fiduciary funding of public expenditure and currency depreciation that economists today recognise as the most likely path to success from the Great Depression.

To no avail.

The Great Depression scarred but taught important lessons to leaders who had been defeated by it, most importantly John Curtin and Ben Chifley. As wartime prime minister and treasurer rallying and organising Australians for the defence of their country, they were determined that Australians would never return to the unemployment and misery that had been the fate of many in the 1930s. Their vision of better lives for all Australians was enforced by the analysis and rigour of the Department of Post-War Reconstruction and the 1945 White Paper on Full Employment.

What followed was a quarter-century of full employment with rising living standards and, after a brief burst of high inflation at the beginning of Menzies' long reign, low inflation.

Success came from the vison of the enlargers and the effective support of the straighteners. It grew from building policy on foundations of economic analysis and knowledge; making equitable distribution of benefits of growth a central objective; expanding public knowledge of the policy choices; and protecting the national interest in policy from vested and other private interests.

Menzies succeeded politically first of all because he retained the Curtin/Chifley focus on full employment. The leading straighteners from the old Department of Post-War Reconstruction retained major public sector roles into the 1960s.

The full employment with low inflation and rising incomes of the Menzies' years and their immediate aftermath was followed by a decade of entrenched high unemployment and inflation. This ended with the election of the Hawke government. The reform era from 1983 to the end of the century gave Australia its best decade ever of productivity growth relative to other developed countries in the 1990s, and then the longest period of economic expansion unbroken by recession ever in any developed country, ending in the pandemic recession of 2020.

While the content of policy was different, the success of the late-twentieth-century reform period was built on the same elements as postwar reconstruction:

- It was built on articulation of an inclusive vision of a prosperous and fair society, in which equitable distribution was a centrally important objective.
- It was based on sound economic analysis, prepared to break the boundaries of orthodoxy if an alternative path was shown to be better. It was based on public education as a means of building support for difficult change.
- It was based on preparedness to hold firm to the public interest against vested and sectional interest. It was based on effective use of a professional public service.

These were the two periods when Australian governments faced up to large problems for the welfare of ordinary Australians, and set the country on a better path. In *Reset* I contrasted these episodes of successful reform followed by a long period of broadly based prosperity with the failures of the 1920s and the decade between postwar reconstruction and the Hawke reform area.

Reset noted that the twenty-eight years of economic growth that ended in 2020 were not all of a kind, or even closely similar. I described the 1990s as the productivity boom, the start of the twenty-first century to 2012 as the China resources boom, and 2013 to the pandemic as the Dog Days.

Reset discussed a number of the causes of Australian economic underperformance in the Dog Days. One was monetary policy mistakes that prevented us making progress towards full employment. A second was change in our approach to immigration, where we allowed relatively free immigration of temporary workers with on average low skills who were not on a path to being Australians. The latter was a radical change in immigration policy in the twenty-first century, from that of the second half of the twentieth century. The new approach had the effect of meeting rising demand for labour whenever it occurred by increasing immigration. As a result, increased demand for labour was not reflected in increased wages.

The Dog Days were characterised by the increased distorting influence of vested interests on policy. The overwhelming influence of corporate vested interests led to the removal of carbon pricing. It led to serious corruption of the taxation system that diminished our capacity to raise public revenue in ways that avoided distortions in the allocation of economic resources. And the Dog Days was a period of increasing difficulty in honest and accurate discussion of public policy. The new media, the information technology and the role of News Corp all had an important effect on distortion of information in Australian public policy discussion.

When the COVID-19 pandemic hit in 2020, it sent all economies into deep recession. In the first half of 2020, we experienced the first decline in output in successive quarters in twenty-eight years.

The Australian authorities responded with a radical easing of monetary policy and expansion of public expenditure. Some of the increase in expenditure was directed well, towards people with low incomes. Whereas in the Dog Days our monetary policy had been tighter than other developed countries even when our economy had been weaker, we moved closer to the monetary policy stance of other developed countries. There was a forced change in immigration, as borders closed. Changes in monetary and fiscal policy and the closure of our borders to immigration led us for the first time in nearly half a century to move close to full employment. Unemployment went down to 3.4 per cent in July 2022.

Some people wonder why wages are not rising when unemployment has fallen so much. There had been an expectation that lower unemployment would cause real wages to rise in Australia after a decade of stagnation. There is no conundrum. The reason is simply that while unemployment is much lower, we haven't reached full employment. Sadly, the Reserve Bank of Australia gave up on full employment before we got there. So we don't know how low unemployment could have gone without being the cause of accelerating inflation. And at this time in history, we may not learn how low unemployment might have been with full employment.

As a young man at the ANU, I had the privilege to discuss the postwar full employment policies with Nugget Coombs and Jack (Sir John to us) Crawford and others who had been in the rooms where it happened. Full employment with low inflation and rising incomes continued until the beginning of the 1970s. Coombs and Crawford and others working with them had themselves been young men. They didn't know how low unemployment would go when they set out to create a set of policies that would give Australia full employment. They were surprised that for twenty years, unemployment averaged a touch below 2 per cent without inflation. There's no very good reason now why we couldn't hold out hopes, if not expectations, of moving much closer to that 2 per cent.

The two decades of full employment with low inflation was followed by a decade of entrenched high unemployment and inflation. The new circumstances were as much a surprise to policymakers at the time as postwar full employment had been.

The pandemic recession was an opportunity to get right many of the things that had gone wrong in the Dog Days and to set Australia up for a new period of sustained growth and prosperity. As I described in *Reset*, a fundamental change was required in many areas of policy. It required a new approach to monetary policy – in particular, not keeping monetary policy tighter than the rest of the world when our economy wasn't stronger than the rest of the world.

Policy reform would have to overcome some big barriers in the path of economic growth in the new circumstances. Export growth and investment in the export industries had been very important in the twenty-eight years of economic expansion. Now we faced big blockages to export growth. One barrier was the breakdown in the open multilateral trading system – to a significant extent, the result of initiatives of the Trump presidency. The breakdown of our trade relations with China was a big barrier. So was the reality that the world was not going to provide a growing market for the second- and third-largest export industries – coal and gas – because of concern for climate change. Production in these industries, which have been important sources of growth in the twenty-first century, had to decline eventually to zero. So there were some big questions about whether we would have the access to the export growth that would be necessary to enter a period of renewed sustained, increasing prosperity.

Those international barriers might have blocked the return to Australian full employment with rising incomes but for one other change. That change was recognition of Australia's opportunity to be the renewable energy Superpower of the zero-emissions world economy.

It was clear by late 2021 that the Coalition government was not going to use the opportunity of the pandemic recession comprehensively to reset Australian policy and grasp the new opportunities. The recession had provided a missed opportunity for such a reset. The partial grasping had taken us closer to full employment than we had been in fifty years. But otherwise, opportunities were let go to waste.

The election result in May 2022 represented a change in the Australian political landscape of immense dimension. It made things possible that hadn't been possible before. The election outcome wasn't the usual oscillation between conservative and labour that had contained Australian politics ever since the fusion of free trade and protection parties under Deakin way back in the first decade of our national story. This was something bigger. The loss in electorates in the richer parts of Melbourne, Sydney, Brisbane and Perth that had provided the Liberal Party's strongest support represents a fundamental change. The election outcome provides a political base for changes in economic policy and in the integrity of our democratic political system. It has the potential to make impossible things possible.

History throws up the unexpected. Whatever difficulties that Australia faced with its reset were greatly complicated by the Russian war.

The Russian invasion of Ukraine suddenly triggered increases in oil, coal and gas prices that left to themselves, would very substantially reduce the Australian standard of living. There is a haunting similarity between what is happening in the very first days of this Labor government to what happened to Scullin back in 1929.

It is of crucial importance to the prospects of Australia that the government elected in May 2022 understands the big international forces playing on the Australian economy. It is crucial for Australia that the new government manages these pressures in a way that resets Australia at first for maintenance of the standard of living and then for broadly based growth.

So the new government and parliament have to deal with all the challenges I discussed in *Reset*, plus one more: insulating the Australian standard of living from those very large increases in coal, gas and therefore electricity prices.

Monetary orthodoxy as it has developed in the twenty-first century leads to a kneejerk tendency towards increased interest rates when the rate of inflation measured by the CPI and other broad-based indexes rises. Increased electricity and gas prices lead fairly automatically to higher interest rates. We've seen that happening in recent times.

I have been worried about the rigidity of the new monetary orthodoxy since the early days of the China resources boom. In a talk to the annual dinner of the Canberra economic society late in 2005, I expressed my concern that a rather rigid approach to inflation targeting had begun to emerge in the early twenty-first century. I called that presentation 'Is Macroeconomics Dead?' and it was published late in 2005 in the *Oxford Review of Economic Policy*. I expressed concern that an inflation standard was replacing the gold standard as a source of rigidity in monetary policy.

You can see why I was concerned by what is happening now. If we continue to tighten monetary policy – raise interest rates – because inflation is higher than the target range, then we will diminish demand for many goods and services in ways that seriously disrupt the economy. High inflation is undesirable, and it is important to avoid entrenched high inflation. But not all inflation is entrenched at high levels. And inflation is not the only undesirable economic condition. There is a danger that we will replace continuing movement to full employment with rising unemployment. Perhaps sustained unnecessarily high unemployment. That would be a dreadful mistake, one that can be avoided with thoughtful policy.

The blessing in the current situation is that truncating the unnecessary increase in energy prices at a time when the economy generally is slowing may give the Reserve Bank the rationale to change its monetary policy stance. That suggests a need to drive a wedge between international and domestic coal and gas prices.

Monetary orthodoxy could lead us to rising unemployment without good purpose

I have an awful echo in my head of the worst ever error of British monetary policy. The chancellor of the exchequer, Winston Churchill, arranged in the 1925 budget that the United Kingdom would return to the Gold Standard at the prewar parity in 1925. This was the conventional advice from the Bank of England, the City of London and the top of the Treasury. This ignored an awful fact of the world in 1925: the massive monetary expansion to fund British participation in World War I made acceptance of higher postwar prices inevitable and a necessary part of the adjustment to the monetary expansion to fund the war. So I picked up Keynes' *The Economic Consequences of Mr Churchill*. Here are a few sentences from his concluding paragraphs:

> The monetary policy announced in the Budget [of 1925] being the real source of our industrial troubles, it is impossible to recommend any truly satisfactory course except its reversal. Nevertheless, among the alternatives still open to this Government, some courses are better than others.
>
> One course is to pursue the so-called 'sound' policy vigorously, with the object of bringing about 'the fundamental adjustments' in the orthodox way by further restricting credit and raising the bank-rate in the autumn if necessary, thus intensifying unemployment and using every other weapon in our hands to force down money wages ... If this policy can be carried through it will be, in a sense, successful, though it will leave much injustice behind it on account of the inequality of the changes it will effect ...
>
> The question is how far public opinion will allow such a policy to go. It would be politically impossible for the Government to admit that it was deliberately intensifying unemployment ... Deflation, once started ever so little, is cumulative in its progress. If pessimism becomes generally prevalent in the business world, the slower circulation of money resulting from this can carry Deflation a long way further, without the Bank having either to raise the bank-rate or to reduce its deposits. And since the public always understands particular causes better than general causes, the depression will be attributed to the industrial disputes which will accompany it, to the Dawes Scheme, to China, to the inevitable consequences of the Great War, to tariffs, to high taxation, to anything in the world except the general monetary policy which has set the whole thing going.

A furtive restriction of credit by the Bank of England can be coupled with vague cogitations on the part of [the prime minister] as to whether social benevolence does not require him to neutralise the effects of this by a series of illogical subsidies ... The Budgetary position will render it impossible for the subsidies to be big enough to make any real difference. And in the end, unless there is a social upheaval, 'the fundamental adjustments' will duly take place.

Some people may contemplate this forecast with equanimity. I do not. It involves a great loss of social income whilst it is going on, and will leave behind much social injustice when it is finished. The best, indeed the only, hope lies in the possibility that in this world, where so little can be foreseen, something may turn up – which leads me to my alternative suggestions. Could we not *help* something to turn up?

The prime minister's economic summit the day after tomorrow is a chance to help something turn up.

Manning wrote in *The Age* in 1981 on the morning of that last Saturday of September, Collingwood again in Carlton's path: 'If the game is close, there may be more than I can endure in my season of the sere and the yellow leaf ... as the Carlton players make me feel as though my love has come to me.'

For the record, Carlton was again way behind in the third quarter, and won by a similar margin to that of eleven years earlier, in the 1970 grand final. Manning's love had come to him.

*

In comments after this lecture, Professor Frank Bongiorno noted: 'Manning Clark said he was weak on backdrop in his history. By backdrop, of course, Manning meant the economy and the kind of material factors that are so important in helping to produce that civilised society that Ross just referred to in relation to taxation. Ross has made a comparable impact, certainly in scale, to Manning Clark's on this country. Both Ross and Manning, of course, have been significant influential and visionary public intellectuals. Both have been animated by their vision of the good life and of the civilised society. Neither is a technocrat. And I guess we're reminded tonight that another man who wasn't a technocrat was John Maynard Keynes. What a splendid quotation that was at the end of Ross's lecture. Again we were reminded of a vision of a good and civilised society.

'Both Ross and Manning understood that Australia would need to find its way in Asia. Manning was in some ways the public intellectual who pioneered that idea in the 1950s. And of course, Ross's work in that line has been deeply influential over the last several generations. Both also realised that Australia could not shut out the modern world. Manning's term, which he borrowed from Angus Wilson, was that we couldn't afford to be "darling dodos". Ross's public career and the words tonight have been a reminder that Australia has to make its way in the world.

'That's an important message, because the temptation to shut out the world has often been overwhelming during the years of the pandemic. Australia got through that pandemic, in a lot of ways, by not shutting the world out, despite the impression we left on others. We kept those borders open, in terms of our exports. The situation we're in now, as difficult as it is, would be a lot worse if not for that.

'Manning would recognise Ross as an enlarger not a straightener. And he would have admired the sweeping vision of Australian history that we've had tonight: from Deakin through Theodore, Scullin, the postwar reconstruction, Whitlam, Hawke, right through to Albanese.

'Ross has been innovative in inviting us to rethink the periodisation of contemporary Australian history. In my own writing I have already relied on the notion of the "Dog Days". It's a really powerful concept, capturing that moment between the China boom and the pandemic.

'I appreciate the references to the Scullin government. Scullin's was a much under-appreciated government. In my view, it wasn't the dreadful failure that has been presented over the years. As Ross said tonight, it was overwhelmed by circumstance. Its instincts were broadly correct. Its official policy, after all, was the Theodore plan. The lack of cooperation from the Commonwealth Bank and the Senate prevented it from pursuing that.

'Finally, I have to express appreciation for the references to the 1981 Grand Final. I remember it so well. I was twelve at the time. Carlton was indeed twenty-one points behind with a few minutes to go in the third quarter. I couldn't watch it anymore. It was too painful to contemplate going back to school Monday morning to all those awful Collingwood supporters. I decided that was the time for a solo kick-to-kick out on the road with the football. Then something magical happened. The magician was the great Mike Fitzpatrick, who took command of the game as Carlton's captain. I've never seen leadership on a sporting field like that. I sometimes think of it in other contexts too. As Ross pointed out, Carlton won that game much to Manning's delight and much to mine as well.'

5

THE ECONOMIC CONSEQUENCES
OF MR TRUMP AND MR BIDEN*

Max Corden's last publication was his 2018 joint article with me in the *Australian Economic Review*, 'The Economic Consequences of Mr Trump'. If we were writing today, the title might be 'The Economic Consequences of Mr Trump and Mr Biden', as there has been continuity across the two presidencies in the fiscal and trade policies that we discussed five years ago. President Biden in practice has taken the Trumpian combination of increasing budget deficits and trade protection a step further in his *Inflation Reduction Act*, while increasing incentives for decarbonisation of the US economy.

This chapter, originally a lecture in Max Corden's honour, applies the approach that Max took to analysing economic problems to one big question: should Australia emulate Mr Biden's *Inflation Reduction Act* and the policies in which it is embedded?

Max was the economics profession's teacher. His published work and his lectures were always models of clarity and precision. His book *Trade Policy and Economic Welfare* half a century ago precisely and clearly set out nearly the whole of what is important for policy in economic thinking

---

*   This chapter was first presented as the 2023 Corden Public Lecture in the Faculty of Commerce and Economics at the University of Melbourne on 10 October 2023. It was published as Ross Garnaut, 2023, 'The Economic Consequences of Mr Trump and Mr Biden', *Australian Economic Review*, vol. 56: 417–30.

about international trade (Corden 1974). His *Inflation, Exchange Rates and the World Economy* forty-six years ago applied the best of international macroeconomic theory to understanding the new problems of a world disrupted by floating exchange rates and shocks from suddenly higher energy prices (Corden 1977).

Max always worked on the big economic issues of the day in the real world. His focus on protection and trade policy in the first two decades of his career was directed by the central Australian economic policy question of those days. His shift in focus at Oxford in the 1970s to unemployment and inflation in a world of disrupted global energy markets was to the big practical questions of that time. Over the past decade he took a close interest in climate change and decarbonisation.

In Max's early years at ANU when he was working on protection in the 1960s, I knew him as a teacher as well as a stimulating author and presenter about protection. On his return to ANU after Oxford, we were colleagues with shared interests in Australian and international macroeconomic policy. After Max's return from Johns Hopkins and my move to Melbourne one and a half decades ago, I knew him as a close friend with shared interests in and concerns about the governance of our country and the world, alongside our longstanding economic policy interests.

In launching Max's autobiography *Lucky Boy in the Lucky Country* (Corden 2018), I described him as a conservative liberal social democrat. For small minds, these four words together mean nothing in particular. In Max's case, each of the words adds content to a precise and rich concept. A democrat, because in the end public choice should give similar weight to the preferences of all people. A social democrat, because society works better for its members if the state intervenes to raise the living standards of its poorer members. And in any case, democracy does not work in practice unless there is reasonably equitable distribution of incomes and access to the civilising services. Liberal because the preferences and freedoms of individuals of all ethnicity, beliefs and circumstances should be respected and defended against the preferences or decisions of a democratic majority when these threaten to oppress individuals and minorities. And conservative, because poorly considered large change carries risks of unhappy unintended consequences, and because people prefer change from established conditions to be gradual and comprehensible.

The conservative, the liberal, the social and the democrat were all in the front of Max's mind through the last Melbourne decade, as he reflected on his first ten years, as a boy in Germany. He now identified as a member of a German centre that could not hold in the 1930s. He was deeply disturbed by the rise and rise of Donald Trump but took comfort from Trump lacking the strategic focus and intent of *him*. But what if a more disciplined and focused leader should come to power with the political views and values of Mr Trump?

The economic consequences of Mr Trump

Max maintained his characteristic self-discipline in his only writing about Mr Trump, our article in the *Australian Economic Review*. Never write about anything in which you are not deeply expert. That has been his creed and practice. And when you write about that, be clear and precise; mean exactly what you say; and make sure that your readers have no doubts about what you are saying.

We noted in that 2018 article that the Trump administration had implemented two major initiatives in economic policy: cutting rates of corporate and personal income tax, leading to an increase in the budget deficit; and increasing barriers against imports. The increased protection was greatest against countries with which the United States had large bilateral trade deficits, notably China. These initiatives were meant to reduce US trade deficits, increase growth in the US economy as a whole, and especially increase employment and incomes of workers employed in manufacturing in the 'rust belt' states. We sought to answer the question: what will be the effects of these policies?

The consequences of Mr Trump's large tax cuts funded by a larger budget deficit are primarily macroeconomic, affecting broad economic aggregates. The consequences of the increases in protection are essentially microeconomic, affecting the allocation of resources across different economic activities.

The Trump policy changes came after a long, slow but reasonably steady increase in US economic activity and a reduction in unemployment after expansionary monetary policies were adopted during and following the Great Crash of 2008. At the time of Trump's election, the budget deficit had been falling with economic expansion but remained high for the advanced stage of the business cycle and the relatively low unemployment. Public debt as a ratio to GDP had by 2018 reached levels unprecedented except in wartime or its immediate aftermath. Easy money after the Great Crash had supported a relatively low dollar exchange rate. This helped US export industries, but a large trade deficit continued.

In the period leading up to Trump's election in 2016, low interest and exchange rates assisted a moderate expansion of manufacturing employment, including in the rust-belt industrial states from about 2010. This followed more than two decades of decline of manufacturing employment accumulating to over 40 per cent from 1988. Unemployment had fallen to the lowest level in nearly half a century.

Our 2018 article noted that the increase in the budget deficit and public debt to fund reductions in tax rates leads to an increase in domestic expenditure. Since there is near full employment, the increase in expenditure leads to an increase in inflation and the trade deficit. The monetary authorities respond to higher inflation by raising policy (shorter-term) interest rates. Higher inflation causes market (longer-term) interest rates to rise. Higher interest rates attract capital inflow and place upward pressure on the exchange rate. An appreciation of the real exchange rate – from the combination of increased prices and an increase in the exchange rate – causes an increase in the trade deficit. Total employment remains about the same as before the fiscal expansion, because the starting point is full employment. Employment falls in industries producing tradable goods and services in competition with other countries, including most manufactured goods. It rises in industries producing non-tradable goods and services.

Mr Trump wanted to reduce US trade deficits with China and the world as a whole through restrictions on imports. We noted that the cost of protection is felt by both potential exporters and potential importers. If the United States imposes tariffs on imports from China, it hurts not only China but also the United States. If China then reciprocates by itself restricting trade, it increases the hurt to both countries.

We noted that trade balances are determined by macroeconomic factors and not by protection policies, which affect the allocation of resources across industries. Mr Trump wanted to reduce the trade deficit by protectionist policies, but his macroeconomic policies were in the way. In the United States, investment was greater than savings, and in the rest of the world combined savings were greater than investment. Investment exceeding savings in the US caused the trade deficit. One element of the low savings of the United States was the Trump-determined fiscal deficit.

A trade surplus reflects a tendency for people in a country to value savings more than domestic investment at prevailing interest rates. A deficit in another country reflects a tendency there for people to value investment more than savings. That one country runs a trade deficit and another a surplus may reflect differences between the countries in demography, time preferences or stages of development reflected in differences in opportunities for domestic investment. For the United States, there is little risk that large borrowing from abroad will create financing problems and a financial crisis in the early future, so the matter can be considered as one of preferences. For smaller countries which do not issue the world's international currency, the level of savings relative to investment is not merely an expression of a preference on those matters. Decisions about appropriate levels of borrowing in smaller countries must also take financial stability into account.

Several international reactions to the increase in US protection are possible. Foreign governments may choose not to react. They may choose to reduce their own trade barriers, either to persuade Mr Trump that he should now desist from his own increases in protection, or to increase gains from trade to offset losses from the change in US policy. They may retaliate by raising their own trade barriers, in the hope of forcing a reversal of American policy – or simply to persuade domestic political constituencies that they are 'standing up' to American pressure. The best response by other countries to the change in US policy from the point of view of economic welfare at home, and obviously for welfare in the United States and the world as a whole, is to reduce their own protection. If they do this, they will offset – perhaps more than offset – the losses from the increase in US protection. Doing nothing is second best. At least the costs of Mr Trump will not be compounded by reduced gains from trade as a result of the partner country's own policy decisions.

The worst outcome for the partner countries, the United States and the world as a whole is retaliation through an increase in the partner's protection. This compounds the loss of gains from trade resulting from the American action – in the retaliating countries, and in the United States and the world as a whole as well. We drew on Irwin's history of US trade policy to note the lesson of US protectionism during the Great Depression: US leadership in ideas about policy could be as important as retaliation in other countries' protectionist policies (Irwin 2017).

The US trade deficit is certain to increase as a result of the two policy interventions combined. It will increase as a result of the higher budget deficit and real exchange rate, and will not be reduced by the increase in protection and associated dollar appreciation.

What actually happened

President Trump was true to his word on increasing protection, especially but not only against China. China chose to retaliate by increasing protection against the United States and some of its allies. And as in the early 1930s, trade policy became more protectionist in many other countries.

The trade share of output fell sharply in the United States and fell in the world as a whole. This contributed to some deceleration of growth in productivity and output from the late 2010s in the United States and throughout the world.

The US domestic reality began to unfold as anticipated in our article. The budget deficit rose. Concerns rose about inflation and interest rates began to rise, raising the nominal and real exchange rates. The trade deficit grew. The increase in employment decelerated with the approach to full employment. Total employment in manufacturing increased modestly, but less rapidly than between 2010 and 2016.

Then came the pandemic. The economy quickly fell into deep recession. Employment fell and unemployment rose sharply. The price level started to fall. The pandemic had global reach, so the exchange rate and trade deficit, which are determined by conditions relative to the rest of the world, did not shift by large amounts. The authorities responded by increasing public expenditure, reducing taxes and easing monetary policy at an unprecedented rate and to an unprecedented extent.

President Biden took office immediately after legislation of Trump's second anti-recessionary fiscal package, when there was still anxiety about recession and unemployment. The Biden government retained virtually all the new Trump protection. Debt-funded fiscal expansion was extended with the American Rescue Plan presented to Congress in January 2021 and signed into law in March. The original presidential proposals provided for substantially higher revenues from increases in funding for the Internal Revenue Service and for a minimum level of taxation out of corporate accounting income, but these were pared back in the legislative process. The surviving Biden fiscal packages were massively expansionary. This was followed by the *Infrastructure Investment and Jobs Act* of November 2021, authorising expenditure of about US$1 trillion over a decade. Then came the *Chips and Science Act*, designed to assist production of semi-conductors and large enough to have macroeconomic implications.

By early 2022 the Biden macroeconomic policy had been defined: unabated Trumpian protection and intensified Trumpian fiscal expansion.

The ironically named *Inflation Reduction Act* (IRA) of 2022 came next. This mainly provided tax rebates and subsidies related to production or use of zero-carbon goods and infrastructure. It was strongly protectionist, with many elements available only for sale or purchase of goods with high proportions of US content. There was provision for some revenue-raising measures, but how many of these would survive the legislative process was uncertain. Overall, the package was expansionary. Since many elements were accessible to any resident who met specified criteria, without limit, it soon became apparent that the total budget impact would be much greater than the original estimate.

Recovery from the pandemic recession was swift. Economic growth in 2021 was the strongest since recovery from the early 1980s recession in 1984. Unemployment fell at the fastest rate on record, from 6.4 per cent in January 2021 to 3.9 per cent by December that year and pre-pandemic levels in early 2022.

Supply chains for many goods had been severely disrupted by pandemic restrictions, with COVID-19 lockdowns in China continuing dislocation through 2022. Diminished global supply capacity and policy-induced increases in demand led to sharp increases in inflation, exacerbated by the effects of the Russian invasion of Ukraine on global energy, chemical manufactures and food markets from February 2022. Inflation as measured by the Consumer Price Index reached a peak of 8.9 per cent in the year to June 2022 before decelerating to 6.9 per cent in December and to 3.7 per cent in the year to August 2023. The strong labour market saw wages rising more rapidly than inflation from March 2023 after a year of falling behind.

US monetary policy was tightened more rapidly than ever before. Cash rates were raised from near zero in March 2022 to 5 to 5.25 per cent in May 2023. Tight money and an easy budget lifted the exchange rate. The merchandise trade deficit, which had lifted during the Trump presidency, reached a new high in 2021 and was bigger still in 2022.

Strong economic growth and low unemployment are usually associated with falling and low budget deficits. The continuing fiscal expansion through the Biden presidency made this time different. At the depths of the pandemic recession in 2020, the budget deficit was the highest ever outside the major wars as a share of the economy. It fell with recovery from recession to US$1.38 trillion in 2022 – 5.4 per cent of GDP, then the highest as a share of the economy outside recessions and major wars. It is increasing again. It may exceed US$2 trillion in 2023 after appropriate accounting for Congressional rejection of the university loan repeal. Nothing in sight suggests anything other than increasing deficits in the years ahead, even if the United States avoids a significant economic downturn.

Manufacturing employment is a bit higher than at the end of the Obama presidency (an increase of 4.9 per cent over nearly seven years). It has increased less than under the more open trade policies of the Obama presidency (8.2 per cent over seven years). Manufacturing's share in total employment has continued to fall. One surprise is that employment in the industries most favoured by the increased protection – steel and aluminium – actually fell.

The green Trump: The effects of Mr Biden's *Inflation Reduction Act*

The Biden IRA is likely on balance to accelerate US domestic decarbonisation. The effects in the rest of the world are more difficult to judge. Outside the United States, four effects are likely to be important: influence on international discussion of policy; acceleration of innovation in production and use of zero-carbon goods and services; effects of changes in international trade on costs of inputs into zero-carbon production; and changes in global interest rates.

There are two clearly positive effects on decarbonisation in the rest of the world. First, the strong commitment to reductions of emissions in the United States and the demonstration of progress have positive effects on the international political discussion of movement to net-zero emissions.

Second, the IRA contains incentives for innovation in zero-carbon goods and processes, which will reduce the costs of decarbonisation everywhere.

The third type of effect is constrained by the limited and declining US participation in international trade. The relative resource endowments of the United States suggest that even with free trade, it would not be intensively involved in international trade in zero-emissions products. On capital goods, even when innovation is located in the United States, large-scale export is more likely from Europe and Northeast Asia. The Tesla car is an example – with early production in the United States followed by large-scale exports from China. On goods embodying renewable energy and other zero-carbon inputs, the absolutely large US domestic renewable energy and biomass resources accompany absolutely large domestic demand in an immense economy. The Trump/Biden policies make the United States a less significant player in global trade in zero-carbon products. In particular, the lift in the real exchange rate from bigger budget deficits and protection reduces competitiveness of US production in external markets, and protection reduces the import share of domestic purchases. The weaker participation of US users and suppliers in global markets reduces gains from trade – that is, productivity – both in the United States and in the rest of the world.

The fourth effect comes not from the IRA alone but from the suite of deficit-increasing policies of which the IRA is part. US budget policies are putting significant upward pressure on global interest rates. Higher interest rates systematically increase the costs of zero-carbon energy and goods, because their production is generally much more capital-intensive than traditional carbon-intensive goods. Through the twenty-first century so far, a tendency for higher global savings and lower global investment had been placing downward pressure on global real interest rates. Real interest rates on sovereign borrowing in countries considered to be safe for debt have been around zero in real terms over the past decade, with a downward tendency over the period. The high and rising US budget deficit has been a major factor in recent reversal of these tendencies.

With the United States now representing over a quarter of conventionally measured global incomes and expenditure, the US budget deficit has been heading towards 2 per cent of global incomes and may go higher. Real ten-year interest rates on low-risk sovereign bonds have recently lifted to over 2 per cent. This is a drag on investment and economic growth in all industries everywhere. The drag is greater in the capital-intensive industries of the zero-carbon economy, especially in the developing world.

The US IRA measures have been emulated to some extent and in various ways by other developed countries, notably Canada, the European Union, the United Kingdom, Japan and Korea. The emulations have been less protectionist than the original. They have tended to increase budget deficits and so have contributed to increased upward pressure on global real interest rates.

One other dimension of Trump/Biden policies is potentially of large importance for global decarbonisation: the attempt to reduce trade with countries that are 'strategic rivals' of the United States and to increase trade with 'friendly' countries ('frenshoring'). There would be substantial consequences if these attempts were influential in the trade policies of strategic rivals or friendly countries.

Should Australia emulate or participate in the *Inflation Reduction Act*?

There are strong pressures to emulate the IRA from Australians wanting more action on reducing greenhouse gas emissions and on increasing output in zero-carbon industries. There is pressure:

1. to elevate the priority of reducing emissions
2. to use 'carrots, not sticks' in the form of subsidies that increase the budget deficit
3. to subsidise the products favoured by the IRA to avoid competitive disadvantage

4. to introduce protection for domestic production of some zero-carbon goods
5. to favour participation in supply chains with politically friendly countries over others, including through access to IRA fiscal subsidies to produce zero-carbon goods in Australia.

Standard international economics, of which Max Corden has been the great expositor, provides guidance to the answers. It suggests public provision of services when supply and demand conditions have the characteristics of public goods or natural monopolies; and correction of market failure by making sure that firms pay for the costs that they impose on others and are rewarded for the benefits that they confer on others. And it cautions us to be careful about the balance of taxes and expenditure – about the effects of corrective policies on the budget balance and public debt.

On the first of these pressures, the greater US efforts to decarbonise its economy increase confidence in all countries that they will be part of an effective international effort to reduce emissions. This support for global decarbonisation increases the economic benefits of Australia utilising its comparative advantage in zero-carbon goods. It also increases the economic and international political costs of Australia having weaker emissions reduction objectives than other developed countries, and failing to achieve its own objectives. The US elevation of the priority of climate change mitigation makes a case for elevation of priority in Australia. Through what policies should that higher priority be reflected?

Standard economics urges caution on the second point of pressure for emulation of the IRA – using increases in the budget deficit, 'carrots not sticks', to encourage decarbonisation. Standard Corden analysis tells us that when a large country runs larger budget and trade deficits, other countries should run larger surpluses. Australia's budget, trade and current accounts are now in surplus. That reduces the cost of rising international interest rates driven by US policies. It strengthens our capacity to manage shocks from the international economy, which US budget policies have made more likely. We can spend something on carrots, while acknowledging the large advantages of maintaining reasonable budget discipline as we elevate the priority of climate change mitigation.

Standard international economics also urges caution on the third point of pressure for emulation of the IRA. One country (especially a large one) subsidising output of one product provides a reason for other countries to reduce support for that product. US subsidies for some goods or services weaken the case for subsidisation of those products in Australia.

The fourth point of pressure for emulation – protection of zero-emissions goods – warrants comment in the degraded contemporary state of public policy discussion. The costs of decarbonisation are much higher if a country seeks greater self-sufficiency in the new products and processes. The costs are highest for small economies. Australia is small in this context. The United States is not. And the costs are much higher in countries with relative endowments of renewable energy relative to other economic resources that are very different from global averages. Here the costs of protection would be extremely high for Australia with its exceptionally rich endowments. Again, the costs of protection would be relatively low for the United States, with relative resource endowments close to global averages.

On the fifth point of pressure for emulation – the 'frenshoring' of supply chains – there are lessons from the theory of customs unions. If the United States is set on a protectionist path, exemption of friends from the trade restrictions unambiguously benefits the friends if the preferences are unrequited. But reciprocal preferences will not necessarily be better for the friends than unrestricted US protection. The less important trade with the United States is in the absence of trade preferences, the more damaging mutual trade preferences are likely to be to the friend. The United States would be a relatively unimportant trading partner with Australia in a zero-carbon world economy with open international trade.

There are some circumstances in which the economic losses of fren-shoring need to be balanced against strategic benefits. These limited circumstances can be identified by rigorous analysis. The costs can be measured and weighed against the strategic benefits.

Australia's comparative advantage in the zero-carbon world economy

Australia will generally do best on decarbonisation and development for itself and for the rest of the world if it specialises in production of goods in which it has comparative advantage. What are these goods in a zero-carbon world? They cannot be identified as an output of an economic model. To attempt to define comparative advantage econometrically is a conceit of discredited central planning.

Comparative advantage is best identified through observation of the operation of markets in which distortions have been corrected. The most important corrections in a zero-carbon world are internalising the external costs of carbon emissions, and the external benefits of innovation in the zero-carbon industries. It is also important to provide efficient supply of a range of services from natural monopolies required in the new zero-carbon economy. However, governments must make choices about priorities in allocation of subsidies to encourage innovation, and to provide natural monopoly services like electricity transmission. They cannot avoid forming and acting upon judgements about likely future patterns of comparative advantage. Intelligent general analysis can identify probable patterns of comparative advantage. Australia has the economic endowments to be an immense exporter of zero-carbon products. The densely populated, high-income countries with poor endowments of renewable energy in Europe and Northeast Asia are currently the largest potential markets.

In the opening chapter of *The Superpower Transformation*, I estimated that Australia could directly reduce global emissions by about 7 per cent by exporting zero-emissions goods to countries that could not economically produce them from their own resources. Work is currently being undertaken within the Superpower Institute to refine that estimate.

Australia's specialisation in both exports and imports according to comparative advantage substantially improves the prospects of North-east Asia and Europe decarbonising their own economies. It therefore substantially improves the prospects of the world meeting agreed net-zero objectives. It sets up Australia with potential for a long period of full employment with rising incomes for a growing population.

Policy for Australia as the Superpower

Twentieth-century doyen of American economists Paul Samuelson was once asked to identify one idea in economics that was neither trivial nor wrong. He nominated comparative advantage in international trade. Samuelson was right about the importance of comparative advantage. But a lifetime of familiarity with economic ideas made some important concepts trivial to him that are not so obvious to others. One is compensating for external costs and benefits if markets are to work in the public interest.

Corden's *Trade Policy and Economic Welfare* set out the principles with clarity and precision. One economic activity's provision of external benefits does not in itself make an economic case for protection. It does, however, make a case for taxing the external cost and for subsidising the external benefit. Without the tax or subsidy, we will get too much of activities that impose costs on others and too little of activities that confer benefits.

Two externalities are of special importance in building the zero emissions economy. A carbon price or an alternative is necessary for markets to work in the public interest in the presence of external damage from carbon emissions. The alternatives include bans on the use of carbon-intensive technologies and subsidies on zero-emissions substitutes. And a subsidy or alternative is required to encourage pioneering innovation in the new industries, since the benefits are shared with competitors and others in society.

Australia has committed to reduce net emissions by 43 per cent from 2005 levels by 2030 and to zero by 2050. This is a minimal but nevertheless essential position. Achievement of the Commonwealth government's goal of 82 per cent renewable energy supply by 2030 is essential to the 43 per cent by 2030 and net zero by 2050. To fail would damage the global decarbonisation effort and international acceptance of Australia as a legitimate supplier of zero-emissions goods to other countries.

Without a carbon price, using subsidies comprehensively to internalise external costs of carbon emissions and external benefits of innovation, would impose costs on the public finances that severely damage economic development. A judicious balance of sticks and carrots is required to achieve Australia's decarbonisation objectives.

Internalising the carbon externality for power generation

Australia would be in a strong position to achieve net-zero emissions at low cost and to build the Superpower if we had retained the emissions trading system (ETS) that was operating from 1 July 2012 to 30 June 2014. We would correct the carbon externality. The ETS would provide the revenue for correcting other market failures with subsidies. Historically, the revenue that the ETS generated in the two years of its operation provided the capital for the Australian Renewable Energy Agency and the Clean Energy Finance Corporation for many years. It also funded an increase in the tax-free threshold and increases in social security payments that fully compensated Australians on low and middle incomes for the increases in prices caused by the scheme. The Australian ETS was due to be integrated into the European Emissions Trading Scheme from 1 July 2014 – the day after its abolition. That would have established indelibly Australia's credentials as a legitimate supplier of zero-carbon goods into the European market.

The abolition of the ETS by the Abbott government was economic policy vandalism of incomparable cost. There is currently some discussion of Australia's low productivity growth over the past decade and the need for reform to lift performance. The reversal of the decision to abolish the ETS is the most valuable economic reform available to Australian policymakers. Incomparably valuable, but excluded from consideration for the time being by our recent political history. In the meantime, Australia has a carbon-price-sized hole in the public finances of decarbonisation and building the Superpower.

With the first best policies denied for the time being, Corden's *Trade Policy and Economic Welfare* encourages us to search analytically for the second best.

Second best for the carbon externality in the electricity sector is the Renewable Energy Target (RET), which was introduced by the Howard government in 2000, strengthened by the Rudd government and weakened by the Abbott government. The Emissions Trading Scheme was expected gradually to take over from the RET the burden of providing incentives for renewable energy expansion. The RET would remain in place until 2030 but was expected to be economically unimportant from the mid-2020s.

This RET has provided by far the most important policy support to Australian emissions reduction since the abolition of carbon pricing. The expectation of the RET's end in 2030 has removed this impetus to investment in grid-scale renewable energy. More recently, the RET has provided a mechanism for certification of voluntary corporate action to reduce emissions. The RET's end in 2030 would remove the commercial rationale of bidding solar and wind power into the market at negative prices. Production would be curtailed when generators faced negative prices. Zero would become the lowest wholesale price, and average wholesale prices would rise. The appendix to this chapter explains how negative prices encouraged by positive renewable energy certificate values under the RET reduce average wholesale power prices. Revenue from the RET reconciles low wholesale prices at times when the sun is shining and the wind blowing with continued production at negative prices and continued new investment. Absence of expectation of future RET revenue is an important reason why there has been little new commitment to investment this year. On the current trajectory, Australia will fall well short of 82 per cent renewable electricity supply by 2030.

In the absence of carbon pricing, the extension of the RET beyond 2030 and its strengthening is the best available mechanism for ensuring that Australia meets its 82 per cent renewable energy goal by 2030. It will do this without any increase in the budget deficit, and with substantially lower wholesale power costs now and into the future. Indeed, it is the only available mechanism for achieving 82 per cent renewable energy without large costs and risks. It is a second-best solution to the carbon externality problem in electricity supply.

Carbon externalities in other industries and externalities of innovation

While efficient supply of renewable energy is the foundation stone of the Superpower, it needs to be supported by incentives to avoid emissions and to reward new production processes in many potentially zero-carbon industries.

The government is making a heroic effort to compensate for external costs of carbon emissions outside renewable energy with the Safeguards Mechanism. This has the merit of not requiring budget outlays. It does, however, have problems. Its baselines are inevitably arbitrary, inviting rent-seeking pressure. Credits can be drawn from sources that are subject to price caps that may be below the true economic cost of carbon. The fact that the caps are well below the European Emissions Trading Scheme price is likely to raise issues in exports to Europe from 2026. But the mechanism will substantially reduce emissions. The Safeguard Mechanism may be a long way from first best, but in combination with the extension and strengthening of the RET, it makes a crucial contribution to minus 43 per cent by 2030.

More complex issues arise with Superpower exports. Where the exports are to a country with a carbon price and a zero-carbon premium built into product prices, we can lean on the other country's carbon price in dealing with the carbon externality. Our products will need to be accepted as having low and then zero emissions in their supply chains. Official certification of zero-carbon status is required. The RET certificates will serve for renewable energy and products such as hydrogen in which renewable energy is the essential zero-emissions input. The government is working on certification for products other than renewable energy. European Union members and their neighbours in the United Kingdom and Scandinavia can be expected to police zero-carbon credentials fastidiously. Suppliers of emissions-intensive products to Europe, including Northeast Asian metal manufacturers, will have an eye on European standards in drawing imports from Australia.

How to bring to account the carbon externality in sales into countries – Australia and others – that lack carbon prices? For sales in the Australian market, the costs imposed on carbon emissions by the Safeguard Mechanism are lower than the economic cost of carbon. There may be a case for a subsidy to cover part of the gap. What about export markets without a carbon price? Official and market pressures for decarbonisation provide some incentives. Is there a case for some subsidy to make up for the absence of a carbon price? Yes, but outcomes depend on the quality of policy design.

How to reward the benefits that innovative investors confer on others? The first movers in any new economic activity carry costs to generate knowledge that becomes freely available to all that follow. For this reason, business understands and business schools teach the advantages of being a follower and not a leader in use of new technologies. All Australian suppliers of debt and most of equity are cautious to the extent of aversion to new business models and technologies. There is a strong economic case for public fiscal support for investors in new ways of doing things. That was the justification for the establishment of the Australian Renewable Energy Agency (ARENA). Grant support from ARENA met a high proportion of capital expenditure in the first grid-scale solar projects. Those expenditures are now widely recognised as having contributed large value to the Australian community.

Some of the required funding to support the early movers in each of the new Superpower industries and activities could be made available through established facilities: the National Reconstruction Fund; ARENA and the CEFC with their wider mandates and increased funding; the Commonwealth's hydrogen facility; various state government programs to support innovation. More is required, within the constraints of sound budget management. The best mechanisms will establish general conditions to determine whether there is genuine innovation in new zero-carbon activities. Within well-designed mechanisms, investors will be able to rely on support once they have met specified conditions known in advance.

Max Corden's lesson: Be clear and precise in policy analysis

President Biden's IRA increases the chances of the world meeting agreed international objectives on timely achievement of net-zero emissions, and so increases confidence in Australia's Superpower opportunity. It increases pressure on Australia to meet its domestic decarbonisation targets. Australians are wise to emulate the commitment to achieving targets and increasing ambition. That is as far as emulation should go. Alternative paths to supporting movement to net-zero emissions and beyond that to building the Superpower are available. We can seek guidance from Max Corden's approach to trade policy and economic welfare and international macroeconomic policy.

Clarity and precision in analysis suggests caution in following the United States into increases in debt-funded tax cuts and expenditure increases to support new zero-carbon projects and industries. There is a premium on measures like extension and strengthening of the RET and the Safeguard Mechanism which do not increase the budget deficit. There is a case for support at a cost to the budget where we can identify external benefits, and where supply conditions for services have the characteristics of public goods. Analytic clarity leads us to specialisation in both imports and exports according to comparative advantage – remaining open to the world's most cost-effective equipment and other inputs into the new industries, and seeking open access to all substantial markets. The most effective subsidy programs will establish general and transparent criteria. Established programs can provide some of the required funding. Clarity and precision in identifying recipients of support from the budget allow large progress with moderate expansion of public deficits.

Max Corden's clarity and precision in judicious application of the best of international economic analysis can help us to unlock the immense benefits, for Australia and the world, of building Australia into the renewable energy Superpower of the zero-carbon world economy.

Appendix 5.1: How the Renewable Energy Target lowers wholesale power prices

Under the RET, retailers and large-scale users of power are required to surrender renewable energy certificates corresponding to their shares of the target. This adds to the costs of power generators using coal and gas. At times when renewable energy is determining prices – a substantial and increasing proportion of the hours each year – the cost is absorbed by the generator. At times when coal- or gas-based power are setting the wholesale prices, the price is added to the wholesale price. The increase in renewable energy supply that the RET induces leads to lower wholesale power prices. This lowers costs to users. The Australian Climate Change Authority undertook detailed analysis and concluded that the overall effect of the RET was to lower the cost of power to users (Climate Change Authority 2015). My assessment is that a carefully calibrated extension and strengthening of the RET from 2030 is likely to reduce costs to users.

Letting the RET die in 2030 as under current legislation would lead to large and immediate increases in average wholesale prices. The upward pressure would rise over time, compared with an alternative of extension and strengthening of the RET. Renewable energy is bid into the wholesale market at its marginal cost, less the value of the renewable energy certificate. The marginal cost is close to zero. With a renewable energy certificate valued at x, the solar or wind generator will continue to supply power into the grid until the wholesale power price falls to minus x. In the absence of a positive value for the RET's renewable energy certificates, the solar or wind generator will spill power rather than sell it into the grid when the price falls below zero.

This appendix illustrates the effect of the RET on average costs to power users with reference to recent South Australian experience. The Superpower Institute's Open NEM provides the data. South Australia is the state in which solar and wind power supplies by far the highest proportion of total generation – on average 71 per cent in 2022 and 79 per cent in the September quarter of 2023. SA wholesale prices were negative for 19 per cent of the time in 2022 and 31 per cent in the September quarter of 2023. The average negative value during these times was −$58.6 per Mwh in 2022 and −$59.1 in September 2023. The negative prices reduced average wholesale prices in South Australia by $11 per Mwh in 2022 and $18.3 in September 2023 – compared with average wholesale prices if the price had been zero in all the periods in which they had been negative. The mandatory requirement to surrender certificates under the RET added around $8.4 per Mwh to costs of thermal power generators over the past year (average LGC price of about $54).

In the absence of the RET, solar and wind generators would spill power whenever the price fell to zero. Renewable energy supply would immediately fall, and average wholesale prices rise. Far from making progress towards 82 per cent renewables by 2030, there would be a sudden reduction in renewables supply to the grid. And there would be no incentive for additional investment in solar energy and greatly reduced incentives for investment in wind. The resulting removal of negative prices would greatly reduce incentives and break strong current momentum for investment in grid-scale storage.

South Australia is the most advanced state in renewable energy supply. Its high renewables share reveals the direction in which other states will move in future.

Figure 5.1 demonstrates the reductions in average prices of solar power in South Australia as renewable energy supply has increased over the past decade. The falling price of solar power (in 2023 prices) contrasts with the rising price of gas generation in the state over this period of rising gas prices. The increase in renewable energy supply has greatly moderated the effects on average wholesale power prices of large increase in wholesale prices for gas and coal power.

Figure 5.2 shows that there have also been downward movements in average wholesale wind prices, although not so strongly as for solar prices.

Figure 5.1

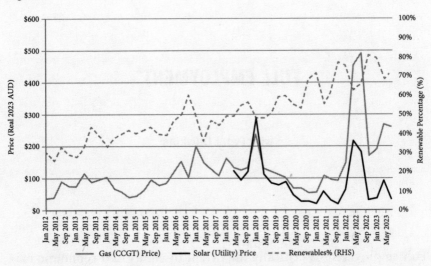

Figure 5.2

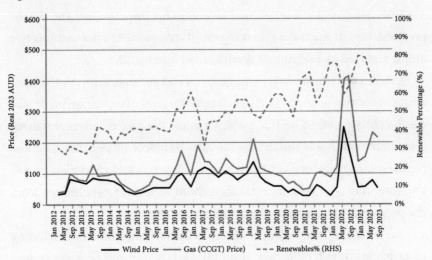

6

FULL EMPLOYMENT*

with Peter Dawkins

Full employment is critically important to equity and economic efficiency. It was the primary objective of national economic policy for several decades after World War II but has mostly fallen from view over the past half-century. It is essential for economic development and democratic success in Australia that it regains its old place as a policy objective and is restored as a feature of Australian economic life.

Evidence from the fiscal and monetary expansion through the pandemic recession of 2020–22 suggests that the level of unemployment that can be considered to be full employment – the rate of unemployment consistent with stable inflation – can now be below 3.5 per cent, as it was for the quarter-century to the early 1970s. The conduct of monetary policy from May 2022 was undertaken without regard for new lessons from the pandemic experience with the labour market.

Achieving full employment along with reform of education including in early childhood, childcare, training, and the tax and transfer system

---

* This chapter was originally a presentation at the Melbourne Institute's 60th Anniversary Symposium and was first published in Peter Dawkins and Abigail Payne (eds), *Melbourne Institute Compendium 2022: Economic and Social Policy: Towards Evidence-Based Policy Solutions*, Melbourne Institute of Applied Economic and Social Research, Melbourne, pp. 32–45.

would increase labour force participation, productivity and real incomes of Australians, and distribute income more equitably.

Return to full employment

In 1998, with Michael Keating, John Freebairn and Chris Richardson, we developed a proposal to reduce unemployment and increase labour force participation (Dawkins, Freebairn et al. 1998). This was widely discussed and became known as the 'Five Economists' Plan'.

In December 2021, in a presentation to the Melbourne Economic Forum (Dawkins and Garnaut 2021), we revisited the Five Economists' Plan of the late 1990s and drew lessons for the current Australian labour market. We commended the Reserve Bank of Australia (RBA) and the then treasurer, Josh Frydenberg, on their recently renewed commitment to full employment and noted that expansionary fiscal and monetary policy was moving us closer to that goal. We also argued that as we approach full employment, a policy agenda focused on raising labour force participation and productivity is critical to ensure growth in total output and increasing real wages (Dawkins and Garnaut 2021). We outlined promising avenues for achieving this.

This chapter expands that discussion. We note the primacy of full employment as an economic policy objective and the importance of a balanced approach to fiscal policy and monetary policy in managing aggregate demand to promote full employment. We discuss possible reforms of the tax and transfer system to promote participation and the growth in after-tax real wages, while paying particular attention to living standards at the bottom end of the income distribution. We also comment on the importance of education and training to enhance workforce skills.

Our analysis was presented immediately after the Albanese government's Jobs and Skills Summit of September 2022. The Summit had five themes:

- maintaining full employment and increasing productivity
- boosting job security and wages
- lifting participation and reducing barriers to employment
- delivering a high-quality labour force though skills, training and migration
- maximising opportunities in the industries of the future.

We hope that the summit marks the beginning of a new era of evidence-based economic reform. This should focus on achieving full employment, raising productivity and participation and increasing real wages, with a view to achieving sustainable growth in living standards and ensuring a fair distribution of income.

Full employment was the first objective of Australian economic policy for several decades from the end of World War II. Full employment was built into the legislated objectives of the RBA early in this period and remains there today. Unemployment was rarely above 2 per cent and mostly well below until 1974, when a sharp contraction during a global recession precipitated by the first oil price shock took it above 4 per cent. It rose above 5 per cent through the immediately following years, and above 10 per cent in the recession of 1982–83. It stayed above 4 per cent, and nearly always above 5 per cent and often much higher, until the massive fiscal and monetary expansion and restriction on immigration during the COVID-19 pandemic took it down to 3.5 per cent in mid-2022.

Full employment was largely overlooked in discussion of monetary policy after the 1980s. Holding down inflation became the dominant objective of monetary policy. Attention has focused on the non-accelerating-inflation rate of unemployment, the NAIRU, which was estimated or presumed to be 5 point something or higher. This remained the case even as actual unemployment in Australia as a whole briefly fell to 4 per cent without accelerating inflation from labour market pressures during the China resources boom. At that time, unemployment fell below 4 per cent in the large states of New South Wales and Victoria.

Acceptance of unemployment rates around or above 5 per cent continued after the end of the China resources boom in 2013, as fiscal and monetary expansion in the United States saw the unemployment rate in that country fall from almost twice Australia's in the aftermath of the global financial crisis to 3.5 per cent on the eve of the pandemic.

The Australian government's 1945 White Paper on Full Employment discussed the risks of inflation. Interestingly, the average unemployment rate fell to lower than the authors had in mind, to below 2 per cent for two decades, without accelerating inflation. This begs the question – how low can unemployment go without accelerating inflation? To descend into the jargon of economists, we are asking what the NAIRU in contemporary and various prospective conditions is. We differ from the RBA in recent decades and from many private economists in thinking about the NAIRU as an observable reality and not an estimate generated from an economic model based on historical data and some presumed relationships.

It may be possible for the Australian unemployment rate to fall to or below 3.5 per cent without generating accelerating inflation – the rate in the United States on the eve of the pandemic.

Full employment disappeared from the RBA's discussion of monetary policy through the decade of persistent unemployment that preceded the pandemic recession. There were signs of change late in 2019 and in the first year of the pandemic. A senior officer of the RBA said in a public lecture at the University of Melbourne that the NAIRU may be 4 point something, rather than the 5 point something that had long been presumed (Ellis 2019). The governor mentioned full employment in monthly public statements after board meetings from October 2019 through 2020. In 2022, full employment receded from view again. It did not get a mention during the period in which there was a number of 0.5 per cent interest rate increases. We were pleased to see it make a brief reappearance in the October 2022 statement.

In the months in which full employment was regularly discussed by the RBA during the pandemic's first year or so, the governor said that monetary policy would remain highly expansionary, with the cash rate steady at close to zero, until sustained wages growth above the inflation rate was accompanied by sustained general inflation above the range of 2 to 3 per cent. That would be the signal that full employment has been reached.

As unemployment fell in 2022, there were no signs in the Australian Bureau of Statistics (ABS) data of sustained high rates of increase in wages placing upward pressure on inflation. By June 2022, the data had established that the NAIRU was no higher than 3.5 per cent, but not exactly how low. Faced with significant price but not wage inflation, the cash rate was raised quickly from 0.1 per cent to 2.35 per cent between May and September 2022 and markets and RBA commentary suggested that further tightening would follow. RBA and Treasury statements accept that the unemployment rate will rise to 4 per cent during 2023.

There has been much discussion of why real wages have not risen in Australia in 2022, as unemployment fell below levels once presumed to be full employment. The simple explanation is that Australia does not have full employment. Faced with significant price inflation from abroad, the RBA abandoned its strategy of resisting tightening monetary policy until we reached full employment before we learnt what the NAIRU really was.

There is no sign of a virulent wage-price spiral of the kind that emerged in the 1970s and 1980s.

The definition of full employment

In 1945, both the United Kingdom and Australia, in that order, published white papers on full employment. The United Kingdom paper, by William Beveridge, defined full employment as the level of unemployment where the number of vacancies equalled the number who were unemployed, but argued that we should try to keep unemployment below that level if possible. The Australian white paper produced by John Curtin's government was less precise in defining full employment but implied something similar. The Beveridge paper postulated that full employment would occur at about 3 per cent unemployment, with all that unemployment being 'frictional': that is, people moving between jobs.

On this definition the United Kingdom and Australia achieved full employment for most of the period from the 1940s to the mid-1970s, with unemployment in Australia averaging 1.9 per cent over that period (Borland and Kennedy 1998). The concept of the Phillips curve emerged during this period, which suggests a trade-off between inflation and unemployment. Estimates of the Phillips curve for that time suggest that unemployment around 2 per cent could be achieved if policymakers were willing to accept inflation around 2 to 3 per cent.

Then, in 1974, supply shocks led first to increases in food prices and then to higher oil prices, resulting in substantial increases in the cost of living in Australia. In the institutional circumstances of that time, this led to a wages breakout and increased interest rates, and a period of stagflation in which both unemployment and inflation increased dramatically. The Phillips Curve was seen as having shifted, and 2 per cent unemployment combined with 2 to 3 per cent inflation now looked unobtainable.

In the inflationary era that followed, internationally as well as in Australia, the term 'full employment' went out of fashion. It was replaced by the NAIRU concept, which in the 1980s and 1990s was estimated to be in the order of 5 to 7 per cent in Australia (Gruen et al. 1999), and increasing over this period. It was understood that inflation expectations had increased and been built into wage setting. Less discussed, but of large significance in Australia, institutional and regulatory pressures led to substantially higher real wages and real-unit labour costs in the 1970s and early 1980s, which increased the NAIRU.

The Hawke Labor government's Prices and Incomes Accord from 1983, followed by labour market reforms and reduced trade union power, led to lower inflation. The decisive fall occurred during the deep recession of 1991–92, following misjudged tightening of monetary policy. The Reserve Bank shifted its approach to monetary policy to 'inflation targeting' in the early stages of recovery from recession, and this was formalised in an exchange of letters between the treasurer and the governor of the RBA early in the life of the Howard Coalition government, in 1996. In the 2010s, earlier labour market deregulation, lax enforcement of law, more open immigration policy, reductions in inflation globally and excessively tight monetary policy took inflation below the RBA's target range.

For a considerable period from the late 1970s, high unemployment itself lowered the value of labour and increased the NAIRU. Unemployment remained persistently high through the 2010s, when it was falling in the United States. Garnaut (2021) and Gross and Leigh (2022) suggest that excessively tight monetary policy caused inflation to remain below the target range and kept unemployment unnecessarily high, with large, unnecessary loss of output, incomes and public revenue.

By July 2022 much lower unemployment was accompanied by higher labour force participation rates (Martin 2022). The number of unemployed persons was approximately equal to the number of vacancies – Beveridge's definition of full employment. But remember Beveridge said we should aim to keep unemployment below that level. There was no sign of excessive wage inflation as measured by the ABS. The NAIRU, no higher than and possibly below 3.5 per cent in mid-2022, could be expected to continue to fall with experience of low unemployment.

The underlying relationships determining the NAIRU change over time and with economic circumstances. We cannot know what the NAIRU is until unemployment has fallen to the point where we observe rising wages in the market as a cause of accelerating inflation. Our experience teaches us to be wary about using estimates based on analysis of data from other times and circumstances.

The Five Economists' Plan

During the 1991–92 recession, unemployment rose to over 10 per cent. It was still just a little under 8 per cent in 1998, which we regarded as Australia's major economic and social problem. The Five Economists' five-point plan presented to John Howard aimed to reduce unemployment to 5 per cent while also increasing labour force participation.

The prime minister called a special cabinet meeting, and the RBA held a conference on the subject. We based the plan on the best available evidence and while it was not fully implemented, it had some influence on policy in the years that followed.

The five elements of the Five Economists' Plan were:

1. steady fiscal and monetary policy and continued microeconomic reform aimed at strong and stable growth
2. replacing living wage adjustments for the time being with earned income tax credits for earners of low wages in low- income families
3. a long-term commitment to reduce effective marginal tax rates, especially for low- and middle-income families
4. a systematic approach to labour market programs
5. upgrading of the education and training systems over the longer term.

The centrepiece of the plan was the wage–tax trade-off, which aimed to support real incomes of low-income workers while reducing labour costs to expand employment. The trade-off was focused especially on low-skilled workers, who had the highest unemployment rates. The tax credit would ensure that workers earning low wages in low-income families received an increase in their real incomes while real wages fell. We argued that the increased labour demand from the wage restraint, combined with an on-going commitment to productivity and output growth, should lower unemployment to 5 per cent and keep it there. Steady productivity and output growth would come through steady monetary and fiscal policy, productivity-increasing microeconomic reform, labour market programs to support the most disadvantaged members of the labour force and upgrading the education and training system to increase labour force skills over the long term.

Various assessments of the employment impact of the plan (see Borland 2002, Richardson 1999, Dixon and Rimmer 2000, Dawkins 2002) came to a range of conclusions about the expected size of the employment effects, though they all concluded that they would be positive.

While the wage–tax trade-off was not formally adopted, what transpired over the next twenty years was a steady reduction in real-unit labour costs, alongside attention to the tax treatment of low-income families, through a family tax benefit and the low-income tax offset (LITO).

Monetary and fiscal policy did not prioritise full employment for more than two decades. Once it did during the pandemic recession, it contributed to movement towards full employment with much higher rates of labour force participation.

Monetary and fiscal policy

Expansionary monetary and fiscal policies during the pandemic were centrally important to bringing unemployment down to 3.5 per cent in mid-2022. This was accompanied by a sharp increase in international prices which eventually found their way into domestic price indexes. Supply chain shocks from COVID-19 dislocations were exacerbated by sudden withdrawal of large amounts of food and fossil energy from world markets with the Russian invasion of Ukraine. Several-fold increases in global gas and coal prices were transmitted fully into the Australian market. Historically unprecedented increases in gas and electricity prices to domestic producers and consumers followed. The sharply increased consumer prices had not been reflected in ABS data on wages by August 2022, with the basic measure still showing average wage increases at 2.4 per cent. The treasurer's statement on the economy in July 2022 estimated a fall in real wages of 7 per cent in the two years to June 2022. This was subsequently confirmed in the official data. This was by far the largest two-year fall in average wages ever recorded in Australia. The acceleration in Australian inflation was not caused by wage pressures.

The RBA raised cash interest rates from 0.1 per cent to 2.35 per cent between early May and early September 2022. The RBA said that it needed to subdue demand to avoid large increases in inflationary expectations and a virulent wage-price cycle. Australia's tightening of monetary policy over these five months was the largest of developed countries over a comparable period. New Zealand started earlier and had gone further by mid-2022. The Australian tightening was close to that of other English-speaking countries with much higher inflation rates (the United States, the United Kingdom, New Zealand and Canada), all of which were thought by financial markets to face a high probability of recession in response to the tightening cycle. We note in reading this paragraph in 2024 that the United Kingdom and New Zealand have indeed experienced recession, and Canada and Australia a prolonged 'per capita recession' (falling output per person). The US economy has continued to grow reasonably strongly, because of the most expansionary fiscal policy ever outside war and recovery from deep recession.

We note that as this chapter went to print in late 2024 the RBA had not increased rates between November 2023 and July 2024. Its officers made a number of references to avoiding increases in unemployment as inflation rates were brought down. We encourage the RBA to continue to comment on the expected impact of its interest rate policy on the objective of full employment in the years ahead. The central banks of the two largest developed country monetary systems outside the United States, the European Union and Japan, had policy rates of 0.5 per cent and −0.1 per cent in early September 2022, though the European Central Bank has since increased them to 1.25 per cent.

Is there a risk of a wage-price spiral?
The RBA has said it is worried about a wage-price spiral of the kind that occurred in the 1970s. But the labour market is not producing increases in wages that are a source of accelerating inflation. In 2022, after a submission from the incoming government calling for a 5.2 per cent increase

in regulated minimum wages, the Fair Work Commission significantly increased them. Corporate profits are at unprecedented highs, and many businesses find it expedient effectively to index wages of senior personnel. Public institutions are loathe to let salaries fall markedly in real terms – and are under trade union pressure to this effect.

We will see higher average nominal wages in the ABS data. But for as long as wages lag behind average prices, they are a response to, and not a cause of, accelerating inflation. At some time in the future the international pressures for price increases will ease and exercise downward pressure on Australian average prices. This will have its own moderating effect on Australian nominal wage increases.

The possibility of a return to a virulent wage-price spiral of the kind established three and four decades ago cannot be ruled out. However, there are no signs of it now. The tightening of monetary policy would bring forward by a small amount and a small time the reduction in Australian inflation that will follow international developments.

The RBA published data from its own liaison survey of companies – less scientific but coming out more quickly than the ABS data – that 60 per cent of surveyed firms are expecting wages to grow by more than 3 per cent over the next year. But with price inflation much higher, real wages will fall at an unprecedented rate. Pressures from the labour market do not seem to threaten a serious wage-price spiral. Nor do data on inflation expectations suggest this as a source of pressure for accelerating inflation. The greater risk is that the tightening of monetary policy will lead to rising unemployment before full employment has been achieved.

Balancing fiscal and monetary policy for full employment,
low inflation and the right amount of debt
It matters how we get the jobs that take us to full employment. Increased employment comes from both domestic and trade-exposed industries. Employment in domestic industries is expanded by higher government

expenditure, lower taxes and lower interest rates. Employment in trade-exposed industries is driven by competitiveness – by currency exchange rates and by Australian relative to international productivity and wages. Too much domestic demand and too little export growth can lead to full employment with undesirably high levels of debt. There must be a judicious balance between domestic and trade-exposed industries.

The level of domestic demand calibrated to achieve full employment without accelerating inflation can be achieved by various combinations of fiscal and monetary policy. If reductions of demand are achieved with tighter money and looser budgets, the real exchange rate will be higher. More of the growth in employment will come in domestic and less in trade-exposed industries. Full employment will be achieved with larger amounts of public and international debt. That will reduce future relative to current living standards.

Full employment with low inflation and the right amount of debt requires judicious balancing of fiscal and monetary policy. At a time of peacetime record highs in public debt and immense fiscal challenges, we are relying too little on fiscal and too much on monetary tightening to reduce demand. With unemployment the lowest in forty years, and terms of trade the highest ever, one would expect budget surpluses. But the Treasury is projecting deficits forward as far as we can see. (We note that budget surpluses did emerge for 2022–23 and 2023–24, as we suggested they should, although this was not anticipated in the official forecasts.)

Strong growth in export industries depends on access to international markets for goods and services, as well as on competitiveness. Here we face barriers from the breakdown of the multilateral trading system and our relationship with our biggest trading partner, China, and from the coming climate-change-induced decline of coal and gas. Fortunately, Australia's potential as the energy Superpower of the zero-carbon world economy can allow us to bypass these blockages.

Minimum wage adjustments

What adjustment to the minimum wage should be made in 2023? In 2022, the Commonwealth supported a 5.2 per cent increase to compensate for inflation. Subsequent comments by the RBA governor have opposed maintenance of real minimum wages while inflation is well above the target range.

The annual rise in the CPI is likely to be well over 5 per cent at the time of the 2023 national wage case decision. That could also be a time of weakening demand and rising unemployment following the tightening of monetary policy from May 2022. (We note that the Fair Work Commission awarded an increase in the minimum wage of 5.75 per cent in 2023 and 3.75 per cent in 2024.)

In that situation the government would do well to consider the use of an earned income tax credit, or more fundamental change based on integration of taxation and social security arrangements around a minimum basic income payment, as an alternative to a substantial rise in nominal minimum wages to support low-income families. This was part of the Five Economists' Plan back in 1998 and was put forward by Hamilton (2022) for the Jobs and Skills Summit in 2022.

There is mixed evidence about the impact of rising minimum wages on employment (Hamilton 2022; Holden 2022). The most famous studies of the effects of minimum wages on employment have been in the United States, including those by Card and Krueger (1994) and by Neumark and Wascher (2000). The former found positive and the latter negative impacts. Each study deals with particular situations, using particular methodologies. Generalisation of conclusions to other circumstances requires caution. One challenge of evidence-based policy is to exercise wise judgement about what evidence is relevant in each situation. There is no question that if minimum wages are raised beyond some limit, employment will be lower than it would be otherwise.

Australia's minimum wages have fallen as a percentage of the median wage since the Five Economists' Plan. They remain high by international standards. The Fair Work Commission will no doubt consider the effect of a large increase in minimum wages on employment at a time of policy-induced rising unemployment and weakening demand.

An earned income tax credit could be designed to provide a larger benefit for low-wage earners in low-income families than a wage increase. It could be designed to have a more positive effect on labour supply than the low and middle income tax offset (LMITO), which is due to be removed and which benefits those on middle incomes rather than those on low incomes.

Productivity, real wages and labour's share of national income

The contemporary world and Australia are experiencing an unprecedented abundance of capital as planned private savings exceed planned investment even at low or negative real interest rates. This is reflected in historically low real interest rates. Together with a declining natural increase in the global labour force, the standard neoclassical models would suggest rising real wages once we approach full employment. The opposite is happening in Australia.

Other factors can intervene. One is immigration. Immigration affects the link between productivity and real wages. Unlimited immigration would take us into a world in which economic output and productivity can rise strongly without lifting real wages (Lewis 1954).

A second factor is oligopoly. We have to think about the increasing role of economic rents in our economy. Productivity is reduced and the profit share of income increased by monopoly and oligopoly. In parts of the economy where competition is not possible or would not lead to efficient use of resources, we must rely on taxation of economic rent or regulation of investment and prices to secure the public interest.

Reforming taxes and transfers to enhance participation, productivity and the distribution of income

Effective marginal tax rates and labour force participation

Since the Five Economists' Plan, labour force participation has risen significantly. In June 1998 the seasonably adjusted labour force participation of those aged fifteen to sixty-four was 63.4 per cent (ABS 1998). In June 2022 it was 66.4 per cent. This is higher than in the United States (61.6 per cent in 2022, down from 63.7 per cent in 2012), the United Kingdom (63.1 per cent) and Japan (63 per cent). However, international benchmarking indicates that it could be higher. The labour force participation rate in mid-2022 was 70.1 per cent in New Zealand, 73.1 per cent in Norway and 75.1 per cent in Sweden.

A major focus of the Five Economists' Plan was the depressive effect of high effective marginal tax rates (EMTRs) on participation. High EMTRs from our tightly means-tested social security system create disincentives to work, especially for low- to middle-income families. The five economists' suggestion of an earned income tax credit (Keating and Lambert 1998) was designed to boost the income of low wage earners in low-income families in compensation for pausing living wage adjustments, and also to raise labour force participation and hours of work. We also argued for a long-term commitment to reduce effective marginal tax rates, especially for low- and middle-income families.

With this in mind, the Melbourne Institute developed the Melbourne Institute Tax and Transfer Simulator (MITTS) to model the labour supply effects of changes in income taxes and social security payments, and the feedback effect on government revenues (Creedy et al. 2002).

While there have been piecemeal attempts at reform, high EMTRs causing disincentives to work remain critically important. Increasing labour force participation is more important to economic growth as we approach full employment. High EMTRs are caused by the interaction of the tax on marginal employee wages with the withdrawal of:

- the LITO and LMITO
- means-tested family payments
- JobSeeker
- childcare payments.

EMTRs of the order of 70 per cent are common. Some are significantly higher. For example, a parent in a two-earner family with two children in 2016 faced EMTRs of well over 100 per cent for working beyond three days a week, due to the combination of income tax, the withdrawal of family tax benefit and the net costs of childcare (Stewart 2018). There was no financial incentive to work beyond three days. Changes made to income taxes and childcare benefit by the Morrison government in 2018 and then in 2021 reduced EMTRs (Stewart 2018; Stewart and Plunkett 2022). But they remain around 70 per cent for such a family, higher for a sole parent, and much higher for some categories of workers.

Childcare and early childhood education

This takes us naturally on to childcare and early childhood education. The labour force participation and hours of work of parents (especially mothers, who carry a disproportionate burden of childcare responsibilities) is noticeably lower in Australia than in many other developed countries. The elasticities of labour supply of mothers with children are high. Mumford et al. (2020) use HILDA data to estimate elasticities.

Wood et al. (2020) and Dixon and Hodgson (2020) show that public investment in childcare would substantially increase labour supply and GDP. It could potentially pay for itself in the government's budget. Wood et al. (2020) analyse the impact of cheaper childcare, making reasonable assumptions about the elasticity of labour supply. Dixon and Hodgson (2020) analyse data on the hours unpaid carers say they would like to work and estimate the cost of boosting care to enable that to happen.

The Centre for Policy Development (2021) has proposed a policy agenda: Starting Better: A Guarantee for Children and Young Families.

Investment in childcare raises economic output by both increasing the labour supply of parents and improving the health, wellbeing and educational achievement of children and later their lifetime careers and productivity. The policy agenda proposes, among other things, a guarantee of three days' free or low-cost early education from birth until school, with more days available at low cost. This would shift the emphasis from childcare to early childhood education, while reducing the costs to parents of paying for childcare to enable labour force participation. The proposal includes more shared paid parental leave. Wood et al. (2021) show that this would also boost the labour supply of mothers and increase their lifetime earnings, while boosting GDP by $900 million a year.

Later, we discuss research that would help to test the validity of the findings of the studies reported above.

A possible overhaul of the tax transfer system

Childcare and early childhood education looks like the single most promising avenue for boosting labour force participation. It would also be timely to undertake a comprehensive review of the tax transfer system and its impacts on labour supply and the distribution of income, with a view to increasing disposable incomes of low- and middle-income Australians while promoting participation in the labour force and employment of low-skilled labour.

There was a moderate increase in inequality in the distribution of household income in Australia in the late twentieth and early twenty-first century (Wilkins 2017; Productivity Commission 2018; ABS 2022). Increasing wage inequality had driven inequality upwards, while the progressive tax and transfer system and employment growth in low-income households tended to drive it down. Wage inequality and a large decline in the wage share of incomes and the absence of initiatives in the tax and transfer system may have exacerbated the tendency to greater inequality more recently – with the important temporary exception of the early period of the pandemic, when the JobSeeker intervention was highly egalitarian.

In the several years from 2007 there was actually a slight reduction in inequality of household disposable income, but this was much less influential than increases in housing costs, disproportionately affecting low-income households (Coates and Chivers 2019). One response would be policies to reduce the cost of housing. Another is to make the tax-transfer system more generous to low-income households.

It was noticeable that in the period of the higher JobSeeker payments, financial stress among low-income families diminished significantly and this led to calls for ongoing significant increases in JobSeeker payments, which had been indexed to CPI and not to average weekly earnings like many pensions and benefits. There was an increase of just below 10 per cent in the JobSeeker rate in April 2021 – the first real increase since the mid-1980s. Apart from budgetary and funding costs, increases in the unemployment benefit rate in the absence of other measures risks increasing EMTRs for part of the relevant income range and therefore negative effects on labour supply.

Equitable income distribution, as well as optimal economic growth, require steady full employment. They would be assisted by comprehensive reform of the tax-transfer system to increase the incomes of low-income families while increasing labour supply and reducing pressures for employment-inhibiting increases in regulated minimum wages.

Guaranteed minimum income (GMI)

The idea of a guaranteed minimum income (GMI) has been explored from time to time since the early years of the Melbourne Institute in the 1960s. Dawkins, Johnson et al. (1998) used NATSEM's microsimulation model STINMOD to model a universal basic income / flat tax system, which provides a guaranteed basic income, combined with a flat tax on all income earned, without any income or assets tests. This could be administered through the tax system, with the basic income provided as a tax credit. Payment would be made regularly into bank accounts, whether or not recipients are unemployed. Dawkins et al. did not allow for any increase in labour force participation from reductions in EMTRs and required complete short-term fiscal neutrality. The flat tax (which is also the EMTR in this system) was found to be 57 per cent – much lower than some of the highest EMTRs in the pre-existing system, but unacceptably high.

Other versions of negative income taxation systems were also modelled, incorporating varying tax rates, the tapering out of tax credits, and some restrictions on the granting of tax credits. This made negative income tax feasible with lower marginal tax rates.

Once the Melbourne Institute developed the MITTS, modelling the labour supply effects became possible. Scutella (2004) used MITTS to model the basic universal income flat tax system, concluding that for revenue neutrality and a single tax rate, a flat tax of over 50 per cent would still be required to coincide with current benefit rates. While increasing equity, the system as modelled would reduce labour supply. Positive labour supply effects required a lower basic income.

The early estimates of the costs of a form of guaranteed minimum income were premised on 'revenue neutrality' – that is, comparing revenue receipts with what would have been received in the absence of the changes. Past episodes of taxation reform in practice have not been 'revenue neutral'. For example, the package accompanying the introduction of the GST in July 2000 had a net revenue cost of about 1 per cent of GDP – corresponding to about $25 billion per annum today.

Conditional minimum income with an employment conditional supplement

Dawkins et al. (2003) modelled a variation on this approach using MITTS in 2003. Their model was built on the then current structure of payments in Australia's social security system, with significant differences. It included an employment conditional supplement (which has a similar effect to an earned income tax credit). Minimum payments would not be guaranteed – mutual obligation conditions on receipt of the payment would remain. It did not seek to incorporate the current disability support system or the age pension. This model gained a significant positive labour supply response at a net cost of $1.5 billion due to the fiscal dividend from the increased labour supply.

Australian income security

In Ross's Australian Income Security proposal (Garnaut 2021), he revisits the idea proposed in his paper 'Investing in Full Employment' (Garnaut 2002) in his Australian Income Security (AIS) proposal (Garnaut 2020). The arithmetic in this proposal preceded the April 2021 increase in the JobSeeker rate. To contain the cost, Garnaut suggests excluding from basic payments resident non-Australians and people whose wealth and incomes remove any close connection between withdrawal of the basic payment and incentives to work (say, income over $250,000 and net assets above $2 million). Assets could be shared among family members who have a legal right to ownership of assets. Marginal taxation rates would remain at the current higher rates for people on high incomes. On the presumption that Australia would move to full employment, increases in labour force participation would be reflected directly in greater economic output and public revenue.

All eligible Australians would receive a basic payment equivalent to the JobSeeker allowance plus supplements that are reflected in the current social security system. For example, the basic payment would be supplemented for children, disability (to the extent recognised in disability pensions) and age (as reflected in age pensions). He also proposes a supplement for being unemployed at times of high unemployment, which would not be necessary when there is full employment. Income would be taxed at the basic rate from the first dollar.

The budgetary costs of the AIS would be much lower than at the time of Dawkins et al.'s (2003) modelling because of the large increase in the tax-free threshold in the intervening years. Garnaut (2021) suggests that the budgetary cost of this proposal could be modelled using MITTS.

Pending that detailed modelling, he suggests that the net revenue cost of the scheme at the time of the proposal, when there was still high unemployment, would be about 2 per cent of GDP, falling to about 1 per cent of GDP as labour force participation increases.

A well-designed reform of taxation and social security would substantially increase labour force participation at a time of full employment, thus increasing domestic and national output and income. It would be progressive at a time when market outcomes were placing downward pressure on real wages and increasing the profit share of domestic income to unprecedented levels. The increased participation would be largest for workers subject to the highest EMTRs, including mothers preferring to work more hours but facing powerful disincentives to doing so. The replacement would supplement wages of low-income workers. This would reduce pressures on equity grounds to raise regulated wages and so reduce growth in employment at the lower end of the labour value spectrum.

Rent and externality taxes, as an alternative to wage regulation for equity

The Australian Council of Trade Unions (ACTU) and major unions participating in the Jobs and Skills Summit drew attention to the unprecedentedly high profit and low wage share of income and the unprecedentedly low real-unit labour costs in Australia in the first half of 2022. This was seen as supporting higher regulated wages and changes in institutional arrangements for wage negotiations that would lead to higher rates of increase in wages.

The steady reduction in the wage share and real-unit labour costs over the past decade, and its acceleration in the aftermath of the pandemic recession, are undoubtedly of significance for income distribution and long-term economic performance. Changes in wage regulation and institutional arrangements for setting wages discussed in the Jobs and Skills Summit should be considered on their merits, for their contributions to equitable income distribution and the rate of increase in productivity, output and incomes. Those contributions depend on the origins of the low and declining wage share and on the impact of various corrections on the unemployment rate that can be achieved at full employment, on growth in labour productivity, and more generally on growth and distribution of income.

Garnaut (2022, and Chapter 2 this volume) observed at the Jobs and Skills Summit that failure to achieve full employment, the level and composition of immigration, and the rising share of rents and declining share of competitive profits in domestic incomes all contribute to the falling wage share. Conscientious pursuit of full employment, refocusing immigration on high skills and permanent residence, and reform of competition policy to reduce the power and influence of oligopolistic arrangements would contribute to reversal of the declining wage share without raising the NAIRU. They would contribute to increased average incomes of Australians. However, much of the increase in profit share resulting from increasing oligopolistic income is likely to remain, as it is associated with changes in the structure of the Australian economy that are impervious to changes in competition policy. These include the increased share of mining income following the increase in the relative prices of mineral products in the twenty-first century – taken much further since the disruption of the global energy trade by the Russian invasion of Ukraine in early 2022.

Much of the adverse distributional impact of the increase in the share of oligopolistic, mineral and other rents in profits is more efficiently corrected with changes in taxation than by increases in wages resulting from changes in regulation and institutional arrangements for setting wages. Shifting the base for corporate income taxation from conventional accounting income to cash flow would allow an increase in taxation of rents while increasing incentives for corporate investment and productive innovation (see Garnaut et al. 2020). A higher rate of taxation on cash flows could be applied to mineral rents – some variation on the proposals suggested by the Henry Tax Review.

More generally, in contemporary Australian economic circumstances, there is a strong case for seeking more equitable income distribution through fiscal rather than labour market interventions. This is likely to generate lower unemployment and higher growth in household living standards. Fiscal interventions with a net cost to the revenue but advantages for economic efficiency would include increased public expenditure on childcare and early childhood education and the shift to AIS.

In this context, a second theme from the Henry Review warrants new consideration: the potential for taxation of external environmental costs, including carbon externalities to contribute to public revenues while enhancing economic efficiency.

Skills, education and training

Meeting the future skills needs of the Australian economy was a central issue at the Jobs and Skills Summit in 2022. Mike Keating, one of the five economists, suggested in the lead-up to the summit that 'low wage growth can contribute to low productivity growth' because low wage growth depresses consumer demand and in turn investment in new plants and machinery (Keating 2022). If we could address the structural causes of low wage growth, he argued, it is entirely possible that we could 'accelerate wage growth and consequently consumer demand, which would accelerate productivity growth, giving us wage growth without a wage-price spiral'. He argued that 'technological change and globalisation have hollowed out routine middle level jobs, depressing pay in these occupations relative to higher-paid occupations'. He quoted Thomas Piketty: 'the best way to increase wages and reduce wage inequalities in the long run is to invest in education and skills' (Piketty 2013).

Skills shortages were much discussed at the Jobs and Skills Summit. The reductions in unemployment between mid-2020 and mid-2022 were accompanied by strong increases in the number of vacancies. Employers said that they had difficulties in filling vacancies. Areas of skill shortage that have been widely publicised include teaching, nursing, aged care and IT workers, to name a few. Employers' difficulties in recruiting unskilled workers at wages that they are prepared to pay are receiving similar attention, for example, farm labourers and general workers in the hospitality and care sectors. Employers have become accustomed to recruiting unskilled and skilled workers alike from developing countries with low wages and poor conditions in the twenty-first century and especially in the years immediately preceding the pandemic. Many businesses depended on continuing inflow of immigrants on conditions inferior to established Australian levels. These businesses are in difficulty as immigration policy again focuses on people with reasonable prospects of contributing to increased economic welfare of Australians, and to enforcement of established Australian laws and practices. Many will not survive scrutiny of immigration from an Australian national perspective and will release demand for labour to more productive enterprises able to offer higher wages and conditions.

A genuine shortage of skills would survive a disciplined adjustment of immigration to the needs of the Australian economy. The National Skills Commission, to be superseded by Jobs and Skills Australia, produces a skills priority list, based on its assessment of skills shortages and ongoing analysis of trends in the labour market to support education and training policy,

There is also a very strong case for strengthening the education and training system to meet skill needs, enhance workforce productivity and increase real wages. It is necessary for growth in productivity and output. The case for investment in skills is stronger with full employment. Employment forecasts indicate that most jobs of the future will require a tertiary education qualification of some type, that is, a vocational education and training (VET) qualification and/or a higher education qualification. We will need a high-quality tertiary education system, available to all, offering both initial tertiary qualifications for school leavers and qualifications and microcredentials to reskill or upskill mature-aged workers.

While on most measures the higher education system is of high quality by international standards, it is only average when it comes to collaborating with industry (Bean and Dawkins 2021). This provides considerable scope for investment in the system that will enhance the value of higher education qualifications.

The VET system, which has had a tradition of working closely with industry, has been in decline, suffering from inadequate funding and excessive numbers of low-quality providers not adding much to the skills of its students. This has resulted from inadequate regulation and poor market design. The VET system needs more investment and a greater focus on quality assurance and improvement (Hurley and Picher 2020).

A review by Noonan et al. (2019) of the Australian Qualifications Framework (AQF), which applies to both the VET and higher education systems, finds that the AQF is not fit for purpose for the workforce of the future. Alongside a reformed AQF, Bean and Dawkins (2021) propose the development of a national skills taxonomy with rich skill descriptors, which can blend with the AQF. They have proposed an associated national credentials platform that enables students, employers and employees to define more clearly the skills they need and the credentials that will foster them.

These proposed reforms to the architecture of tertiary education would help ensure that education and training providers more effectively meet the needs of students, employers and employees, and enhance the market for skills and qualifications.

Differences in funding models for higher education and VET, and differences between different jurisdiction in the funding of VET, as well as the lack of income contingent loans for VET courses, also create distortions in choices between VET and higher education. Noonan and Pilcher (2015) and Higgins and Chapman (2015) have explored funding reforms to remove these distortions and create greater harmony between VET and higher education.

The Mitchell Institute and others (see, for example, Dawkins et al. 2019) have been undertaking a major program of research to help design such a new tertiary system, much of it led by the late Peter Noonan. A joint project of the Mitchell Institute and the Centre for Education and Training at the Australian Industry Group draws this together into a flexible plan. This should provide an evidence-based policy agenda to enhance skills and productivity in Australia.

Conclusions and the need to develop the evidence base

Australia needs a major economic reform agenda to get to full employment and to raise productivity and participation, to enable sustained economic growth and enhanced real wages. This must be undertaken while restoring the strength of Australian public finances in the face of challenging international economic and geopolitical circumstances and domestic demographic tendencies. This will inevitably require a substantial increase in the share of taxation revenue in GDP, alongside public expenditure reductions in areas that have low or negative benefits for equity and economic efficiency. We need tax reform to raise productivity and participation and to increase public revenue.

Economic policy needs clearly defined objectives, a theory of how policy works and evidence against which to test and refine that theory and the policies that flow from it. Policy needs to be constantly evaluated. That is how we see evidence-based or evidence-informed policy.

Evidence-informed policy is multidimensional. It requires well-defined objectives. It takes advantage of empirical evidence about how previous policies have worked, natural and deliberate policy experiments, and simulation modelling.

In suggesting reforms to deal with contemporary economic and social challenges, we have drawn on earlier studies of the likely effect of similar policies. More detailed estimates of the likely effects of such policies can be obtained through simulation modelling. The Melbourne Institute and the Centre for Policy Studies have put together a proposal to join the Melbourne Institute's MITTS and CoPS dynamic CGE model-ling to simulate the economy-wide effects of such policies. MITTS would need to be integrated with the HILDA Survey. HILDA provides data on childcare costs and labour supply, which will enable MITTS to estimate labour supply responses to changes in childcare costs.

Such analysis would also consider the constraint that would be imposed by a limited supply of childcare workers and early childhood educators. This should guide the speed of introduction of such policies and suggest the wage increases that may be required to secure the early childhood workforce to make this policy work. The same modelling tech-nology can also be used to examine the likely effect of an overhaul of the tax-transfer system to reduce effective marginal tax rates.

We have covered many other issues in this chapter and drawn on a range of evidence in proposing policy directions. In considering these suggestions, policymakers would be wise to draw on modelling and sometimes policy experiments.

7

MONETARY POLICY FOR FULL EMPLOYMENT WITH LOW INFLATION*

with David Vines

The Australian economy has performed badly for most Australians over the past decade. Real output per person has grown at well below the OECD average and real wages fell. Over the seven years preceding the COVID-19 pandemic recession, unemployment was stuck at over 5 per cent and underemployment rose strongly when unemployment fell elsewhere in the developed world. We argue that the RBA has not used its key policy instrument – the interest rate – to achieve the best possible outcome for *both* of its objectives, inflation and employment.

The pandemic and its aftermath brought radically different circumstances and policy. Unemployment fell to 3.5 per cent after fiscal and monetary restraint were abandoned during the pandemic recession. Inflation rose to well above the target of 2 to 3 per cent that had been followed through the three decades of flexible inflation targeting. Subsequent statements from the monetary authorities suggest a view that unemployment will have to rise substantially for inflation to be brought back to the target range. These statements reveal an expectation that the

* This chapter was first presented to the Melbourne Economic Forum at the University of Melbourne on 29 May 2023 and first published as Ross Garnaut and David Vines, 2023, 'Monetary Policy Mistakes and Remedies: An Assessment Following the RBA Review', *The Australian Economic Review*, 56: 273–87.

extraordinary reduction in real wages through the post-pandemic inflation will be sustained.

This was the economic context of the review of the Reserve Bank of
Australia (RBA) initiated by the treasurer in July 2022, and of the discussion of the review after its release on 20 April 2023 (de Brouwer et al.
2023). This chapter discusses the review's conclusions and asks whether
its recommendations would have led to better outcomes.

A central problem in Australia in recent times is that different areas
of policymaking, with influence over different policy instruments, have
not worked well together. This article focuses on monetary policymaking.
Chapter 13 looks more broadly at coordination of policy across the range
of policymaking instruments – what we describe there as the conducting
of an economic policy orchestra.

When we describe ways in which cooperation between the RBA and
other macroeconomic policymaking institutions has not worked well,
we note that not all of this has been the RBA's fault. Furthermore, since
the policymaking has lacked a coordinating centre, the RBA has at times
been drawn into assumption of roles beyond both its knowledge and
its competence.

We begin by sketching the story of economic development in Australia over the past decade. We then set out some of the reasons why policy
has delivered unsatisfactory outcomes. This allows us to suggest policies
that would now lead to improved prospects for inflation and employment
and to rising real incomes. We then go on to observe that although mistakes in monetary policy are part of the reason for the underperformance
of the Australian economy over the past decade, they are by no means the
only reason. Returning to general prosperity will require coordination of
policies in many areas. Closer coordination of monetary with fiscal and
prudential policy is essential for good performance. But excellent performance requires contributions from and coordination of fiscal and monetary policy with trade, competition, labour, climate and energy policies.

In conclusion we suggest that while it is true that the review makes some valuable suggestions, the recommendations from the review may not help much.

2013–23: A lost decade

The RBA review assessed that the RBA and the economy had performed relatively well over the past three decades. Among other things, we had experienced almost three decades of expansion of total economic output without recession.

The long expansion was achieved through a period in which many developed countries experienced two recessions, and New Zealand three. New Zealand is particularly interesting, not only as a neighbour with some similar macroeconomic features (a high proportion of commodity exports and deep economic integration into Asia), but because it is the global pioneer, and in some perceptions the exemplar, of the inflation-targeting monetary policy regime.

Yet the years 2013–19 saw unprecedentedly low growth in output per person. Some growth in total output was maintained despite stagnating output per person only because there were exceptionally large increases in the labour force from immigration – Australia's Dog Days (see Garnaut 2013a, 2021).

Through this third period, several other influences exacerbated the downward pressure on ordinary Australians' living standards that was coming from low output growth. There was an increase in the profit share in national income, and a fall in the wage share. And Australians did not share the reduction in unemployment experienced in the United States and many developed countries. In 2013, unemployment was several percentage points higher in the United States than Australia's five point something. By the eve of the COVID-19 pandemic, seven years later, unemployment in Australia remained at five point something, while underemployment had increased markedly. By contrast, the percentage of the labour force which was unemployed in the United States had fallen to well below that in Australia: about 3.5 per cent.

The four and a half years since the beginning of the pandemic have had their own dynamic that is weaving its way into what threatens to become a new Dog Days story.

Global developments

The disruption of international trade and more generally of global supply chains caused by the pandemic greatly reduced productivity. The disruption of supply chains has only gradually unwound. But as economies have emerged from lockdowns, demand for goods and services has grown rapidly. In the developed economies, accumulated liquid financial balances have been liberated to support consumption expenditure. A combination of low productivity and high demand has driven a strong inflationary impulse through the United States and Europe and from there to the rest of the world. This inflation was pushed to new highs by disruption of global markets as a result of the Russian invasion of Ukraine and the international response to the ongoing conflict there.

Monetary policy has been tightened everywhere and fiscal policy has also been tightened in many countries. By mid-2023, this had brought recession to some developed countries, including New Zealand, and recession is now threatened in others. Throughout the developed world, higher prices were driven by scarcity and by market opportunity, with profits representing an unusually high proportion of inflated prices and incomes (IMF 2022, Blanchard and Bernanke 2023). Sharply higher prices for energy, food and chemical manufactures following Russia's invasion of Ukraine were returning to pre-invasion levels by mid-2023. The restoration of supply chains and easing demand growth were together giving rise to decelerating inflation for traded goods and services generally. But inflation remains well above target levels in large parts of the developed world.

Distinctive policies in the world's two largest economies, the United States and China, have exerted powerful influences on the global economic performance in the aftermath of the pandemic.

In the United States, the Trump administration conducted strongly expansionary fiscal and protectionist trade policies from 2017 until the COVID-19 pandemic. Interest rates began to rise moderately from this time – from levels for nominal cash rates and real long bond rates that were near zero – leaving overall demand growing strongly. Continuing strong domestic demand and more restrictive immigration and trade policies led to a continuing reduction in unemployment to around 3.5 per cent. This was widely seen as being close to full employment – the point beyond which an increase in demand for labour would lead to increases in wages at a rate that threatens to cause an acceleration of the rate of inflation above its target level (see Blanchard and Bernanke 2023).

The United States, like the world as a whole, fell into the pandemic recession with the lockdowns during the first half of 2020. Massive increases in government spending and deficits and monetary expansion through sub-zero cash rates and quantitative easing placed a floor under aggregate demand and unemployment. They also led to an extraordinary increase in private cash balances and liquid financial assets, building a powerful latent expansionary impulse awaiting the return of more normal economic conditions. The COVID-19 disruptions compounded the negative impact of America's turn towards protectionism on productivity growth both at home and in trading partners. The Biden administration added to fiscal expansion from early 2021 as an anti-recessionary initiative, and again with the *Inflation Reduction Act* from October 2022. The federal budget deficit is expected to remain at about 6 per cent of GDP in 2022/23 despite unemployment being historically low and widely thought to be close to full employment. Strong demand, supply-side constraints and the disruption of trade quickly lifted inflation to over four times the official target of 2 per cent (again see Blanchard and Bernanke 2023). Inflation was transmitted abroad by the strong dollar that was induced by fiscal expansion and monetary tightening. But despite extraordinary fiscal expansion at a time of historically low unemployment, US inflation has been decelerating rapidly through 2023. Some commentators have begun to refer to 'immaculate disinflation' – disinflation without an apparent cause.

China is by far the world's largest producer of manufactured goods and contributes parts of the goods supply chain almost everywhere. It is overwhelmingly Australia's largest trading partner. Within China the COVID-19 lockdowns were maintained until close to the end of 2022, extending supply chain disruption and reductions in productivity across the world. Continued disruption of supply chains through the first year of post-pandemic expansion in the rest of the world magnified the global inflationary impact of increased demand. China's own anti-recessionary policies were more restrained than those in the United States and the rest of the developed world so that the end of lockdowns and easing of supply chain disruptions from early 2023 brought disinflation. Producer prices were falling through 2023 and there was discussion of the possibility of general deflation in the absence of new, expansionary fiscal and monetary policies.

The United States and China have both contributed a great deal to pressure for lower inflation in global goods markets through 2023.

The dislocation of global energy, chemical manufactures and food markets by the Russian invasion of Ukraine in early 2022 came as global post-COVID inflation was at a high point. Over the year and a half since the invasion, much of the old volumes of Russian and Ukraine exports have found their ways onto global markets, returning prices for these goods to close to their pre-invasion levels. Together with easing supply chain conditions generally and global monetary tightening, this brought inflation down through the developed world in 2023. But not as fast as some have hoped and thought necessary to remove the risk of raising inflationary expectations.

Pandemic and subsequent developments in Australia
In Australia, the pandemic recession marked the end of twenty-eight years of continuous growth in total output. Federal and state governments

provided unprecedented levels of income support and extended the provision of health and other services to households and subsidies to businesses. The federal and several state government budget deficits as a share of the economy were far in excess of anything previously known outside the two world wars. Policy interest rates (cash rates) were reduced to their lowest-ever levels, at 0.1 per cent. Australia for the first time adopted a policy of quantitative easing (QE) like that which had been introduced in most developed countries in response to the global financial crisis (GFC) and was introduced in all developed countries during the pandemic recession.

The RBA monetised the huge federal and state deficits through QE. It took the unprecedented step of setting a target for interest rates on multi-year bonds and expressed its expectation that it would keep both cash and medium-term interest rates at record low levels for several years.

Suddenly, the historically high rates of immigration which had occurred during the Dog Days period were replaced by net emigration, which caused a marked decline in labour supply. In combination with massive expansion of demand, this reduced unemployment below 5 per cent by late 2021 and to 3.5 per cent in June 2022. This was lower than for half a century, and down to the levels achieved in the United States immediately before and after the pandemic. It has continued at that level through to the latest data available, for June 2023. There has been no evidence of any upward pressure on real wages in the marketplace that would have signalled that the non-accelerating inflation rate of unemployment (NAIRU) had been reached (Borland 2023).

In mid-2023, record high terms of trade, low unemployment and firm fiscal policy generated the first budget surplus since before the GFC for the financial year 2022/23. Together with high inflation, this reduced public debt as a proportion of the economy far more rapidly than had been anticipated in any official or private forecasts. This is a welcome strength of Australia's current economic circumstances, which expands the range of policy options available to governments.

The US and Australian macroeconomic situations are similar in some ways and starkly different in others. Both countries have low unemployment by the standards of the past half century – 3.5 per cent in Australia and 3.6 per cent in the United States in June 2023. Demand for labour is being driven by contrasting combinations of fiscal and monetary policy. The US federal budget deficit is the highest ever in peacetime at a time of reasonably low unemployment. Australia is running a rare budget surplus. Both countries are running the tightest monetary policies since the GFC: cash rates of 5.25 to 5.5 per cent in the United States and 4.1 per cent in Australia. Total demand relative to labour supply is stronger in the United States: real wages have been rising there and falling in Australia. The different combinations of fiscal and monetary expansion in the two countries mean that Australia is in a stronger position to manage the effects of future economic shocks on intergenerational equity, and they have also contributed to Australia's relatively strong competitiveness in trade-exposed industries. The larger US economy and its issue of the world's international currency insulate it at least for a while from the consequences of policies that would be imprudent in Australia.

What happens next?
The RBA says that any tendency for nominal wages to rise to offset the effects of inflation will require further increases in interest rates. If the RBA's declared approach is the only policy response, we can anticipate continuing low economic growth and perhaps even recession, despite the high immigration and much higher unemployment alongside entrenchment of the declines in real wages.

Australia can do much better than this. We think that policies that lead to a post-pandemic Dog Days would be a mistake.

The first way in which things have gone wrong for the RBA: Running an excessively tight monetary policy

Perhaps the most contentious macroeconomic policy question of this century so far is how far the RBA needs to raise interest rates to bring inflation back within the 2 to 3 per cent target range within a reasonable time. We believe the RBA's approach to this question has been misguided and that the thinking underlying its mistakes goes back some time.

The picture that we painted above of the economy as it came out of the pandemic was of disrupted supply, high demand, high prices for traded goods and high inflation. During 2021, 'year to' inflation rose to nearly 8 per cent[1] and by June 2022, Australia's unemployment rate had fallen to 3.5 per cent.[2] The 'year to' inflation rate was still above 7 per cent at the end of 2022.

The RBA's mistakes about the NAIRU

The RBA leadership had been asserting for many years prior to the pandemic that the NAIRU was over 5 per cent. The 2019 Freebairn Lecture at the University of Melbourne was given by an assistant governor of the RBA, Luci Ellis (Ellis 2019).[3] Ellis noted that the NAIRU had fallen steadily through the 2000s and was still falling at the time she was giving her lecture. She noted that the RBA's own econometric models said that the NAIRU had by this time already fallen to 4.5 per cent. She went on to introduce a number of qualifications that we think are important, in particular that these models did not account either for changes in rates of underemployment or for a weakening of workers' bargaining power. She cautioned that the NAIRU cannot be observed directly, noting that 'you can guess that you are below it if wage growth is accelerating'. The deputy governor of the RBA, Michelle Bullock, explained eloquently in June 2023 the benefits of full employment. But she did not spend time on Ellis's qualifications and stated that unemployment at 4.5 per cent would achieve that desirable condition (Bullock 2023).

The latter number informs an RBA view that for inflation not to accelerate, unemployment needs to be 4.5 per cent or above. For inflation actually to be brought down, in the RBA view, the rate of unemployment needs to be above 4.5 per cent to discipline the wage-fixing process. How much above depends, according to this argument, on the steepness of the Phillips curve.[4]

In fact, unemployment has stayed at more or less the same level – 3.5 per cent – for more than a year, and yet inflation has declined. In the June quarter of 2022 the consumer price index (CPI) increased by 1.8 per cent. At the end of July 2023 – a year later – we learnt that in the June quarter of that year the CPI rose by only 0.8 per cent (ABS 2022, 2023). It is thus not at all clear that the arguments put forward by the RBA leadership are correct.

The NAIRU may already have fallen as low as 3.5 per cent. There are many reasons for thinking this. The first is that, even in current circumstances, there is virtually no industrial action. This appears to be because in Australia at present a very low proportion of the workforce belongs to a union and we have been through a period in which there has been weaker enforcement of labour regulations and laws and a further reduction in wage regulation. Second, real wage growth is being held down by technological change, including the effects of the internet, of more sophisticated and powerful computing and now of artificial intelligence. Third, the very rapid increase in immigration has also helped to hold real wages down.[5] Fourth, a long period without large increases in unemployment from recession disqualifies fewer people from employability on grounds of inadequate previous work experience. Finally, higher underemployment changes the relationship between conventionally defined full employment and pressures for higher wages in the labour market. Jeff Borland's careful analysis of actual labour market conditions, focusing on the last of these features, has pointed to the likelihood that the NAIRU may now be as low as 3.5 per cent (Borland 2021, 2023).

But even if we accept that the NAIRU is now no higher than 3.5 per cent, we need to ask another question in the inflationary conditions of 2023. Does unemployment need to be increased *above* the NAIRU in order to bring inflation down, and in particular to prevent the development of a wage-price spiral? Concerns about the possible emergence of such a spiral have been significant globally (IMF Research Department 2022), as well as in Australia.

Some US evidence may shed light on how to think about this question for Australia. In their widely noticed econometric analysis of recent inflation in the United States, Olivier Blanchard and Ben Bernanke (2023) demonstrate two important things. First, they show convincingly that the shocks to inflation in the United States were transitory rather than permanent: that is, they were mainly 'external' shocks that disrupted both demand and supply of all of goods, services and labour, rather than shocks 'internal' to the labour market. Second, US inflation expectations – both through the pandemic and subsequently – remained partly anchored at a low level. Although the very great increase in inflation in 2021 and 2022 appears to have given rise to a sudden upward move in shorter-term inflation expectations, it does not appear to have dislodged longer-term inflation expectations, which have remained very close to the 2 per cent inflation target. In a thought-provoking study, Tomas Michl and Bob Rowthorn (2023) argue that, in such circumstances, merely keeping unemployment at the NAIRU, to prevent inflation from coming under pressure to accelerate, may well be enough to bring inflation down quite quickly, simply because people expect it to come down.

We think that similar circumstances are likely to be relevant in Australia. In Australia's case, the appropriate policy for bringing inflation back down towards its target is not one of seeking to create more unemployment in order to exert discipline on the wage-bargaining process, as argued by Governor Lowe and Governor-elect Bullock. Instead, what matters is that policy ensures that inflation expectations are not dislodged and that these expectations remain at least partly anchored on the inflation target. The necessary containment of inflationary expectations, as well as of inflation itself, is being greatly assisted by the fall during 2023 of the prices for many traded goods that had lifted sharply through the post-pandemic expansion and the Russian invasion of Ukraine.

If anti-inflationary policy is to be conducted in this way, then communications will play a critical role. The RBA will need to make it absolutely clear that it is determined to ensure that the target level for the rate of inflation will not be allowed to slip, even if the return to target takes a number of years. They will do this more credibly if public statements on monetary policy are calibrated accurately against observable economic realities. Such an approach to policy is likely to assist not only in the task of establishing full employment with moderate inflation. It may well also help to hold the NAIRU at a low level, and perhaps even contribute to its continuing fall. This will be a quite different approach to anti-inflation policy from the one being pursued at present.

A gradual approach to returning to the target range of inflation will be essential if unnecessary increases in unemployment are to be avoided. This is because there are strong economic reasons to expect higher-than-average increases in nominal wages for some time. The very rapid inflation over the past two years has led to an unprecedentedly large contraction in real wages. While the CPI increased by 12.35 per cent over the two years to March 2023, the official wage price index indicates that average wages rose by only 6.2 per cent – a fall by 5.8 per cent in average real wages (ABS 2022, 2023). Official forecasts anticipate continued substantial reductions in real wages after March 2023, at least until the end of 2023. But when the economy settles down after this inflationary episode we can expect the level of real wages to return to near its level before the pandemic, because there has been no change in structural relationships in the economy that would point to a reduction of 6 per cent and more in the equilibrium real wage.[6] The low rate of productivity growth means that it may not end up at a level much higher than this, but there is no reason to expect an absolute decline. For such an outcome, wages must grow faster than prices for a period of time. This will be a period in which the increases in traded goods prices that initiated the general inflation will be lower than they had been earlier, and this moderation will be placing downward pressure on the general price indexes. But the natural tendency for money wages to catch up with past inflation means that the inflation rate is likely to come down less rapidly than it would otherwise have done. The calls by Governor Lowe for wage increases to remain below price increases do not seem to recognise the importance of this readjustment process.

In a careful study, Isaac Gross and Andrew Leigh (2022), using the RBA's MARTIN model, find that the interest rate was kept too high during the period from 2016 to 2019, so that during that time inflation fell below the RBA's target band. The authors did this by comparing actual monetary policy decisions to a counterfactual in which the interest rate was set according to an optimal simple rule. They suggest that optimal monetary policy in that period would have required a substantially lower interest rate and would have led to significantly better employment outcomes. 'The failure to implement optimal monetary policy cost the equivalent of approximately 270,000 people being out of work for a year' (Gross and Leigh 2022).

Gross and Leigh confine their analysis to 2016–19, but the phenomenon of unnecessary unemployment was also present at least over the several immediately preceding years. However, the RBA's MARTIN model has embedded assumptions about the NAIRU which we believe are probably inappropriate, for reasons we have already discussed. Bishop and Greenland (2021) note that there is too little data and the data change too much over time for us to be confident about results that are obtained from regressions using historical national time series, as the models do. They themselves draw upon larger numbers of observations using regional data and estimate a lower NAIRU. We think they were right at that time and would be right by a wider margin now. Consequently, the excess unemployment caused by the RBA during the period from 2016 to 2019 would have been larger than the figure quoted above.

The RBA's mistakes about interest rates in the pandemic recession
We make two points.

First, it was a mistake to set interest rate targets other than the cash rates that had hitherto been the focus of policy. Rates for multi-year bonds are necessarily set in deep global markets. Unlike cash rates, they are not within the control of the RBA. It is not surprising that market developments overwhelmed the RBA targets in less than a year, and the policy was cancelled. It was also a mistake to announce an expectation that cash rates would remain at 0.1 per cent until 2024. The future is inherently unpredictable. A central bank loses credibility when it announces an expectation that is soon rendered obsolete by changes in economic circumstances.

Second, the RBA also appears to have the wrong view that the 'natural' or 'neutral' interest rate – that interest rate which is neither expansionary nor contractionary and is consistent with full employment and steady low inflation – is substantially positive. This vew is leading them to a belief that there will be no cost in taking nominal interest rates back to levels that would be substantially above the inflation rate, once that inflation rate is back within its target range. In these circumstances, the RBA seems to think it is simply restoring a normal real cash rate that would have to be re-established sooner or later. The reality is very different: the neutral real cash rate may not be significantly positive for as far ahead as we can see. Of course, this has massive implications for whether the interest rate is being set at the right level at present.

The RBA view ignores the fact that real long-term interest rates, set in capital markets, have been falling steadily for several decades, with an acceleration following the GFC (Blanchard 2023). Real interest rates for low-risk debt are much lower than they have been over at least 700 years, excepting only the inflation with suppressed interest rates during the twentieth century's two world wars (Blanchard 2023). This reflects underlying tendencies in supply and demand for capital: tendencies to lower investment shares in expenditure and higher savings shares in income. The strengthening of these tendencies since the GFC has led to discussion of 'secular stagnation' by Summers (2020) and others. The maintenance of full employment and economic growth at an optimal rate requires real interest rates on low-risk debt of zero or below – and even with zero real interest rates may require large public deficits. Even the immense US, Japanese and other budget deficits of the post-pandemic period have not lifted the neutral real interest rate in developed countries to somewhere above zero.

The IMF speaks of interest rates staying 'lower for longer'.[7] Olivier Blanchard's widely noticed book *Fiscal Policy Under Low Interest Rates* (2023) structures discussion of optimal fiscal policy around expectations that the neutral real interest rate in developed countries will stay near or below zero. This structure is built on the assessment that long-term interest rates will remain low for a long time. We agree with Blanchard.

We are discussing a world phenomenon. But these global developments will have a profound influence on long-term interest rates in Australia, with its deep integration into global capital markets.

Our view that the natural real interest rate is near zero and likely to remain there is not contradicted by the very rapid rise in nominal interest rates which has occurred in the recent past. The inflationary pressures which we describe above have required policymakers to raise interest rates very quickly – although until recently they have remained well below contemporary inflation rates. The forces determining long-term real interest rates, which we briefly described a few paragraphs ago, are very different from those determining interest rates in the recent past, which have reflected the current inflationary pressures.

There is no discussion in the RBA review of the RBA's perception of the 'neutral' interest rate – the real cash rate at which savings and investment are in balance with full employment and moderate inflation. That rate is well below RBA calculations in recent years. This misconception has distorted RBA perceptions. There is an intriguing statement in the review's executive summary that there is 'uncertainty' about future neutral interest rates in a world of growing inequality and demographic change.

There is no acknowledgement that these and other factors have led to the certainty of a lower neutral rate.

The second way in which things have gone wrong for the RBA: A failure to adequately cooperate

In our view, the RBA's biggest error was in running tighter monetary policy than the rest of the world in the seven years before the pandemic, at a time when the Australian economy was not in a strong enough position. Inflation by all relevant measures was on average below the target range over this period. This relatively firm monetary policy caused the Australian dollar exchange rate to be high. The high exchange rate had a large impact on trade-exposed industries other than resources early in the period. Unemployment stayed well above the lowest level consistent with low inflation during this whole period. A failure of coordination of monetary with prudential (APRA) and fiscal (Treasury) policy contributed to the mistakes.

Between 2013 and 2019, there was some public discussion from time to time of the RBA being inhibited in lowering interest rates, not because it thought that unemployment was below the NAIRU but because it was concerned about the systemic risks associated with high levels of borrowing for housing and the associated housing asset boom. Gross and Leigh pick up this point in relation to their discussion of the period between 2016 and 2019: 'the RBA was concerned about financial stability and accordingly set interest rates higher than inflation and unemployment alone would warrant'. They are very critical of such a policy stance. They say that, on this point, the literature is remarkably clear-cut. 'A strategy of using monetary policy to constrain asset price growth, dubbed leaning against the wind, has been found generally to fail any reasonable cost benefit test' (Gross and Leigh 2022).

Gross and Leigh do not discuss the even greater waste of resources in the earlier period from 2013 to 2016. The period following on from the end of the China resources boom in 2012 saw a large fall in the terms of trade and mining investment. This was also a period in which there was sustained fiscal consolidation of 1 per cent per annum over six years – a massive withdrawal of aggregate demand by fiscal policy – at the very time when external demand for exports had fallen significantly. A number of people, including Stephen Grenville in his submission to the RBA review, have criticised this fiscal consolidation. During this period, the RBA recognised that aggregate demand in the economy was too weak to generate satisfactory levels of economic activity, and the RBA governor at various times urged the federal government to loosen its fiscal stance.

Others have argued that this fiscal contraction was appropriate and necessary, given how public sector debt had been massively increased in the response to the GFC, and given the exposure of the Australian economy to significant international shocks. But whatever one's view about the fiscal position, this was a time when aggregate demand was contracting very significantly. Lower policy interest rates would have directly facilitated demand expansion and led to higher incomes and investment in the trade-exposed sector via a lower exchange rate.

Apparently there were significant discussions about this issue within the RBA throughout the period from 2013 to 2019. According to one view, the lower interest rates which would have been economically appropriate would have led to a damaging increase in asset prices, which APRA would have been powerless to prevent. A second view was that APRA should have been trusted to fulfil its prudential task. The first view appears to have had more influence. Greater cooperation between the Treasury, Reserve Bank and APRA would have produced a much better outcome.

Would the recommendations of the RBA review have actually helped?

Our answer to this question is: not very much. The review makes recommendations on structure and process. Some of the institutional reforms recommended by the review have merit. But it is not obvious to us how they would have led to superior economic outcomes, except in one important respect which we identify below.

Overall, we are comfortable with the review's restatement of monetary policy objectives to give equal and exclusive weight to full employment and price stability. Actually, the equal weighting of currency stability and full employment is already in the law under which the RBA operates, which was legislated by the Menzies government in 1959. The exchange of letters between governors and treasurers since 1996 has been interpreted as, and may have led in practice to, inflation being given priority over employment. The review's approach simply restores respect for the established law.

However, the review barely touches the performance of the economy. It shows that inflation and unemployment have been lower on average over the past three decades of flexible inflation targeting than in the two preceding decades. True enough. But there is no comparison with the two decades that preceded the past five, when performance was far superior. And it treats the last three decades as a single period by averaging them, and so hides the distinctive underperformance of Australia after 2013. In particular, the review does not assess underperformance on unemployment compared with the United States and some other developed countries over the past decade.

In fact, the review says much too little about the failings in monetary policymaking which we have discussed in some detail in this paper. The review also says too little about the coordination of monetary policy and fiscal policy. And it says almost nothing about the interaction of monetary policy with other areas of policymaking. In particular, given the mistakes we described earlier, we think it a weakness of the review that it did not make recommendations for the reintegration of prudential and monetary policy – the return to the RBA of the prudential function, from whence it was taken two decades ago.

We now turn to the discussions in the RBA review of institutional culture and its recommendations about structure and decision-making processes. Here, we have three points to make.

Independence

We think there are advantages in independence and believe these have been fully realised over these past decades. Nevertheless, the existing legislation gives government the power to overrule RBA decisions – providing, however, that the government follows a set of carefully specified procedures. The review recommends ending this power. In our view that would be a mistake.

The relevant current provision of the legislation governing the RBA had its origin in the Commonwealth Bank's resistance to Treasurer Theodore and the Scullin government's (as it turns out, well-judged) expansionary policies, supported by currency devaluation. It is now widely accepted that the costs and distress of the Great Depression in Australia would have been substantially less if the Theodore/Scullin policies had not been blocked by the chairman of the Commonwealth Bank, Sir Robert Gibson. Lessons were carried from that experience through Chifley's participation in the Royal Commission on Banking in the 1930s, and then by Coombs' advice to the Menzies government on the wording in the current law.

The law allows for the government to override the RBA on a policy matter but requires it to provide an explanation to the parliament. That power has never been used, although we note former treasurer Keating's recent statement that he once threatened its use (Hutchens 2023). Since the governorship of Bernie Fraser during the Keating prime ministership (1991–96), there has been an understanding that the RBA would act independently, and that it would seek to hold inflation at an average of 2 to 3 per cent over time. This understanding has taken the form of a written agreement since the exchange of letters between Governor Ian Macfarlane and Treasurer Peter Costello in 1996. Of course, no such agreement between two parts of executive government can override the law.

In our view, the current arrangements have the relationship where it should be. In normal circumstances, the government leaves the RBA to do its job independently. However, if the democratically elected government forms the view that the RBA is wrong, and wrong to an extent that warrants taking the political risk of explaining to parliament and therefore the community why it thinks the RBA's action is wrong, it would be anti-democratic for the government to be blocked from acting in what it judges to be the national interest. In this context, we note that the strong commitment to the idea that governments should never have any role in monetary policy was brought into the policy discussion of the democratic world by the Austro-Hungarian economists with their roots in a pre-democratic political economy (see Chapter 3).

Separating 'governance' from 'monetary policy'

We see no harm and possibly some good in the separation of the governance responsibilities of the RBA from the Monetary Policy Committee (MPC). If there is such a governing board, it should be clearly superior to the Monetary Policy Board (MPB).

What would the governance board actually do? At the Bank of England, the Court has prestige but does not do much. It oversees compliance with the law and management of conflicts of interest, looks after the Mint, organises surveillance of the gold reserves, and provides supervision over bank pensions and terms of employment. All this might become possible in the case of the RBA governing board. A Canadian expert, David Dodge, has said to us that having such a board in the Bank of Canada has been valuable.

A Monetary Policy Committee

We see merits in the shifting of responsibility for monetary policy from a board of generalists to a board with greater specialist expertise in monetary analysis and policy. The authors of the review argue that this would lead to a better understanding by the board of the options for policy, to better discussions at board level, and better actual decisions about policy. We agree that their proposals might lead to such an outcome, if amended in the way we suggest below. Doing this might help the RBA to avoid making the kinds of mistakes which we have described in this chapter.

We think it a good thing that the review recommends that the secretary of the treasury remains a member of the board, in their personal capacity. But we see a large problem in finding in our small country six external economists with the necessary specialist expertise and practical experience – especially if they are to be rotated periodically in the way of well-managed boards. Care would have to be taken about conflicts of interest between board members with continuing access to RBA staff, expertise and data, and their part-time commercial employment. That leaves economists employed by universities and specialist research institutions, and people with the appropriate expertise who are prepared to avoid conflicting commercial employment (perhaps parents temporarily out of the full-time labour force, people retired from public or private sector employment or employed in non-commercial private roles). The relevant qualifications must include wisdom on the operation of the real economy. Knowledge and experience are necessary to participate helpfully in discussions of monetary policy. And confident judgement may be required when the real-world economy is generating outcomes that diverge from the output of econometric models.

It may be realistic to find two suitable academics and two other appropriately qualified people with no current commercial roles as board members on a continuing basis. We doubt that more people than that of the required quality would be available on a continuing basis. If there were four RBA appointees, plus the governor as chair, a dynamic with four external appointees could work well, so long as the externals had access to the data and knowledge of RBA employees, and staff support to carry out their own investigations, and so long as a political culture of open discussion was established anew. This is the setup in relation to the MPC in the United Kingdom. If only three appropriately qualified external members were available, the number of RBA full-time employees could be reduced to three, plus the governor as chair. The proposal made in the review for six external members of the board, and only the governor and their deputy from within the RBA, seems wildly unbalanced, since it would deprive the discussions of the detailed knowledge that senior internal officials can bring.

We are sure that one day a week is too short a period of time for the external members of the MPB, who are meant to be expert in the details of the models and the data, to devote to the task. There was no explicit statement about this in relation to the MPC in the United Kingdom when it was established, but the amount which the members of the MPC are paid, and the expectations of what they are to do, means that it is thought of as a three-day-a-week position. Not full-time but much more than a day a week. It has been said to us that very few of the existing six external members of the RBA board would be prepared to devote three days a week to membership of an MPB. But maybe that says something about the kind of person that needs to be found to serve on the board.

The review suggests that external board members should be required periodically to make their own public statements about monetary policy. If this recommendation is adopted in practice, care will need to be taken that public discussion of economic policy is not dominated by reporting of divergences of view within the MPC, at a large cost to coherence in policymaking and communications on policy, and to the exclusion of debate over issues that are fundamentally important to the Australian standard of living.

Improved development and coordination of policy

It is clear that the large mistakes of the RBA that have contributed to economic underperformance will need to be corrected by improvements in economic analysis and discussion. The RBA review makes useful suggestions as to how this might be done, with its proposal for greater research capacity on the macro-economy, greater external interaction with stronger economic research institutions outside the RBA, and joint use of the output of this research by both the Treasury and the RBA.

Such developments would help to improve thinking about policy, and also help lead to better coordination between fiscal and monetary policy and to better cooperation across a number of areas of policymaking.

A central requirement will be the strengthening of the professional capacity of Treasury and other policy departments, after a decade of cuts in recruitment and staffing numbers and outsourcing of policy analysis and advice to private consulting groups. The denuding of professional capacity was much less important in the RBA than within the economic policymaking departments of state; the RBA was able to protect its access to professional resources, while other areas of policymaking were vulnerable to decisions on arbitrary reductions in numbers of officials across the board.

However, the biggest changes required if Australia is to achieve sustainably full employment with rising incomes for a growing population are in the wider economic policy discussion. An RBA fit for the future will help. But it will not avoid the need for clearer coordination of policymaking across a range of policymaking institutions to do with all of: trade policy, competition policy, labour market policy, and policies to do with climate and energy.

Beyond this there is a need for clearer public discussion of the fundamental policy choices facing Australia. In particular, it is necessary, for a strengthening of the national democratic culture, to allow leaders committed to the Australian national interest to pursue that interest with wide comprehension of what is at stake across the community. In this wider context, improving the performance of the RBA is a necessary condition for success, but far from the only condition.

Some observers are resistant to this argument, claiming that interest rates depend fundamentally on monetary policy and on the risk premia set in financial markets. That is, of course, true in the short run, in the way that we have discussed, especially at times of supply constraints and demand surges, and at times of crisis when the risk premia imposed by financial markets may well be large. But as we have discussed, when crisis is over, and inflation is back under control, then it is the supply of savings and the demand for investment that will matter for the determination of interest rates. This is fundamentally because monetary policymakers will need to set interest rates which ensure that these two things are in balance so as to ensure full employment without inflation, and – of course – because pandemic-related risk premia will have largely adjusted in those circumstances.

8

FREE TRADE AND A TAX ON RENT*

It's remarkable that the Henry George Society has an annual dinner and lecture 132 years after the great man visited Melbourne and Sydney. We don't have a Parkes, Reid or Lyne lecture. Those three premiers of New South Wales through the 1890s were substantial historical figures. Neither do we have a lecture to remember any of the five Victorian premiers of that decade. In this chapter, I will explain why the ideas George explained all that time ago warrant our attention today. They remain relevant to Australian democratic prosperity.

Bede Nairn's brief entry on George in the *Australian Dictionary of Biography* marks George down as a minor figure. That's not right. George's *Progress and Poverty* sold several million copies. There is no near comparator for a book about economics. The world population then was one-fifth of what it is today and the literate proportion of the total much smaller.

The main ideas in George's work seem to me to be broadly right now, as they were then. George supported free trade. That's as important now as ever for global development and Australia's prosperity and place in the world. He wanted to tax land and other rent as the main source of government revenue. Rent taxes raise revenue without sacrifice of total

---

* This chapter was originally presented as the 132nd Henry George Oration on 7 September 2023 in Melbourne.

income and output. Back then, Australian discussion of rent focused on the great agricultural and pastoral properties that had passed into private ownership with small payments unrelated to actual economic value.

Governments spend a lot more now than then. Then there was no Medicare. No government then thought about spending $369 billion on nuclear submarines. It may have been realistic to think of rent taxes raising most government revenue back in the 1890s. We need other sources of taxation today, but we would be better governed if taxation of rent contributed a much higher proportion of the total.

George also wanted to promote competition and break up monopolies whenever possible. He noted that some economic activities are not suitable for competition and so are natural monopolies. It wouldn't be economically efficient to have multiple electricity suppliers running multiple transmission lines down the same street. George wanted natural monopolies to be held in public ownership. Railways were the most important natural monopolies in the 1890s.

Where the activities of one firm impose costs on others, George wanted to tax them to deter the activities and balance the cost. That's relevant to climate change: markets will deliver poor outcomes for society without taxation of the costs that one firm's carbon emissions impose on others.

Australia had a very good carbon price for two years, from 1 July 2012 to 30 June 2014. I've worked on many areas of public policy over a lot of years and have learnt that modelling of economic effects of new policy is usually only the roughest of guides to what actually happens. In the case of carbon pricing, the modelling jointly for my Climate Change Review and the Commonwealth Treasury predicted outcomes accurately: the increases in prices of goods and services as reflected in the Consumer Price Index; the tax cuts and social security increases to make sure that there was no reduction of real incomes for people on low and middle incomes; the assistance for trade-exposed and emissions-intensive industries; and the reductions in emissions.

The Gillard government, through Minister for Climate Change Greg Combet, reached agreement with the European Union to merge the Australian and European emissions trading schemes from 1 July 2015. The second Rudd government brought the date forward to 1 July 2014. That would have equalised carbon prices in Australia and Europe; provided Australia with secure access to European markets for products of what we are now recognising as Superpower industries; and ensured that competitors in third countries who were not facing similar incentives to reduce emissions did not receive an unfair advantage. Prime Minister Abbott got rid of carbon pricing the day before we were due to join the EU ETS, on 30 June 2014.

Without the Abbott Blot, the Commonwealth government could be collecting many tens of billions a year from the ETS with today's European carbon price and exchange rate, and this year's expected Australian carbon volumes. We could pay for the nuclear submarines with less than half the proceeds of the carbon price from the time of the announcement of the agreement with the United States and United Kingdom, and first delivery of a vessel. We would pay for Medicare with much left over to go towards the NDIS. We could cut every personal tax rate from the highest to the lowest by over a fifth. Some members of the Australian parliament support raising the GST rate to pay for cuts in income tax rates. Reintroducing the European-linked carbon price would give all the presumed economic benefits of a higher GST – and efficiently reduce carbon emissions as a bonus.

We wouldn't raise those many tens of billions per annum forever from a carbon price. The government wants Australia to have net-zero emissions by 2050. The carbon price revenue would phase out over a generation. In a talk to the Melbourne Energy Institute earlier today, I said we would be richer if we got to zero emissions by 2035. If we did, the carbon revenue would phase out more quickly. In the meantime, it would pay for a lot of tax reform.

In the past, the government finances have had to pay for tax reform. When John Howard introduced the GST, the compensating income-tax cuts and expenditure increases cost over 1 per cent of GDP more than the GST raised. In today's GDP, that's an increase in the budget deficit of more than $25 billion to make the GST package politically more acceptable. The really hard part of tax reform to improve equity and increase efficiency is the transition. Carbon price revenue that fell to zero as we removed carbon emissions could fund the transition to a more equitable and economically efficient taxation system. By the time we had zero net emissions and so ceased to receive revenue from carbon pricing in 2035 or 2050, the new and more efficient tax system would be generating large economic benefits that would make their own case for continuing with it.

George's protection or free trade, rent and the historical Australian case for protection

Back in 1986, Kym Anderson and I published a book on Australian protection. We noted George's influence in the attractive policies of the NSW Free Trade governments supported by Labor in the 1890s. The young Labor Party was strongly committed to a more equitable distribution of income and wealth. Premier Reid and the Free Trade governments secured the support of the Labor Party by collecting more revenue from sale and leasing of land and using part of that to introduce Australia's first old-age pensions and some other social security payments. Victoria headed in another direction, favouring protection and collecting less revenue from land. That led to a battle between Free Trade and NSW interests led by Reid and Protection and Victorian interests led by Deakin through the first decade of Federation.

There's no doubt about the Georgist influence on the excellent innovations in trade and financial policy in New South Wales in the 1890s. And there's no doubt about the Georgist influence through Marion and Walter Griffin on the financial model applied to Canberra from its commencement in 1927. The Griffins supported Henry George's views on land taxation. Canberra had in place for several decades a fiscal system with no private freehold land, long leases of land from the government, and payments for land leases that were adjusted periodically to reflect economic value. Prime Minister John Gorton corrupted the arrangements in the disappointed hope of winning the Canberra seat in the House of Representatives. In the twenty-first century, only the teals, independents, Greens and Labor win Canberra seats. I hope that John Gorton's ghost regrets his 1969 policy.

Free trade became anathema or curiosity or joke to most Australians in the generations that followed Federation. Hancock's marvellous book *Australia*, published almost a century ago, has a chapter about Australia's love of protection. Australians loved even the word itself with all its friendly connotations.

Three economists from Tasmania – Giblin, Brigden and Copland – and one other were commissioned to write a report on the Australian Tariff for the Bruce government. The Brigden Report actually advised caution on the level of the tariff. But it is famous for developing what came to be known as the Australian case for protection. The idea is that in a country whose main exports depended on land, protection effectively placed a tax on export revenue and therefore on the rent of land used to produce exports. It increased demand for labour in the import-competing industries. Increased demand for labour either put upward pressure on wages or allowed employment of more immigrants. Protection was an indirect tax on rent, which paid for higher wages or more employment and immigration.

The logic of the Brigden Report is sound as far as it goes. But it misses the point that if higher wages and employment are the goal, you could get more at the same cost to owners of the land used for exports, or the same amount at less cost to exporters, if you tax rent directly and use the proceeds directly to support labour in one form or another.

Protection in practice was very costly for Australia. On the eve of World War I we had the highest average real incomes and wages in the world. People in other economically advanced countries wrote about Australia being the working man's paradise. We lost that favourable position through our poor economic performance as protection rose between the wars. Per capita real income in the United States and several other countries rose above levels in Australia. The slide down the per capita real income table continued after World War II. Gradually economists and others noticed that protection was contributing to the slow rate of increase in living standards relative to other developed countries. The critique of protection grew from the 1960s. The Whitlam government implemented the 25 per cent tariff cut in 1973 but introduced new protectionist measures when unemployment rose for other reasons in 1974 and 1975. The Fraser government greatly increased protection in the most protected industries, mainly through quantitative restrictions on trade.

The Hawke government opened the Australian economy by combining economically efficient trade policies with use of the budget to raise general living standards. It reintroduced Medicare after its abolition by the Fraser government. It extended and strengthened the social security system, including through expanded family payments. The Keating government extended the superannuation system to cover almost all workers. There was a big increase in expenditure on education, with large increases in the proportion of children finishing high school, and the proportion going on to tertiary education. In response, total factor productivity grew faster than in any other developed country in the 1990s for the first time since Federation.

Despite the successes from the reform era of the late twentieth century, Australians tired of open trade. We have been drifting back to protection in recent years. If we partially reverse the reform policies that gave us sustainable increases in living standards, don't be surprised if we reverse the increases in living standards as well. I don't cite Milton Friedman on everything but he's sound on free trade. Here is Friedman citing George: 'It's a very interesting thing that in times of war we blockade our enemies in order to prevent them getting goods from us. In times of peace we do to ourselves by tariffs that which we do to our enemies in times of war.'

Samuelson, Solow and the erasure of land rent in neoclassical economics

Kym Anderson and I discussed the Australian and international literature on the Australian case for protection in that book four decades ago.
Marion Crawford Samuelson published an article that put the Australian case clearly. Then her husband, Paul Samuelson, the most influential
American economist in those decades, developed an elegant neoclassical model that purported to present the Australian case for protection.
In the model, in a country that had an abundance of capital and a shortage of labour relative to the rest of the world, protection would shift the
distribution of income towards labour as anticipated in the Australian
case for protection. But Samuelson's model was a huge oversimplification of what had been a different Australian case. There was no land
in the Samuelson model, yet the core of the Australian case was that
protection operated as an indirect tax on land. Samuelson omitted land
from his simple and elegant model because the algebra didn't work if you
included a fixed factor of production.

Samuelson was a colleague at the Massachusetts Institute of Technology of the young economist Bob Solow. Solow was working on a theory
of economic growth based on the Samuelson-type neoclassical model, in
which there was free movement of capital and labour, automatic adjustment of labour and capital to changes in wages and interest rates (and
therefore no unemployment) and no land.

At the same time, in the 1950s, Trevor Swan at the Australian National
University was working on growth models of a similar kind (Vines, forthcoming 2025). Swan and Solow are recognised as having both developed
the model that is the foundation of subsequent growth theory. Swan tried
to keep land in his model to make it more realistic. He recognised that
economic growth would be associated with rising land rents and their
effects on income distribution and the growth process.

Solow's model without concern for a fixed factor of production was
simpler, more elegant and less realistic, and it won the Nobel Prize for

Economic Science. It set economics on a wrong course. Half a dozen years ago my close friend and colleague Max Corden showed me a letter that he had just received from Bob Solow. Six decades after Solow's article, Bob wrote to Max:

> We conventionally allocate all of the value added to either compensation of labour, or return to capital as debt and equity. That would be fine if there were perfect competition. In reality there is a third component, monopoly rent. It gets allocated to labour and capital in unknown proportions. What one would like to see is a three-way breakdown in market return to labour, market return to capital and rent.

The changing role of rent

Henry George in the nineteenth century focused on agricultural and urban land rents in the United States, where rising incomes and a rapidly growing population were raising the rent value of land. Moving from New York to California helped George to recognise the pivotal role of economic rent in economic growth. Growth in population and demand for goods and services in New York had made land more expensive. George foresaw that Californian land would eventually be expensive like New York land. He started to think about how a tax on the increasing value of land could generate value for the community rather than delivering windfall benefits to individuals.

George focused on agricultural and urban land rents. But at other times and in other places other sources of rent have been important. Piketty's *Capital in the Twenty-First Century* presents the results of painstaking statistical work using the official records of the major developed countries. In the couple of decades before the Civil War, half of the value of capital in the southern states of the United States was the capitalisation of the rent value of slaves. At different times in history, different sources of rent have been important.

The rent share of income has become much more important so far in the twenty-first century. We are seeing this in many countries. The rising profit share of national income is especially prominent in Australia. The large increases in the profit share have emerged alongside a falling price of capital in competitive markets. That doesn't happen in that old Solow growth model. In that model, the price of capital falls as the amount of capital rises, the economy adjusts to use more labour-saving technology, and wages rise. A pity that reality doesn't work like the model. More of a pity that much conventional economic policy analysis presumes that the world works like the model and not reality.

Keynes on the falling cost of capital

Ninety-three years ago, John Maynard Keynes, the world's greatest public intellectual in the twentieth century, wrote an essay for his Cambridge students: 'Economic Possibilities for our Grandchildren' (Keynes 1930b). The context of the time was high unemployment; social division; the rise of fascism in Europe; and the attraction of fascism and communism in Britain. It was a time for holding out hope of progress in a capitalist democracy. Keynes discussed the implications of continued capital accumulation and technological progress over the hundred years ahead. Putting aside the effects of unnecessary wars and economic depressions, the economy's productive capacity would increase many times. Savings out of increased income would provide an abundance of capital. Investment would decline as a share of the economy. Capital would be abundant. Interest rates would fall to very low levels. No-one would have a very high income simply because they owned a lot of capital. High incomes would come only from innovation and entrepreneurship – producing new goods, or old ones in more productive ways. Labour would be scarce and expensive. The real rate of return on low-risk investment would be low.

The real rate of return on competitive low-risk investment in the twenty-first century has fallen much as Keynes anticipated. The average interest rate on long sovereign debt in most developed countries has been lower than the inflation rate over the past decade and a half. The real cost of long-term safe debt has been near zero.

In Solow's model, with perfect competition and no rent, this abundance of capital would lead to lower returns on business investment and higher wages. But exactly the opposite has happened. We have experienced wage stagnation, an extraordinary increase in the profit share of income, and higher returns on business investment.

The only explanation for such a divergence between the rate of return on competitive riskless capital and actual business rates of return as reflected in the profit share of GDP is a rise in rent.

What has caused the rise of rent? There is extensive recent literature on this question, especially in the United States. There is also extensive recent literature on the fall in real interest rates in competitive markets.

The increase in the profit share and the fall in the wage share is actually bigger than the statistician makes it look. Executive remuneration is mostly classified in the wages and not the profit share.

There has been an explosion of executive remuneration this century, starting in finance and other high-rent parts of the private sector and extending into the public sector including the universities. It has gone much further in Australia than in Europe or Japan. It emerged in the United States before Australia but has caught up in Australia over the past decade.

Much of the increase in executive remuneration is really the sharing of rent between owners and managers of businesses in rent-rich sectors.

The increase in rent is happening in the other English-speaking developed countries but seems to have gone furthest in Australia. Why?

One reason is the huge growth in the role of minerals and mineral rent in the economy. That followed the growth in Northeast Asian and especially Chinese demand for our minerals. From 2002 until 2012, the then most populous country on Earth experienced the fastest sustained rate of growth over a decade of any substantial country ever. And the Chinese pattern of growth was highly complementary to our resources. Chinese growth required iron, fossil energy, other metallic minerals, wool and other raw materials in immense quantities. There was a huge increase in demand for Australian exports and a big lift in prices and profitability of Australian export commodities, especially the minerals. This was Australia's China resources boom.

The boom eased from 2012 with changes in China's pattern of growth and is changing again post-COVID. But much of the boost to global demand for minerals remained. Prices eased from the giddy heights of 2012 but remained much higher than before the China resources boom. On average and in real terms, the price of iron ore over the last half dozen years is several times as high as it was in 1990s. After all the fluctuations and adjusting for inflation, coal and gas prices in normal conditions are on average also several times their levels in the 1990s. The last year and a half have been abnormal and prices much higher, through the disruptions following the Russian invasion of Ukraine. Prices of many other mineral commodities behaved similarly.

The large miners were making good profits from their established Australian mines in the 1990s, There has been a huge increase in rent for anyone with an established mining business. Already in the 90s, rising demand for minerals in China and other Northeast Asian countries had lifted mining exports to about 5 per cent of Australian GDP. That ratio has increased to 15 per cent since then.

Late last and early this century, exports of manufactures, services, minerals and agricultural products were of similar value. Now minerals are twice the value of exports from all the others put together.

Payments for labour are very much lower for mining than for the other sectors. In the last quarter of 2022, mining profits exceeded those of all other sectors of the Australian economy added together. Yet mining employed only about 2 per cent of the Australian labour force.

Taxing mineral rent

The increase in the annual value of mineral sales since early this century is over $200 billion per annum in today's purchasing power. High proportions of the increase in annual sales value would be rent. The corporate income tax collects a modest minority of the rent for the public revenue. We apply the corporate income tax at 30 per cent of the value of accounting profits – after artificial deductions for costs attributed to offshore 'marketing hubs' and services of other kinds in low-tax countries. A general reduction in the corporate tax rate, as sought by the Business Council of Australia on behalf of big foreign and Australian business, would reduce the tax on mineral rent with very little positive impact on the level of investment or output in the mining industry.

The states have constitutional rights to minerals and powers over mining royalties. They have the rights and responsibilities to require payments from private companies equal to the value of the resources for access to mineral resources. The states apply royalties in various forms and at various rates. These collect rent, but usually take forms that reduce investment and output in marginal activities as well. The rates are generally low, so the balance between avoidance of distortion and collection of rent is calibrated in favour of avoiding distortion.

The Australian system of horizontal fiscal equalisation reduces states' incentives to extract the rent. Under the principles applied by the Commonwealth Grants Commission, the state receiving royalties eventually retains only its national population share of total payments for mineral leasing. Western Australia's objection to this principle led to the Morrison government's agreement on a floor to Western Australia's share of the GST pool. The issue will arise in Queensland as the Grants Commission brings the state's new coal royalties to account in distributing GST revenues. Mining companies now use the redistribution of state royalties under the Commonwealth Grants Commission in arguments against economically rational pricing of access to mineral resources.

Western Australia applies a 5 to 7 per cent royalty to the value of iron ore sales. This might have corresponded to a reasonable share of the mineral rent in the 1990s but represents a small proportion of the total today.

The Queensland government has raised significant total royalties from coal mining from low royalty rates. When coal prices rose strongly in response to the Russian invasion of Ukraine, it raised royalty rates – with a maximum ad valorem rate of 40 per cent applying to a substantial proportion of revenue when prices were at their peaks in 2022 and early 2023. This favourably transformed Queensland budget prospects. A large part of the increased revenue was used to fund energy infrastructure for the transition to zero net emissions. Part was used to shield power users from energy price increases that would otherwise have followed from the Russian invasion of Ukraine. Part strengthened the long-term fiscal position by reducing public debt.

NSW mines contribute a substantial proportion of Australia's coal exports. The government raises significant revenues, but at rates that leave most of the rent with the mining operators. So far governments have chosen not to increase the proportion of rents going to the public revenues as payment for public resources being depleted by mining. (I note that after delivery of this lecture, the NSW government increased coal royalties, although by less than Queensland).

The Commonwealth administers mining leases only offshore. The Hawke government came to office committed to introduce a national resource rent tax. It mostly limited its application to offshore petroleum when the states declined to cooperate for onshore resources. Western Australia joined the Commonwealth to application of a resource rent tax in one onshore petroleum field. The Commonwealth's resource rent tax raised substantial taxation but was rendered much less effective by changes in deductions for processing not directly related to exploration and mining in the early 2000s.

The Henry Tax Review commissioned by the Rudd government proposed the comprehensive taxing of mineral resources by the Commonwealth government. This was linked to a recommendation to lower the rate of corporate income tax. It would have had the effect of shifting a substantial part of the tax burden from the general corporate taxpayer to the mining industry. As minerals prices have turned out, it would also have greatly strengthened the Commonwealth's general fiscal position.

The Henry Review recommendation on resource rent taxation had several weaknesses. It introduced a novel taxation model without the prior public discussion that would have allowed the building of support within the community. The novelty made it easy for vested interests to misrepresent its character and effects. Extensive public discussion and understanding is a precondition for successful reform. And the tax contained one structural weakness. It proposed to balance the 40 per cent tax on positive cash flows (the rate of tax in the Hawke government's resource rent tax), with a payment for unsuccessful exploration and development expenditure. Such a payment for negative cash flows is sound in principle and is a feature of the reform of business taxation that is advocated later in this lecture. But delaying payment until surrender of the mining lease required the investor to believe that the taxation regime would remain stable over a long period. Some would have discounted the value of the payment for the chance of changes in the regime.

There is no more important issue in Australian taxation reform than replacing current arrangements by efficient mineral rent taxation. That requires large analytic effort and effective political leadership. Success would bring high rewards to the Australian polity. I expect that it would bring electoral rewards to the government that is seen as being responsible for a good outcome.

The Henry Review proposals and carbon pricing were both defeated by massive campaigns by vested interests, harnessed by the Commonwealth Opposition of the day led by Tony Abbott. Abbott's electoral success in 2013 is widely interpreted as establishing that vested interests' investment in the political process leads to defeat of proposals for reform in the public interest. This is not a reasonable interpretation of what happened in 2013. Australian democracy remains better than that.

But the distorted public memory inhibits the development of policy in the public interest.

I have spent a lot of time in this lecture on mineral rents. They are more than half the rents in the contemporary Australian economy. I will run through more quickly the other main sources of rents.

The network and intellectual property rents of information technology

The new information technology industries draw rents from two sources – networks with characteristics of natural monopolies; and intellectual property protected by patent. They are the source of much of the increase in global rents in the twenty-first century. Once established, major information technology companies are well protected from new competitors by the usual network economies. Once established, they serve new customers at very low marginal costs and with little incremental fixed expenditure. Their sales account for a large and rapidly growing share of expenditure everywhere. They contribute to the low share of investment in expenditure.

Australia cannot expect to establish a competitive supply of IT services. The ACCC has identified some measures that can improve the competitive environment, without fundamentally changing the oligopolistic structures. We should do what we can to increase competition. More importantly, Australia can ensure that the public revenue receives a reasonable proportion of the rent generated by sales within Australia. This is best achieved by using the cash-flow base for business taxation that is summarised below.

Urban land rents

The increases in land and housing costs in Australia over the past couple of decades have transformed unfavourably the lifetime economic prospects of younger Australians who do not have the support of wealthy relatives. That is a tragedy. There are two sources of higher house prices.

One is the increased rent value of land, which is capitalised in the asset price. The other is the increase in the capital value of a stream of rents that has come with lower interest rates.

It is worth discussing why the rent value of land has increased, as well as how it should be taxed. The value of land in a good urban location is the difference between the cost of the land on the frontiers of the city – the open fields being subdivided on the way to Ballarat, Mandurah and Goulburn – and the value of the land in good locations.

That differential, which sets the value of land in the attractive areas, is very much affected by the quality of transport and communications. We haven't invested in transport infrastructure in line with the growth of our population. We are starting to catch up in recent years but have a long way to go. The new transport infrastructure increases the value of some urban land, while reducing the scarcity or rent value of other property. Taxation on the increases in land values resulting from improvement in transport infrastructure is an important source of public revenue in some of the countries and cities that have managed the transport infrastructure problem best. Changes in urban planning that allow denser housing near the centres of urban employment and the transport nodes will also reduce land scarcity and rents throughout the city.

High population growth from immigration increases the scarcity and rent value of land – especially if it has not been carefully calibrated to expansion of supply of transport, other urban infrastructure and housing. Australia and Canada currently stand out with immigration rates that are extremely high by international and our own historical standards. Immigration brings many benefits for Australians. But the rates since its resumption after COVID have been beyond the capacity of our infrastructure to absorb. It is much of the reason for the extraordinary shortage of housing and increases in land values and rents.

Let's make sure we tax land rents in the public interest, but let's also think more strategically about the contributions of immigration and underinvestment in transport infrastructure to the increases in land prices.

Standard monopoly and oligopoly are more serious here than elsewhere

So the larger role of mining and higher population growth are two large reasons why the rent share of income has risen more in Australia than elsewhere. A third is that standard monopoly and oligopoly are more serious and have deteriorated more in Australia than elsewhere.

Increased concentration of banking business is a large problem. I worked with Hawke on the liberalisation of the financial system in the mid-1980s. That was meant to increase competition. It did for a while. The older participants in this meeting will remember the state banks, the building societies, the credit unions that played a large role in accumulating household savings and providing housing loans forty years ago. Most of them have now been absorbed into the four big banks.

The increased concentration in banking has its parallels in many sectors. Australians have been in denial about increasing oligopoly and the rise of rents. *The Great Reversal* by American academic Thomas Philippon, discussing how much less effective competition is in the United States today than in Europe. Europe has done much better than the United States. Among other things, the European Union has had stronger antitrust laws and enforcement. Philippon says that many countries becoming part of the one market disrupted the organisation and effectiveness of national business lobbies that place pressure on the policy-making and enforcement process.

The problem is much greater in Australia than in the United States and has probably deteriorated more in recent times. In America, there has at least been much serious analysis and discussion of the problem in recent years. Our discussion in Australia hasn't been so rich. There have been lonely minds and contributors in discussion in the Henry George Society, in and around the ACCC, and in our few genuinely independent think tanks.

It is a big step forward that the oligopoly problem has been taken seriously by the Commonwealth Treasury and its ministers. I am encouraged by two splendid speeches on the issues in mid-2023. One was by Andrew Leigh, Minister Assisting the Treasurer on Competition Policy. Leigh was a highly reputed professor of economics at the ANU before entering parliament and is still a highly productive contributor to Australian economic analysis. He spoke about the Australian oligopoly problem at the Conference of Economists in Brisbane in July 2023. Drawing on the international literature, he illuminated the ways in which more powerful oligopoly has increased profit margins and placed downward pressure on wages. The second was by Rod Sims, former chair of the ACCC. He presented data in awful detail on the reduction in numbers of suppliers in many Australian industries, to levels that are inconsistent with effective competition. It is good news that the treasurer established a review of competition policy, to which Leigh and Sims will contribute in different ways. The review had not been released at the time of preparing this book for publication.

Add up all the opportunities for economic reform to reduce economic rents or to tax them efficiently and equitably and you have a transformational economic reform program to increase productivity and equity. Resource rent taxation. Tax on carbon externalities. Tax on land and housing rent – and urban infrastructure and planning and immigration adjustments to reduce urban land rents. Increased competition. And to provide an overarching framework for raising revenue from business rents, the replacement of standard corporate income tax with a tax based on cash flow.

Cash-flow tax

Craig Emerson, Reuben Finighan, Stephen Anthony and I proposed the replacement of the standard business income tax by a cash-flow tax in a paper in the *Australian Economic Review* in December 2020. The cash-flow tax would be a tax on economic rent.

The cash-flow tax, or business rent tax, would:

- allow immediate deduction of any capital expenditure
- provide a cash credit at the tax rate for negative cash flows
- deny any deductions for interest or any other payments for financing
- deny a deduction for imports of services, unless those imports of services related directly to provision of the service within Australia.

The paper proposes various practical details and costings, and suggests transitional arrangements.

On average, companies in competitive businesses would pay little or no tax. The successful would pay tax at the designated rate; the unsuccessful would be reimbursed their losses at the tax rate. Competitive businesses include Australian cities' marvellous restaurants, most of whom struggle to survive, many without surviving. Those who are actually making losses would be reimbursed at the tax rate. Those who are making profits would pay tax.

Companies that are innovating would pay less than under the established corporate income tax. For the innovator with limited secure profits, there is asymmetry between treatment of success and failure. Success is taxed, and failure is not compensated. This is different from the company with a secure flow of rents. If a company with established cash flows makes some investment and is unsuccessful, expenditures are deducted against other income for corporate income tax purposes.

The cash-flow tax also reduces the tax burden on companies that are investing, at the expense of companies that are simply receiving income from past investments.

We calculated, based on public information, that at a 30 per cent tax rate the cash flow would be roughly revenue neutral over time, even if the expected positive effect on investment, innovation and output did not materialise. The suggested transitional arrangements would make it revenue negative in the early years and revenue positive in later years. Any decision on application would require analysis of revenue impacts from information available only to the tax office.

Companies that are innovating and investing at high rates would pay less tax than under current arrangements. Companies that are receiving high rents and not investing much would pay more. The tax is less vulnerable to international tax avoidance than the corporate income tax in its current form.

Now is the time for the cash-flow tax and for other reform measures to make Australia a more prosperous and equitable economy and society and successful democratic polity. There is a lot of work in turning these broad thoughts into a program for effective reform, in explaining and in building support for the program. That is a task for this venerable society in its 133rd year, Prosper Australia. There is a large challenge of political leadership in making it happen.

Some of the policy disappointments of the twenty-first century so far may discourage ambition for Australia. The lesson of our longer history is that our democratic polity is capable of productive change when some Australians are prepared to put the necessary effort into development of ideas, public education and political leadership.

In this chapter, I have pointed to a few indications that after a dark decade, the prospects of reform to increase prosperity and equity in Australia might be turning a little bit. Australians who have been thinking about these problems for a long time can help those prospects turn for the better.

THE ECONOMIC PUBLIC INTEREST
IN A WORLD OF OLIGOPOLY*

The structure of the economy changes gradually. Structural change accelerates from time to time with big social, political, economic and technological events. Over the years, the changes accumulate to an extent that renders some old approaches to analysis unreliable and misleading. Most observers notice some unexpected outcomes, make small adjustments within familiar approaches to policy, and are surprised when we do not see the expected improvements in understanding and anticipation of change. Bigger minds realise that something important has changed and develop new analytic frameworks.

So it was with Adam Smith at the beginning of modern economic development; with Marshall and the founders of neoclassical economics rewriting the classical approaches that had led to the dismal conclusions of Malthus and Marx; and with the Keynesian revolution from the 1930s.

Sometimes innovative thinkers realise that structural relationships have changed, but don't see the whole of the new world and prescribe incomplete remedies which make some problems worse while contributing to easing others. So it was with the influential Austro-Hungarian

---

* This chapter was first published in *Economic Papers* 43(1), March 2024. It is an edited version of the 2023 Bannerman Competition Lecture, 3 May 2023, Sydney, hosted by the ACCC and the Law Council of Australia. The author acknowledges the numerous discussions with David Vines.

response to stagflation from the 1970s, from von Mises via Hayek and Friedman, with political economy roots in Emperor Franz Joseph's empire and its glittering capital Vienna (Garnaut 2023, and Chapter 3).

Big trends in economic development and thought about economic policy are sometimes global in their reach, or shared across substantial parts of the world economy. But there are always national variations on the global themes. Unusual national institutions and structural characteristics require different frameworks for thinking about the economy and approaches to policy. Successful policy requires national differences to be reflected in ideas about policy. Thus there is an Australian national history of ideas about economic development, interacting with the global narratives and relating well or poorly to the Australian reality through different historical periods.

Most of the value of economics is generated in the fresh thinking every now and then – both globally and nationally. The rest, occupying the working lives of most economists, is incremental adjustment to established interpretations of reality. The marginal adjustment works well enough until big structural change again requires more fundamental re-examination of how it all works.

The modern Australian economy was born rich, with its abundant natural resources relative to population, and economic institutions adapted creatively from the young industrial revolution in its British homelands. It never faced the pressures on living standards from growth in the labour force that overwhelmed improvements in productivity through the first generations of the industrial revolution in Europe. Democracy with a broad franchise emerged earlier in Australia and New Zealand than in the European and later American heartlands of the industrial revolution. The Australian Settlement of economic institutions and policy in the early twentieth century was a creative response to our labour scarcity and to our democracy with a nearly universal franchise.

There have been big changes over the twenty-first century that greatly affect Australia's capacity to deliver rising standards of living to most citizens in a growing population. One major component of those changes has been a large increase in economic rent as a proportion of national income. The increased mining share of income has contributed an important part of the rise of rent but not the whole. Its consequences have included a historic shift in income distribution, and a contribution to a decline in the rate of productivity growth. Together, a shift in income distribution and lower productivity growth have contributed to stagnation, and recently decline, in real disposable income of wage-earners. The downward pressures on real wages and their large political implications have come later than in the United States and United Kingdom but are now evident.

In the past, high terms of trade (that is, high export prices relative to import prices) have been associated with pressures for higher real wages. Australian terms of trade over the past year have been higher than ever before. Yet real wages in Australia fell more through 2020/21 and 2021/22 than in any other two-year period in our history. The profit share of income is higher than ever, and the wages share lower.

On average, the Australian economy has performed reasonably well since flexible inflation targeting was introduced in the early 1990s. But that average includes the extraordinarily strong performance in the 1990s after the recession of 1990–91. It hides close to the lowest growth in productivity, output per person and real per capita household income among developed countries over the past decade.

To understand these developments, we must look afresh at the role of economic rent. After we have come to understand the changes in the structure of the economy that have produced these outcomes, we can see how restoration of economic dynamism and growth in ordinary Australians' standards of living is going to require policy coordination across parts of the economy that have been thought about and managed separately.

My special focus on policy related to management of economic rent has close relevance to competition law and policy. But I will look at competition law in a wider context.

Productive responses to large structural change require contributions from many institutions in different areas of policy, and coordination across them. As John Maynard Keynes once said, we need an orchestra with a range of instruments, and a good conductor. At such times we can admire a virtuoso performance on a single instrument, but it will not realise the potential of the time and place.

Competition policy is an important instrument and the ACCC an important player in the response to the increasing role of rents. They will have their greatest value as part of the orchestra with that good conductor. Excessive focus on one instrument and one player leaves out the many advantages of calling on a whole orchestra. Let me make the point with reference to energy prices and competition in the energy market.

Higher oil, gas and electricity prices were the largest contributors to a higher consumer price index (CPI) over 2022/23 – electricity prices up over 15 per cent and gas over 26 per cent. The RBA with interest rates as its only instrument thinks of raising them. How would a conductor who could call on any policy instrument go about reducing upward pressure on domestic energy prices? She wouldn't think of raising interest rates first or second, or maybe at all. She would be aware that for many household users of power, the charges for using poles and wires represent about half the power bill. Prices are regulated by arrangements that guarantee specified rates of return on past investment. The rates of return rise with higher interest rates, so higher interest rates feed directly into higher power prices. To the extent that higher interest rates reduce demand for power – and the RBA sees rising interest rates reducing inflation because they reduce demand – the reduced use of a fixed quantum of investment in poles and wires requires an increase in prices to compensate for lower volumes of sales. The conductor with access to all the orchestra's instruments would look at regulatory arrangements that set prices for the distribution and transmission of power.

In addition to the cost of poles and wires, the remainder of the cost of electricity to users is in the generation of wholesale electricity, and the costs and profit margins for retailers. The increase in wholesale generation costs has been driven overwhelmingly by the higher international prices for coal and gas that accompanied and followed the Russian invasion of Ukraine. Higher interest rates reduce domestic coal and gas prices a bit – because they raise the foreign exchange value of the Australian dollar. But this effect is small compared with reductions that could come from driving a wedge between domestic and international prices. Placing caps on coal and gas prices as agreed by the national cabinet in December 2022 is one way of doing that. Alternatively, state governments onshore or the Commonwealth offshore could increase royalties, or the Commonwealth could increase profits-based taxation, to support compensatory payments to some or all users of power. On retail margins, there are a few dominant retailers in each state electricity market, and much scope for oligopolistic pricing. So our conductor would be doing what she could to reduce or at least avoid increases in market concentration, and to make sure that retail margins were not markedly above those that could be justified in a competitive market.

Thus, for electricity and its large contributions to the CPI and community concern, raising interest rates is not an obviously economically efficient instrument for reducing prices. Raising interest rates may even raise prices for many users of power. Good policy would bring in a range of instruments, with competition policy playing an important role alongside others.

High profits and low cost of capital

The historic lift in the profit and fall in the wage share of income are challenging facts. The shifts are the more striking because they have come at a time when the real cost of capital available in competitive markets is the lowest it has ever been. The real cost of long-term debt has been close to zero over the past decade.

The low real interest rates suggest that, in this respect at least, we may be living in a world that resembles the one that Keynes described ninety-three years ago (Keynes 1930a). One of the economist's aims was to give

Cambridge students hope that there could be an attractive future in a market economy, at a time when democratic capitalism was engaged in a competitive struggle for hearts and minds with authoritarian political systems. The essay explained that the accumulation of capital and technological improvement over a century would lead to such a surplus of savings beyond the profitable opportunities for investment that the real interest rate on low-risk capital in competitive markets would fall to zero. If we avoided unnecessary wars and economic depressions, no-one a century forward from 1930 would have a high income simply because they owned capital. We would see the 'euthanasia of the rentier'. Ordinary citizens would be liberated for the challenge of using time for good purpose. There would still be reward for invention, innovation and entrepreneurship, and therefore enhancement of the material human condition. People who earned high incomes would derive them only from using capital, labour and technology in new ways, and not from simply owning capital.

Real interest rates on sovereign and other low-risk debt in Australia and other developed countries have fallen steadily through the twenty-first century. Over the past decade, average real returns on low-risk capital in competitive markets have been around zero. This is such a striking departure from historical returns to capital that most economists, businesspeople and officials either deny that it is true, or think it results from public policy that must change. They await the early return of 'normal' real interest rates – the variations around about 5 or 6 per cent that prevailed through most of the past half millennium (Blanchard 2023, pp 28–32). They don't understand the world in which they live.

The reality of near-zero real returns on low-risk debt has been temporarily obscured by inflation following the supply disruptions and monetary expansion of the COVID years. The rise in nominal interest rates driven by the new inflation over these past eighteen months is not a return to old real returns on low-risk capital. Nothing of the sort. Nominal policy rates remain well below the rate of inflation – so real rates are negative. The rates on longer bonds, set in competitive markets, remain strongly negative.

Durably low real interest rates

Real interest rates in competitive markets are near zero or negative because in the world as a whole private citizens are tending to save higher proportions and to invest lower proportions of their incomes. The changes in savings and investment propensities reflect changes in the structure of economies, including the rise in rent and associated increase in inequality in income distribution.

Why are savings high? The twenty-first century in the developed countries has seen a falling share of total income going to people on low incomes and without wealth who depend on wages to live and spend almost all of their incomes. An increasing share has gone to the wealthy, who spend a much smaller part of their incomes. These effects are exacerbated by the increasing proportion of incomes held by the wealthy in international tax havens, accumulating without taxation or drawdowns for consumption. Developing countries that happen to have unusually high savings rates – first of all China – have increased their shares of global income. More of the world's income growth has been concentrated in developing countries where incomes have been growing rapidly, and it takes time for consumption patterns to adjust upwards to higher incomes. In the developed world and China, ageing populations want to provide for longer retirement.

Among factors reducing investment, the increasing share of services in the economy has reduced investment in buildings and equipment. Information technology has allowed more efficient use of capital. A higher proportion of investment is in intangible assets like intellectual property and does not require capital expenditure on fixed assets. Lower rates of productivity growth in the developed countries have reduced the rates of obsolescence of old plant and the need for investment in replacements. IT network services now represent a higher proportion of consumption, requiring little capital and also operating expenditure in comparison with the value of sales.

The increasing role of economic rent

Returns to low-risk capital in competitive markets are close to zero in real terms, and yet returns to business investment are higher than they have ever been in the developed countries. In Australia, the profit share of income is far higher than it has ever been, at least over the period for which reasonably reliable data are available. The increased profit share is impossible to explain without recognising the increased role of economic rent in the Australian economy.

Economic rent is income above that which is necessary to attract the economically optimal amount of investment into an activity. It persists where competition in the supply of a particular good or service is imperfect or, in some cases, non-existent.

I am not talking about the profits from innovation and entrepreneurship to use capital more productively in a competitive economic system. These are what nineteenth-century economist Alfred Marshall called quasi-rents. Quasi-rents are the temporarily high profits that follow changes in economic equilibria, which take time for competition to erode.

Economic rent arises whenever high profits in an economic activity fail to induce expansion of supply to reduce prices and profits to normal or competitive levels. The restriction on entry may arise because production requires a specific resource, the supply of which cannot be augmented by investment. Examples include urban and agricultural land and mineral resources. Land and mines that can produce valuable product at lower costs than others, or which are favourably located, cannot be reproduced through investment. The restriction may arise because there are overwhelming economies of scale that make it impossible for a newcomer to compete – as in a network, or an economic activity where the scale of production at which unit cost is lowest is very large compared with the size of the market. They may arise because incumbents have established an oligopolistic position in the market and protect their market power with anti-competitive behaviour. The restrictions may exist because government law or regulation blocks new entrants.

Different sources of rent can interact with and reinforce each other. Rents from any source can be invested in influence over public policy and its implementation to maintain and extend oligopolistic positions.

Economic rent is sometimes but not always associated with economic inefficiency. Regulatory barriers to competition that serve no public interest reduce economic efficiency. It is in the public interest to eliminate inefficient sources of rent by removing barriers to competitive entry, or by actively promoting competition.

However, some rent emerges from restrictions on competitive investment that increase economic efficiency. This is often the case with exclusive ownership of a specific land or mineral resource – the allocation and enforcement of private property rights. In the absence of this restriction on competition, over-investment in the use of the resource would reduce economic value. For example, a lot of labour and capital is wasted in a gold rush – when as much or more gold might have been extracted with much less labour and capital if one firm had been allocated an exclusive right to mine the deposit.

On access to urban land, planning regulations are necessary to restrict investment to levels that maximise economic value. In the absence of planning restrictions, there may be over-investment in favourable sites, to the point where total economic value is diminished. Here a judicious balance must be struck between the public interest in full use of the resource and the public interest in avoiding dissipation of value in over-investment.

A second category of efficient rent results from government protecting private use of intellectual property resulting from scientific or technological or intellectual or artistic creation. The restriction increases incentives for economically productive investment in innovation, at the same time as it restricts the social value generated from access to each creation. As with urban planning, a judicious balance between competing sources of value is necessary for economically optimal outcomes.

A third category of efficient rent is 'natural monopoly', associated with ownership of a network, or a physical asset with overwhelming economies of scale, or the two together. Examples of network monopolies are provided by the main information technology and social media platforms. Examples of the two together include electricity transmission, gas pipeline and telecommunications hardware systems – and in the zero-carbon economy, infrastructure for the storage and transport of hydrogen. Duplication of investments in a natural monopoly would usually waste resources. But the acceptance of monopoly allows the owner of the established assets to maintain high prices and profits at the expense of community welfare.

Some activities generating efficient rent can be subject to regulation of investment or price to increase total economic value. Whatever the source of rent, and however rent may be constrained by regulation, rent can in principle be subject to additional taxation without sacrifice of economic value. The economically efficient taxation of rent is the subject of our paper on the cash-flow basis of corporate taxation (Garnaut et al. 2020).

The share of rent in national output and income has varied widely in the course of modern economic development. Such variations have had large effects on political systems. Generally high proportions of economic rent in total incomes and the inequality of incomes with which it has been associated have blocked the establishment and undermined the maintenance of democratic political systems.

The rent of agricultural land was at the heart of classical economics (Ricardo 1817) and the economic and political systems from which it grew. Mineral rent has been the main source of income in some resource-rich countries since the beginnings of the modern economy and was important globally in the immediate aftermath of the oil-price leaps in the 1970s. Rent from the concentration of private ownership of business assets was at the centre of the great fortunes of late nineteenth and early twentieth century America, and its reduction the policy focus of President Theodore Roosevelt. In the early twenty-first century, rent has expanded its share of total income everywhere, notably in Australia.

In Australia, a high and increasing proportion of incomes has emanated from rent-heavy sectors, especially mining, but also urban real estate, information technology, financial services, media and large-scale retailing. For confirmation of the Australian trends, look at the role of mining, banking and other rent-heavy sectors in market capitalisation on the Australian stock exchange. Profits of mining, with economic rent contributing a considerable proportion, were larger than the whole of the rest of the economy in the final quarter of 2022. Profits from mining were larger than the total from financial, business and legal services, hospitality, accommodation, construction, health, education, media, transport and all the rest, although mining accounts for less than 2 per cent of employment.

In the United States, where the macro and micro evidence base is developing most rapidly, a range of recent economic analyses has identified an increasing proportion of rent in income from the early 1980s. From 1980 to 2016, returns in excess of normal profits as a share of GDP grew between four and fivefold. The increasing importance of economic rent was the central focus of Olivier Blanchard's Presidential Address to the American Economic Association in 2019, before COVID diverted our minds. The rise in rent accompanies increases in market concentration, especially in banking, healthcare and ICT. The US economy has bifurcated into an abundance of firms with low returns and a narrow band of firms with super-profits: returns for firms that were in the top 10 per cent by profitability rose from 20 per cent per annum in the mid-1980s to around 100 per cent per annum in recent years. Rent has become more persistent: the odds of a super-profitable firm still being super-profitable ten years later have doubled since the 1990s to 85 per cent. The pattern of growing rent is present in many countries. De Loecker and Eeckhout (2018) present analysis to show that global average mark-ups increased by 52 percentage points from 1980. The increase in G7 countries ranged from around 30 to almost 150 percentage points (see also de Loecker and Eeckhout 2020).

Finighan (2023) has analysed the massive increase in opportunities for rents arising out of asymmetry between information available to concentrated producers and atomistic users – an asymmetry rendered much more economically important by the increased capacity of large-scale data analysis. These same developments in information technology and artificial intelligence are increasing knowledge asymmetries between specialised large companies seeking to increase market power, and the government agencies seeking to regulate them in the public interest.

Ingles and Stewart (2018) referred to various Australian and US estimates suggesting the normal return on investment represents between 30 and 60 per cent of the corporate return, with various rents constituting the remainder. Murphy (2018, Table 2) estimated that 41 per cent of Australian corporate income tax revenue was from rent.

All these empirical observations precede the COVID disruptions of supply chains and the energy price increases following the Russian invasion of Ukraine. Many precede the increased restrictions on open international trade introduced for protectionist or geopolitical reasons by President Trump in the United States and broadly maintained by President Biden, and followed to greater or lesser degree by many other countries including Australia. They precede the Chinese geopolitical restrictions on trade over the same period. These developments have substantially increased the role of rents over the past few years.

It is time for these important developments to enter the mainstream of our discussion of the economy and economic policy.

The place in the orchestra of competition policy and the ACCC

When the Australian economy is playing by new rules, it is time for thinking from first principles about the role of our instruments and how they can best be played. Competition policy is important to achieving all of Australia's economic objectives: full employment with moderate inflation, rising incomes and reasonably equitable distribution of income. But it cannot deliver any of them on its own.

Greater competition can sometimes be the most effective means of expanding economic activity in an industry, and so of economically increasing employment. It can sometimes be the most efficient way to reduce prices of a product and therefore to contribute to lower inflation. It will usually contribute to greater dynamism in an industry and therefore to productivity growth and rising incomes in the whole economy. It is a source of greater equity in income distribution.

But greater competition is not always possible; and where possible, not always the lowest-cost way of making progress towards an economic objective. Sometimes it is better to recognise that monopoly or oligopoly is economically efficient, or that its removal through application of competition policy would impose costs that exceed the benefits. The national interest then requires restructuring of taxation to increase its incidence on rents and reduce its incidence on competitive activity.

The orchestra of economic policy needs an instrument that comes in when greater competition is both possible and the best means to an important end. The ACCC is the regulatory rather than policy agency. But it understands better than other parts of government what can work, what is best left alone, and how to make things work. It can assist the conductor in her choices of instruments and in the timing of calling them into play.

Let me conclude with a few suggestions on the role of the ACCC and competition policy. Mostly this reinforces approaches that have already been established, but there are a few lessons from this chapter's discussion of unusual features of our contemporary economic story.

First, we should accept that there are important natural monopolies, in which the presence of massive economies of scale prevents economically effective competition. This includes the transmission and distribution of power and gas, and now the storage and transport of hydrogen.

The lesson for the future is to avoid private ownership of new assets where these can be separated commercially from established private systems. We can at least apply the lessons of analysis and experience and keep storage and transport of hydrogen in public hands. Where the horse has bolted into private ownership, as in electricity transmission and distribution in the three south-eastern mainland states, we should invest greater analytic effort into regulation of investment, access and pricing. The setting of the rules is immensely complex and depends on information that is available more completely to the operating company than the regulator. One simple rule, which is necessary but far from sufficient for good outcomes in the public interest, is to separate ownership and management from use of the utility. This is easily applied, but always contested in practice by operating companies.

Second, network information services have some characteristics of natural monopolies, but some opportunities for competition at least at the margins of each company's business. Much of this is new territory for competition agencies everywhere. The ACCC has established itself as a leader in the space. Australia needs more sector-specific rules to promote competition and prevent the worst abuses of market power in the digital economy, along the lines that are currently in the process of being implemented in the European Union and soon the United Kingdom. In September last year the ACCC proposed new up-front rules for application to designated digital platforms in particular sectors. This has merit. If Australia does not act on this, we will fall behind other countries in promoting competition and protecting consumers in these areas. The application of sound rules in the Australian public interest will require Australian governments to stand up to great pressure from large foreign companies and influential governments.

Third is the well-established regulation of competition. Avoiding additional concentration of ownership and management in industries in which genuine competition is possible is more important than ever. The challenge of introducing effective competition is greater for the asymmetry of information between consumers and producers, increased beyond recognition by the new information technology and artificial intelligence. It's a small change, but I welcome the shift in focus currently being discussed in relation to the role of the ACCC, from focus on a substantial lessening of competition to a significant lessening of competition. More fundamentally, Australia needs to rethink its merger laws in the light of the discussion in this chapter. The changes recently recommended by ACCC chair Gina Cass-Gottlieb appear to be steps that a government seeking to increase welfare-enhancing competition would want to implement.

Fourth, we should accept that there are large areas of the economy in which restrictions on entry are important for economic efficiency, and others in which increased competition is difficult to achieve or carries risks of negative economic effects of other kinds. Resource rents are extraordinarily important in our economy. While other rents are smaller, urban land rents, network rents, and rents in natural monopolies in which private ownership will be difficult to unwind are all important. Here we need to recognise the limits of competition policy, to accept the continued presence of the rents associated with them and build forms of business taxation that raise substantial revenues from rents and relatively little from competitive economic activity.

My fifth point is crucial to full employment, rising incomes and equitable income distribution for a growing Australian population. This relates to the interaction between trade and competition policy. Free trade in goods and services is necessary to provide globally competitive access to inputs along the whole supply chains for export-oriented industry. We can be confident that free trade will severely constrain the use of oligopolistic power in goods in which Australia is a substantial exporter. Constrain, but not remove. As we have learnt in relation to gas pricing over the past few years, where there is oligopoly within Australia, free trade is consistent with a wide range of prices for exportable products, between import and export parity. (Import parity is the price in other exporting countries plus the cost of preparation and transport to Australia. Export parity is the price in importing countries less the cost of preparation and transport for export.) For much of our history, import parity pricing was the norm for many exports that were also inputs into domestic manufacturing. For example, Australia was a major exporter of base metals, but prices for these products were typically set as the price in London plus the cost of export to Australia. The difference between export and import parity prices is important to global competitiveness of Australian manufacturing and processing activity based on Australian energy and material inputs. The ACCC's role should include ensuring the availability of exportable products within Australia at export parity pricing. This will be crucially important to building Australia as the zero-carbon Superpower of the future world economy.

10

CHINA, GLOBAL ECONOMIC DISINTEGRATION AND THE CLIMATE CHANGE CHALLENGE*

The international community's success in controlling human-induced increases in temperature depends on Chinese approaches to decarbonisation at home and abroad, and on the rest of the world's approach to trade with China. In turn, the Chinese government's success in achieving its development goals depends on the world managing effectively the challenge of climate change.

This chapter examines the role of China and its interaction with the rest of the world in the global response to climate change and then discusses Chinese economic development as the apotheosis of the international trade and development system established at the end of World War II. Rapidly increasing trade within an open global trading system underpinned extraordinary Chinese growth in output and incomes in the four and a half decades following the gradual shift from autarchic central planning to market exchange and international economic integration commencing in 1978. China having relative resource endowments very different from the average for the world caused the gains from open trade to be exceptionally large. A large, rapidly growing country's reliance on fossil carbon for energy and industrial inputs raises their cost with

---

* This chapter was first published in *Oxford Review of Economic Policy* 40(2), Summer 2024, pp. 374–86.

successful economic development, placing a brake on global economic development. Dealing successfully with the climate challenge by breaking the connection between economic growth and fossil carbon use removes what would have emerged as a barrier to continued economic growth on the model of the twentieth century: the increasing cost of fossil carbon as a source of energy and industrial inputs with depletion of the natural resource stocks that can be exploited at lowest cost.

I then discuss China's vulnerability to climate change and its national interest in finding a global solution. China is centrally important to the problem and the solution. It is the world's largest emitter of greenhouse gases, and by far the world's main producer of most of the capital goods that are essential for timely achievement of zero global emissions. It has played an important role in international discussion of solutions. Global success is possible only if it continues to do so. But progress will be challenged by tensions and tendencies in the contemporary system of relations among states. I discuss how China has become the world's largest trading country and the largest bilateral trading partner of most countries. Specialisation in line with comparative advantage has underpinned Chinese economic success. It will be crucial to success on climate change. Then I examine major elements in Chinese domestic policies to reduce greenhouse gas emissions. The foundations for suitable policies have been laid, but major policy development is necessary.

Cooperation between the United States and China is necessary for successful mitigation of climate change. After initial progress during the Obama administration, there was a dangerous stand-off under President Trump. I discuss how productive relations on climate change have been re-established under President Biden, although they remain vulnerable to geopolitical tensions and require continuing effort for success. I examine what can be done to establish a framework for wider international cooperation on climate change when direct Sino–US relations are constrained and periodically disrupted by geopolitical and geostrategic tensions. I then look at some particular challenges to climate change cooperation emerging from the COVID-19 crisis and the Russian invasion of Ukraine.

Finally, I conclude by acknowledging the case for despair but recognising as well episodes in earlier periods of global geostrategic tension and the recent history of climate change cooperation that encourage continued effort.

The context provided by global and Chinese economic development

China's economic development over these past four and a half decades is the apotheosis of the system of open international economic exchange that was established after World War II. Chinese participation was delayed by the Cold War restrictions on open multilateral trade and the autarchic central planning policies of the communist government of the People's Republic of China after 1949. Two interrelated developments in the 1970s underpinned China's productive integration into a global economy. Belated recognition in the early 1970s by the United States that China was not indelibly aligned strategically with the Soviet Union, and shared strategic interests with the West, allowed countries allied with the United States and then the United States itself to remove barriers to trade and investment. And by the late 1970s, dominant elements in the Chinese leadership had come to understand the failures of autarchic central planning and the economic development advantages of open trade and investment. The Chinese reforms to make greater use of market exchange and international economic integration moved onto a higher plain of opportunity with entry into the World Trade Organization in late 2001.

Open trade is more valuable to countries with relative endowments of economic resources that are very different from the world as a whole. Differences increase the gains from trade. China and the other densely populated high-income countries of Northeast Asia – Japan and South Korea – are exceptional today for their high ratios of capital to natural resources, including renewable energy resources. So are the countries of central and northern Europe. Securing the gains from trade was an underlying motive and at times an explicit rationale of European and then Japanese imperialism. The dismantling of the old empires was largely completed in the first two decades of the postwar political and economic system. Global development in the first three postwar decades demonstrated that international trade and investment could be undertaken commercially on a scale vastly greater than anything achieved under imperialism.

China's success greatly expanded the scale of the open international economy. It enhanced conditions for trade expansion and economic development everywhere. It gave Australia its China resources boom, with high terms of trade and by 2008 average incomes as conventionally measured higher than the United States for the first time in a century. The last decade of the twentieth century and the early years of the twenty-first were the most successful ever for growth in incomes in developing countries. The first eight years of the twenty-first century saw rapid trade expansion and rising incomes in most of the developing world, including in many parts of Africa that had previously remained outside modern economic development. Rising labour incomes in China from about 2005, as what had been a Lewisian labour surplus economy entered its turning point in economic development, opened new opportunities for specialisation in simple labour-intensive manufactured exports elsewhere in the developing world (Lewis 1954; Garnaut and Huang 2006; Cai and Huang 2013).

Two sets of economies stand out as being highly complementary to the high-income developed countries of Europe and Northeast Asia. One is the set of countries with large endowments of natural resources relative to population – a few developed countries (first of all Australia and Canada, with large per capita endowments of capital as well as natural resources) and some developing countries. The other is the set of densely populated developing countries, with large endowments of labour relative to capital and natural resources – the economies of South Asia, and increasingly parts of Africa in which past failure of development delayed the fall in fertility and the demographic transition.

Countries with relative resource endowments that are very different from the rest of the world receive the largest gains from trade and lose most from restrictions on trade. Other important parts of the world economy, notably the United States, have relative resource endowments close to the global average, and so receive smaller if still considerable gains from open international trade.

Jagdish Bhagwati's 'The Pure Theory of International Trade: A Survey' six decades ago taught us that differences in relative costs that deliver large gains from trade can come from two main sources. The first is differences in relative resource endowments highlighted by Heckscher (1919), Ohlin (1933) and Samuelson (Stolper and Samuelson 1941). The second is differences in relative technological efficiency across countries and industries. Bhagwati called these 'Ricardian' sources of comparative advantage, since the classical exemplification of comparative advantage by Ricardo did not depend on differences in relative resource endowments (Ricardo 1819). All countries gain from increased trade and specialisation in production of products in which they are relatively efficient. Such differences can depend on differences in economic history, industry policy, education, capacity for innovation or chance. All countries also gain from the technological improvement that comes from trade across international borders in technology and goods embodying new technology. All countries generally gain from the greater domestic competition that comes from integration into open international markets.

The postwar international trading system supported expansion of trade and growth in incomes of unprecedented scale and geographic breadth in the six decades after World War II. It has come under great stress since the global financial crisis of 2008 (see Guzman and Stiglitz 2024). Protectionist pressures have become more influential throughout the developed world. Their influence plumbed new depths in the United

States in the Trump presidency from 2017 to 2021, with nearly all restrictions being retained by President Biden.

One source of these pressures is the contraction of employment and depression of labour incomes in some industries that have faced increased import competition. These adverse distributional effects can be offset by distributional measures funded out of higher incomes from increased foreign trade. Where they were so offset, support for open trade has been stronger. Where distributional issues were ignored, protectionist pressures were more effective (Susskind and Vines 2024).

Growing strategic rivalry between the United States and China increased pressures for trade restriction. As Robertson (1938) observed of the interwar period, once trade restriction is said to be associated with military advantage, policymakers concerned with the wider national interest are pushed to the margins. While a larger economy is generally associated with greater military capacity, there may be circumstances in which some economic loss from restrictions on trade can be justified on strategic grounds. Circumstances in which this may be important warrants analysis case by case.

The world faces a great challenge in removing reliance on fossil carbon and hydrocarbon over a few decades. That change will be secured with greater certainty and much lower cost if it occurs within an expanding international trade and investment system. That system has been weakened by developments over the past decade and a half. The world faces urgent demands for international cooperation and exchange to limit damage from climate change at an inopportune time.

Close cooperation between China and the rest of the world will substantially reduce the costs of decarbonisation in both. This will occur through three main mechanisms: China supplying capital goods for the new energy and industrial technologies; countries with relatively abundant and rich solar and wind resources and reasonably low cost of capital supplying China with zero-emissions goods embodying renewable energy; and China, alongside the currently developed countries but quantitatively as important as all of them together, supplying capital, capital goods, and technology for zero-emissions development through the developing world.

China benefits from timely global achievement of zero net emissions by avoiding the immense economic, political, and environmental costs of extreme global warming. It also receives large benefits of other kinds from a successful global transition. First, reduction in global coal, oil and gas use reduces what would otherwise be large increases in world prices (see below). This constrains the associated deterioration of China's terms of trade. Second, the increasing use of zero-emissions energy reduces China's dependence on imports of energy raw materials from countries that are potentially politically or economically unstable or strategically problematic from a Chinese perspective. It therefore enhances energy security. Third, as the country with the strongest comparative advantage in producing the capital equipment for the zero-emissions economy, China's economic development can be strengthened by exports of these goods to support the global energy and industrial transition. Fourth, the shift to zero-emissions transport, industry, and residential and commercial heating reduces air pollution, which became a source of serious health problems and degradation of the quality of life in many parts of China through the decades of carbon-based economic growth (Chen et al. 2013). Air pollution has become politically contentious within China. It will be greatly reduced by comprehensive decarbonisation of the economy.

Even if there had been no climate change problem, global development based mainly on fossil energy would have become increasingly difficult through the twenty-first century. Ever-increasing demand would drive ever-increasing costs of oil, gas and coal. The coal, oil and gas resources that have highest quality, that are most easily and cheaply extracted, and that are most accessible to centres of demand, are used and exhausted first. Over time, the fossil carbon mining frontier shifts to more costly resources. World prices rise. The terms of international trade would have continued to move against China and developing countries that have less than their shares of fossil carbon natural resources. The cost of structural transition from backward low-income to modern high-income economies would have increased, and the chances of success diminished.

We saw the process of global development putting upward pressure on fossil carbon prices and threatening to constrain global development in fast forward in the period of exceptionally strong Chinese economic growth in the decade to 2012. World prices of oil, coal and gas rose by 400 and 500 per cent over a decade. The energy transition forced by concern to limit climate change has moderated those increases and removed the likelihood that their resumption will damage global development in future.

The climate change challenge to Chinese and global development

Chinese scientists have identified and published extensively within China on the country's vulnerability to global warming. Attention has been drawn in particular to damage to water supply and agricultural output in the North China plain; the destabilisation of flows in the Yangtse, Yellow and other great rivers from deglaciation of the Tibetan Plateau; and the impact of rising sea levels and the increased intensity of extreme weather events on that large proportion of Chinese economic activity near the river deltas and other low-lying areas of coastal China. China would share with all countries damage from destabilisation of the international political and economic order from impacts of climate change in Southeast, South, Central and West Asia. Chinese scientists have had institutionalised access on climate issues to the Chinese leadership for over one and a half decades. This has informed Chinese domestic policy and participation in international discussions.

China has been part of the UN discussion of climate change from the early years. It played an important role in the Paris conference of the parties of the UNFCCC in 2015 and the Glasgow conference in 2021.

At and immediately after the November 2015 Paris meeting, all the UN members agreed to work together to hold human-induced increases in average global temperatures below 2°C and as close as possible to 1.5°C. Each country would define its own nationally determined contributions, and the conference of the parties would meet every five years to review progress and to strengthen national contributions towards the agreed goals. The operating model is 'concerted unilateral mitigation'. Concerted because many countries are acting towards similar goals at the same time. Unilateral because each takes its own decisions without binding international agreements (Garnaut 2013; Susskind and Vines 2024). The first of the five-year reviews was to have occurred in Glasgow in late 2020 but was postponed until the following year because of COVID disruption at that time. At Glasgow, the focus was more strongly on holding temperature increases to 1.5°C, which would require achievement of net-zero global emissions by 2050 as well as early movement towards that outcome.

At Glasgow for the first time, all developed countries joined commitments to zero net emissions by 2050. Among other countries, several of the largest accepted commitments to zero net emissions by specific dates for the first time (China, Russia and Indonesia by 2060, and India by 2070). China committed to emissions reaching their peak before 2030.

Big as the new Glasgow commitments were, they did not add up to net zero by 2050 for the world as a whole. Meinshausen et al. (2022) have suggested that the nationally determined commitments can be reconciled with the global goals by each group of countries moving forward by five years the time at which they will reach net zero: the developed countries to 2045; China, Indonesia, Russia and other countries at intermediate levels of development and climate ambition to 2055; and India and other lower-income developing countries to 2065.

The arithmetic does not add up for net-zero global emissions by 2050 without China achieving net zero by 2055 or earlier. China is now the country with by far the world's largest greenhouse gas emissions, currently accounting for around 30 per cent of the global total. This is more than all currently developed countries combined. This is not surprising, since China has a much larger population than the sum of developed countries, Chinese incomes have grown rapidly for four and a half decades, and China is now at a stage of development at which energy intensity is particularly high.

China is home to around half of the world's emissions-intensive manufacturing. Steel is the biggest of these industrial activities. China accounts for over half of global steel production and 60 per cent of global steel emissions, with Chinese steel contributing nearly 5 per cent of total global emissions from all sources (Song 2022). The emissions intensity of Chinese steel production is higher than in developed countries mainly because the short history of large-scale steel consumption limits the contribution from recycling of steel scrap (scrap share about 22 per cent compared to about 60 per cent for the European Union and about 70 per cent for the United States).

In 2023, China installed about 42 per cent of the global total of new solar and wind capacity – more than the total in the developed world. China is demonstrating that zero-emissions technologies can be installed rapidly at an immense scale. In the decade to 2023, solar power output increased about sixty times to more than 500 terawatt hours (TWh). Wind increased nearly seven times from a higher base over the decade to nearly 900 TWh. China is the location of nearly half of the fifty-seven nuclear power plants currently under construction in the world. New hydro-electric capacity continues to grow strongly, but annual output varies with rainfall. Zero-emissions energy has supplied nearly all the increased Chinese power generation since 2013 – more than the total for a few years, and less since 2017. Total zero-emissions power generation in 2023 supplied about one third of total grid power supply – corresponding to a bit over two thirds of total US grid-scale power generation and use.

Chinese coal use doubled to over 4 billion tonnes in the decade to 2013. This was virtually all of the increase in global coal consumption, reaching over half the world's total. This was the proximate cause of China accounting for most of the world's increase in greenhouse gas emissions over this period. The rapid deployment of zero-emissions power generation after 2013 saw the stabilisation of Chinese thermal coal use, with the level in 2021 being similar to that in 2013.

China is by far the world's main producer of the capital goods for the zero-emissions economy. It produces about 80 per cent of the world's photovoltaic panels, and about 60 per cent of wind turbines, batteries and electric vehicles. It produces a majority of inverters for turning direct into alternating current, hydro-electric generators, transmission cables, and electrolysers for producing green hydrogen from renewable energy. It produces a substantial proportion of value added in most of the world's new nuclear power reactors. Most zero-emissions capital goods produced in China are deployed in China. At the same time, China's capacity for low-cost production of this equipment on an immense scale expands what is possible in global generation of zero-emissions power and reduces the cost of reducing emissions all over the world.

The new technologies of the zero-emissions world make heavy demands on a range of minerals and metals which were less important in the fossil carbon economy (Sandiford 2022). These include silicon for solar panels, and lithium, vanadium, graphite, cobalt, nickel, titanium, magnesium, manganese, rare earths, and other materials for batteries, electric motor vehicles and other goods. The International Energy Agency has called these 'critical minerals'. Following Sandiford (2022), I prefer the term 'energy transition minerals'. China has become the dominant world processor into usable products of many of these materials. It produces around 90 per cent of the grade of silicon required for photovoltaic panels. In the case of lithium, which is critically important in current battery manufacturing, it processes about 90 per cent of world supplies through relying heavily on imports of raw materials.

Chinese natural resources for many important energy transition minerals are not particularly large or rich, in comparison with Chinese economic size and domestic demand. Its resource endowments do not suggest comparative advantage in their production. For example, the processing of energy transition minerals – notably silicon – makes heavy demands on zero-emissions energy and other inputs into industrial processes that are not relatively abundant in China. Chinese domination of current world production derives from early recognition of the necessity of global transition to net-zero emissions, supported by domestic policy. It makes economic sense for China and the rest of the world for China's net exports of these products to decline and in many cases disappear as productive capacity is installed elsewhere. Diversification of supply would also be healthier for global economic stability and security.

Global output of energy transition minerals will need to increase rapidly to meet global demand. Chinese enterprises and their technology and experience can play a large role in increasing the scale of production in other countries.

China is important to the development of energy infrastructure in the developing world. It is important as a source of capital goods and investment. This is true for both carbon-intensive and zero-emissions electricity. China's official development institutions, like those of Japan and Korea, until recently supported the expansion of coal-based electricity systems in Asia and Africa. Decisions to cease financing new coal-based power stations in the lead-up to the Glasgow UN conference on climate change in 2021 were of large global significance. Even more positively, Chinese financing of new investment in the zero-emissions industry and processes and application of zero-emissions technologies is making a substantial contribution to other countries' decarbonisation.

The Chinese economic development context of the energy transition

The expansion of foreign trade played a crucial role in Chinese economic growth through the first four decades of economic reform. Growth rates of foreign trade were more than twice as high as the extraordinarily high rates of output over this long period (Garnaut 2018). China now is by far the largest participant in international trade. It is the largest trading partner of most countries.

Increased foreign trade supported strong productivity growth. It allowed rapid growth over long periods of China's most productive industries as they changed over time. It eased bottlenecks that otherwise would have constrained Chinese economic growth. Energy and metallic minerals were drawn from abroad in quantities and qualities far beyond what would have been available for Chinese development within the old commitments to self-sufficiency. This was most obviously the case with energy and steelmaking raw materials, where China became the world's largest importer of fossil carbon, and overwhelmingly the world's largest market for iron ore. Supply of engineering equipment and technology from the advanced industrial economies also removed or loosened what would otherwise have been binding constraints on Chinese growth. Imports of knowledge and technology directly or embodied in goods and services made an important contribution to the growth process. Imports of education services were also important, with Chinese becoming major parts of the student population in the English-speaking and some other countries.

Chinese international trade in services as well as goods was important in the early stages of the energy transition in response to climate change. This is illustrated in the transformational reduction in costs of photovoltaic panels from early this century. In the early 2000s, climate policies in the European Union, supplemented by national policies in Germany and some other member countries, greatly increased incentives for the deployment of solar photovoltaic electricity generators. The new demand was initially mainly supplied by domestic production of photovoltaic panels in Europe. At around this time, Chinese graduates from advanced electrical engineering programs at Australian universities were returning home. Several identified a business opportunity in applying their new knowledge commercially to link the growing solar photovoltaic market in Europe with Chinese comparative advantage in manufacturing production at a large scale. Support from Chinese provincial governments facilitated the early development of new companies manufacturing solar panels. Exports to Europe allowed early production at a considerable scale, which reduced unit costs. Lower costs of photovoltaic equipment made solar power more competitive with fossil energy abroad and also in China. That increased sales abroad and at home, further increasing scale of production and reducing costs. Learning by doing and increased scale in manufacturing more than technological change have continued to bring down costs. Now, two decades into the virtuous circle of expanding output and falling costs centred on Chinese manufacturing capacity, the cost of new renewable energy is much lower than the cost of new coal or gas generation in many countries, even after taking into account the cost of storage to balance the intermittency of solar and wind generation. With the high contemporary global prices of coal and gas, the cost of fuel alone for fossil carbon power generation exceeds the total capital and running costs of solar and wind in places with good natural resources for renewable energy. The reduction in renewable energy cost has established a commercial base for decarbonisation of electricity in countries with abundant resources, even in the absence of supportive domestic policies. It has also established the foundation for decarbonisation of many areas of industrial production that had once depended on fossil carbon and hydrocarbon with high greenhouse gas emissions.

So international trade has been of large importance to Chinese economic growth from early in the reform period, and now for the Chinese transition to zero net emissions. It is crucial for facilitating and reducing the cost of the shift from fossil carbon to renewable energy.

The relationship between global growth, energy demand and fossil energy prices began to change about a decade ago.

Chinese and world coal consumption reached a local peak in 2012–14 and fell for a while, as China began to implement a new economic

development model with less emphasis on investment and heavy industry. However, there was partial reversion to the old model as trade
tensions rose with the United States, growth slowed and anxieties about
employment and incomes increased from 2017. Chinese coal use began to
rise again, to a new peak in 2019. After COVID disruption, post-COVID
expansion of old economic activities saw Chinese and global coal use
reach its highest level ever in 2023.

This retrogression from 2017 does not violate China's commitment
to emissions peaking before 2030. It does, however, raise hard questions about the attainability of global climate objectives. Zero net global
emissions by 2050 and holding the average increase to 1.5°C above pre-
industrial levels now requires earlier peaking and sharper declines in
Chinese emissions.

What are the prospects for China achieving peak emissions well
before 2030 and net zero by the mid 2050s? They are good in the established system of power generation – ignoring the great increase in power
use that will be necessary for electrification of industry that currently
uses fossil carbon directly. Now that Chinese wind and solar generation represents a substantial proportion of the total domestic electricity
supply, continuation of recent rates of growth would force large annual
reductions in generation from fossil carbon. When there is excess total
generation capacity, economic forces lead to utilisation of renewable
ahead of fossil carbon electricity, as it does not have high operating costs
from purchase of coal, gas or oil.

The prospects are good for transport, with the combination of electrification of land transport and decarbonisation of electricity supply
providing a fast start. For the world as a whole, production of internal
combustion cars reached its peak in 2017. Since then, more than the whole
increase in demand has come from electric vehicles. In 2022, global sales
of internal combustion vehicles were 20 per cent below 2017 levels. China
is well ahead of the rest of the world. Nearly half of new car sales in China
in late 2023 were fully electric or plug-in hybrid – much higher than the

average of developed countries, although less than in Scandinavia. Decarbonisation of shipping and long-distance civil aviation is likely to require large-scale imports of zero-carbon liquid fuels made from zero-emissions hydrogen and biomass.

The greatest challenge is in industry, in China and the world as a whole. It is bigger and harder in the country which accounts for around half of global emissions-intensive manufacturing. Research, development and commercialisation of new technologies for steel, cement, petrochemical and other emissions-intensive industries are in their early stages. Known technologies can remove carbon emissions from production of almost all goods, or can produce zero-emissions substitutes for them. Few of these are feasible without carbon prices at levels commensurate with the social cost of carbon – something no lower than and perhaps in the vicinity of the current price for carbon allowances in the European Trading System. Some products and substitutes would require fiscal or regulatory support at higher levels. It is likely that commercial innovation in these industries, and large-scale manufacturing of the equipment that will achieve decarbonisation of industry, will lean heavily on developments in China. This is as it was for electricity and transport. Supply of zero-emissions inputs to industry – including green iron for steelmaking; and hydrogen and biomass derivatives for petrochemicals – is likely to require large-scale imports from countries with comparative advantage in producing these materials.

As this book is in final preparations in July 2024, I note that current estimates of emissions for 2024 are substantially lower than actual emissions in 2023. It appears that Chinese emissions may have peaked in 2023, well ahead of the 2030 commitment.

Chinese domestic emissions reduction policies

There are two market imperfections that must be corrected in the process of achieving zero net emissions. The first is the external costs of carbon emissions. Stern (2007) called this the greatest market failure of all time.

The second is the external benefits of innovation in the new technologies required in the zero-carbon economy.

On the carbon externality, China has had extensive experience with an emissions trading scheme (ETS) since it was introduced into a number of provinces and cities in 2017. The scheme was extended to the whole of China in 2022. There are many and wide gaps in product coverage, so that it does not yet secure reductions wherever in the economy they can be achieved at the lowest cost. Many permits are allocated to producers without payment, so the scheme does not raise the public revenue that would otherwise be possible without distortion of economic activity. More permits are allocated than would come from a trajectory defined to reduce emissions to zero at an economically optimal rate. The price of carbon dioxide-equivalent emissions has been well below the level necessary to drive the economy towards net-zero emissions – US$8–9 per tonne through 2021 and 2022 and a bit over US$10 in late 2023.

At least the mechanism can be tightened and extended relatively easily. Higher prices later can increase pressure for lower emissions. The ETS provides a foundation for an efficient set of policies to achieve zero net emissions by 2055. The discussion of international cooperation later in this paper suggests that tightening and extending the emissions trading system could establish a sound basis for Chinese participation in international trade in the goods and services that will be important in the zero-emissions economy. Linkage to international markets will establish and require a much higher carbon price – something like the level now emerging from trade within the European ETS and rising over time.

The second externality – one company's innovation conferring benefits on others – leads to underinvestment in innovation in the absence of public financial support. China has many mechanisms for providing fiscal support for innovation in the zero-carbon economy. Here the task is not to introduce new mechanisms, but to rationalise established schemes across activities. Fiscal support for public-good research in universities and specialised research institutions is warranted and generally provided at relatively high levels. In the early stages of development and commercialisation of new technologies and new approaches to economic activity that significantly reduce emissions, the best economic outcomes will be achieved by all innovative investment attracting similar rates of fiscal support.

High fiscal support for innovation from national, provincial and local governments is accompanied by large efforts to absorb knowledge from innovation abroad, including by Chinese firms investing in companies involved in research, development and commercialisation in zero-carbon activities in Western democratic capitalist countries. This has been controversial in recent years in many countries, so that China may rely more in future on domestic innovation.

China–US climate change cooperation

Cooperation between China and the United States played a significant role in the success of both the Paris and Glasgow conferences. Both meetings were preceded by bilateral agreements that announced substantially increased ambitions for national programs. Both countries took the bilateral commitments into the conference as national programs. China's commitment at Glasgow was particularly important for the global effort. It brought the global goal of zero net emissions by 2050 within reach.

It is worth recalling the main elements of the US–China Joint Glasgow Declaration on Enhancing Climate Action in the 2020s, secured by presidents Biden and Xi on 10 November 2021 – the eve of the Glasgow conference. The agreement between the two countries began by recognising the seriousness and urgency of the climate crisis. The two governments agreed to accelerate actions in the critical decade of the 2020s, as well as to cooperate in multilateral processes to avoid catastrophic impacts. They declared their intention to work individually, jointly and with other countries during this decisive decade, to accelerate the transition to a global net-zero economy.

In particular, the two sides expressed the intention to cooperate on:

- regulatory frameworks and environmental standards related to reducing emissions of greenhouse gases in the 2020s; and in the process maximising the societal benefits of the clean energy transition
- policies to encourage decarbonisation and electrification of end-use sectors; key areas related to the circular economy, such as green design and renewable resource utilisation
- deployment and application of technology such as carbon capture, usage and storage and direct air capture.

The two countries agreed that it is necessary to control and reduce methane emissions in the 2020s. The two countries would cooperate to enhance the measurement of methane emissions; to exchange information on their respective policies and programs for strengthening management and control of methane; and to foster joint research into methane emission reduction challenges and solutions.

The two countries agreed to cooperate on policies that increase shares of low-cost intermittent renewable energy. The United States noted its goal of 100 per cent carbon-pollution-free electricity by 2035. China noted that it will phase down coal consumption during the fifteenth five-year plan (2025–30) and make best efforts to accelerate this work. The two sides recalled their respective commitments to eliminating support for unabated international thermal coal power generation.

Recognising the importance of eliminating global illegal deforestation to reaching the Paris goals, the two countries agreed to collaborate in eliminating illegal deforestation through enforcing their respective laws on imports.

Both countries recognised the importance of developed countries mobilising jointly US$100 billion per year by 2020 and annually through 2025 to assist developing countries on climate goals and stressed the importance of meeting that goal as soon as possible.

A 'Working Group on Enhancing Climate Action in the 2020s' would meet regularly to address the climate crisis and advance the multilateral process, focusing on enhancing concrete actions in this decade.

The US–China joint agreement provided an important support for Glasgow. It anticipated continuing to support progress to net-zero global emissions through the 2020s.

The agreement was suspended in August 2022 by the Chinese government in response to the visit to Taiwan of the speaker of the US House of Representatives, Nancy Pelosi. The Chinese government said this was a breach of the One China principles upon which Sino–US diplomatic relations had been established. Prior to these developments, Sino–US climate change cooperation had continued, even as bilateral tensions escalated. Through 2023 high-level political contact and discussion was resumed, culminating in resumption of active discussion of climate change around the APEC heads of government meeting in San Francisco in November 2023.

None of the Glasgow and subsequent US–China cooperation would have occurred under a Trump presidency. The prospects look bleak in the event of a return to Trump-like policies in the United States from early 2025.

Geostrategic tensions and climate cooperation

Both the United States and China can continue to move purposefully on their own decarbonisation and on emissions reduction with third countries in the absence of formal bilateral cooperation. However, US–China cooperation has been important for successful outcomes in UNFCCC conferences and has the potential to strengthen each country's own decarbonisation efforts and the sum of their respective impacts in third countries. Any breakdown in that cooperation is a setback for the global effort.

The disruption of Sino–US trade and investment under the Trump government has continued generally under President Biden. Strategic rivalry between the United States and China is a fact of the contemporary world. For the time being, it seems inevitable that each country will restrict trade at least in items that seem to have implications for the strategic balance. Global development and prosperity, and more generally the future quality of human society, depend on China and the United States being able to manage strategic tension without war, and without loss of global gains from trade beyond items that have direct, large and clear implications for strategic competition. It is not obvious that restrictions on trade in zero-carbon technology and goods would systematically favour either China or the United States in their strategic competition. It is therefore to the benefit of both and to the world as a whole that mutually beneficial trade and investment relations on the zero-carbon economy continue, with exclusions for strategic reasons following rigorous analysis. In the unhappy circumstances of continued disruption of Sino–US trade and investment related to climate change, it is important that US–China tensions impose minimal damage on the global progress towards zero net emissions. It is important that third countries interact productively with both on reduction in emissions.

Chinese trade and economic cooperation with other developed countries have been disrupted by political tensions over the past seven years. Changes in Chinese political priorities and international policy and inward-oriented policies in the United States have interacted in ways that have damaged confidence in international economic exchange. Some politically motivated Chinese restrictions on trade and investment with third countries have been damaging to established trade and to the confidence required to support expansion. This has inevitably reduced gains from trade, investment and technological exchange related to the energy and industrial transition.

The increases in barriers to US imports during the Trump presidency were greatest against China (Corden and Garnaut 2018). Barriers did not fall under President Biden. Indeed, the *Inflation Reduction Act* (IRA) extended protection of US production of goods that are important in reduction of greenhouse gases (Garnaut 2023). China imposed restrictions on trade with the United States and several other countries during the Trump period and still retained many of them in early 2024.

The international setbacks and the COVID-19 pandemic and the policy response to it slowed without stopping growth in foreign trade and output in China and the developing world globally. Trade in goods and services that are important in the energy and industrial transition to net-zero emissions has grown more rapidly than trade in general, in China, the United States and the world as a whole. It is important to achievement of net-zero emissions in China and the rest of the world that it continues to do so. Continued expansion in trade in goods and services related to the zero-emissions economy lowers the cost of transition and assists its reconciliation with continued global development.

How is the Chinese and global transition to net-zero emissions affected by recent US (the IRA) and EU (the Carbon Border Adjustment Mechanism, CBAM) initiatives affecting trade and decarbonisation? The initiatives are both motivated and shaped by climate, industry protection and China-related political objectives.

The IRA on balance has positive effects on global decarbonisation (Garnaut 2023). Two effects are positive. It accelerates US domestic decarbonisation. US influence on global political and intellectual trends causes this to lift the priority of climate mitigation objectives in much of the rest of the world. It increases support for innovation and commercialisation related to the zero-carbon technologies, with spillover effects everywhere. It has two negative effects. It is strongly protectionist, favouring US production of many zero-carbon goods, and also production in allied countries for energy transition minerals and some other important inputs into production. This reduces gains from trade in goods related to the energy and industrial transition and increases costs everywhere. And the IRA is part of the set of expansionary fiscal policies, commenced under President Trump and extended under President Biden, that has lifted the US budget deficit to by far the largest experienced outside recession or during or in the aftermath of major wars. The US budget deficit this year will absorb about 2 per cent of global incomes or 8 per cent of global gross savings. The US IRA has been partially emulated in other North American countries, in Europe and in the developed countries of Northeast Asia. The combined budgetary effects have been important causes in the rise of global long-term real interest rates on low-risk debt from around zero to over 2 per cent. Virtually all the zero-emissions technologies and processes are highly capital-intensive – much more so than their carbon-intensive competitors. The higher interest rates have increased costs in the energy and industrial transition.

The Trump–Biden combination of protection and budgetary expansion has raised the US real exchange rate and reduced US competitiveness in all other markets. The simple arithmetic says that this has increased the competitiveness of China in the rest of the world's markets.

The European Union's CBAM seeks to impose additional taxes on imports of products from countries that apply less rigorous policies than the European Union to reduce carbon emissions. From 2026, it will impose additional import taxes on goods entering the European Union, to close the gap between carbon taxes and constraints imposed in the countries in which production was located, and carbon taxes that would have been paid on the same activities in Europe. It will systematically favour imports from countries that are doing more to reduce emissions over those from countries that are doing less. It will encourage trading partners to go further with policies that reduce emissions. The CBAM is likely to be highly and favourably influential in the climate change mitigation policies of trading partners. Major trading partners of Europe with strong commitments to climate change mitigation will have incentives to go further in policies to reduce emissions intensity to European levels. For China, the high current emissions intensity would make that a step too far in the near future. The straightforward medium-term response would be to tighten and extend the Chinese ETS to raise the carbon price and to support trade with Europe in goods and carbon credits. It is in the EU's and global interest that a path be kept open for China when its efforts or achievements in decarbonisation are comparable with those of the EU.

There is a risk that CBAM will be applied without regard for announced principles, so that it increases protection in addition to legitimate compensation for differences in carbon policies. Generally favourable effects on the global mitigation effort would then come at a cost to global development.

The CBAM may have a role in resolution of Trump-era US tariffs against the European Union. The 10 per cent US tariffs on aluminium imports from Europe and the 25 per cent tariffs on steel were the subject of discussion in early 2024. The United States has suggested that a 'carbon club' be established – a common tariff region with the EU for these and perhaps other products. One possibility would be for the European CBAM rates of border tax to be applied by both countries, alongside free trade between the United States and the European Union. The rationale would be that with the IRA, the United States is making similar effort to Europe in reducing emissions. Other countries could join the carbon club if they were making similar decarbonisation efforts. The arrangements would be inconsistent with WTO rules. That would not seem to be a barrier on the US side: since early in the Trump presidency the United States has not accepted the application of WTO rules to itself. As a matter of pragmatic judgement, the arrangement would probably be favourable for the global mitigation effort, and have low costs from distortion of resource allocation, so long as the protectionist element of the proposed arrangements was small.

The combination of the IRA and associated US budget expansion and protection, and development of a carbon club between the United States and the European Union, would tend to divide the world into two trading regions, centred respectively on the United States and China. China would be the main focus of exclusion and may not be accepted into the club no matter what its mitigation efforts.

The high budget deficits, protection and real exchange rate would make the United States less competitive in the rest of the world for zero-carbon as well as other goods and services. Some of that high cost structure and reduction of competitiveness would flow through to partners in the club – although less to the extent that the European Union resisted pressures to use the CBAM in a protectionist way. China would become more competitive and increase its share of world markets outside the carbon club. The US-centred and China-centred trading regions would be of comparable size, so both are likely to lose similar amounts from reduction of gains from trade. Countries that maintained open trade with both the carbon club and the rest of the world would experience the largest gains from trade. Arbitrage through them would help to reduce costs of global economic fragmentation in both the carbon club and the rest of the world.

The world has to prepare for the possibility of the election as president of the United States in November 2024 of Mr Trump, or an alternative with similar approaches to policy. This would see a reduction in the positive and an increase in the negative contributions of US policy to the global mitigation effort. It would see a large additional reduction in gains from trade in the United States and the rest of the world, including China. The rest of the world would be wise to avoid retaliation on trade or climate, allowing the possibility of a turn in the US political cycle to policies more favourable for good global outcomes. The rest of the world's best response from the point of view of climate change mitigation and global development would be to reduce protection and to increase efforts to reduce emissions. This would occur within the framework of 'concerted unilateral mitigation' – albeit for the time being a concerted effort of countries other than the United States.

Wider mechanisms for maintaining open trade with China

More generally, there is large advantage for climate change mitigation and global development in maintaining open trade in zero-carbon goods, equipment for building the zero-carbon economy and carbon credits.

The understanding of comparative advantage and the gains from trade have been assimilated into much Chinese development discussion. At the fourth decadal anniversary of reform in 2018, I remarked that China had become a source of education on Ricardian theory and practice (Garnaut 2018). Professor Lin Yifu's Center for New Structural Economics at Peking University was a source of knowledge on comparative advantage, influencing development planning to good effect in some African countries (Lin and Wang 2017). There have been important crosscurrents in Chinese trade policy over the past several years, with anxieties about access to developed countries' markets feeding back into other tendencies to accelerate self-sufficiency in a number of advanced technological products. It is important for global climate change mitigation and Chinese and global development that these tendencies do not extend into high-volume trade in goods that are important in the zero-carbon economy.

In 2011, important steps were taken to support open trade in 'environmental products' at the Asia-Pacific Economic Cooperation heads of government meeting in Vladivostok. It was agreed that fifty-six products, including photovoltaic panels and wind turbines, would be subject to tariffs no higher than 5 per cent. As with all APEC agreements, this was within the framework of open regionalism, characterised by concerted unilateral liberalisation. Participation was voluntary, and its terms not legally binding. Nineteen of the twenty-one APEC members joined. Compliance has been much higher than with 'binding' WTO agreements. Four of the nineteen participating countries have not comprehensively complied with the agreement. Malaysia and Thailand describe themselves as being on a path to compliance. Chile's general tariff of 6 per cent requires amendment to bring tariffs on the fifty-six items down by a percentage point. The United States complied until the Trump tariffs introduced major breaches, which have not been corrected. With the important US exception, the substantial progress under APEC auspices has survived the trade and political tensions of recent years. It would be helpful to extend the early initiatives and to introduce similar initiatives in the WTO. Pending support from all WTO members, plurilateral agreements could be helpful in themselves and encourage wider multilateral efforts.

It is strongly in the interests of China and its economic partners in the developed world that China is not excluded from developed country markets for goods that are currently made with high emissions but which are capable of being made with net-zero emissions. China has a particular interest in open trade in two types of products. One is the capital goods of the zero-emissions economy, where China is currently by far the world's largest exporter. It is prospectively a much larger exporter as the world moves to zero net emissions. The second is goods currently made with high emissions that will embody zero emissions in the new economy – zero-emissions iron, silicon, aluminium and other metals, made with renewable energy or hydrogen from renewable energy in countries with rich mineral and renewable energy resources; or zero-emissions hydrogen embedded in ammonia or in other chemical compounds. Drawing zero-emissions materials from countries with rich renewable energy resources will allow China to remove emissions from its own supply chains at relatively low cost, supporting its continued access to and competitiveness in the markets of developed countries.

Disruption from the COVID crisis and the Russia–Ukraine war

Long-term progress on the energy and industrial transition has been affected by the dislocation of the COVID-19 pandemic and then the disruption of global energy markets from the Russia–Ukraine war.

The global economic recession caused by the COVID restrictions reduced carbon emissions in 2020. There was a sharp increase in emissions in the recovery from recession. We will soon learn whether the latter were temporary increases that had no long-term consequences, or an unfortunate turning point.

The disruption of the global coal, oil and gas markets from the war in Ukraine is a larger challenge to the transition. High energy prices in Europe, spreading to the rest of the world, have elevated the priority of short-term energy security and cost over reductions in emissions. This has been a setback for movement to net zero in the short run, especially in Europe. However, it has drawn attention to the insecurity of reliance on fossil carbon and hydrocarbon imported from potentially unreliable sources. Renewable energy, drawn from local sun and wind, is inherently more secure. Renewable energy embodied in imported products may be similarly or less insecure depending on the country of origin. The long-term effect of the fossil carbon market disruption may be to accelerate the energy transition.

Conclusions

China has an immensely important role in reaching the agreed international goal of holding temperature increases close to 1.5°C by achieving zero net global emissions by 2050. Success is much more likely and will be achieved at much lower cost if there is close cooperation across national boundaries. Within that success, China is a major source of capital goods for the global transition and a major importer of currently carbon-intensive goods that are more economically supplied from countries with richer relative endowments of renewable energy resources. Geopolitical tensions with developed countries are potentially a risk to the required cooperation. China and its partners throughout the world share an acute interest in ensuring that disruption of trade is confined to goods and services in which China or other countries have real and substantial security interests. This would allow the world to continue to benefit from specialisation in line with comparative advantage in goods that are important in the energy and industrial transition to zero net emissions.

An unvarnished examination of the current state of international relations in many spheres may suggest bleak prospects for the global and the Sino–US cooperation that is necessary to contain climate change within bounds that are consistent with the continued good health of human civilisation. War in the Ukraine and Gaza; geopolitical tensions between China and the capitalist democracies; the parlous financial position of the World Health Organization; and the denial of institutional support for the normal functioning of the World Trade Organization. These all caution against hope. But the successes so far in the Paris and Glasgow conferences around the concept of concerted unilateral mitigation, in expanding the boundaries of open trade in environmental products, in Asia-Pacific cooperation and in the maintenance of constructive Sino–US cooperation on climate change through the 2020s so far suggest that continued efforts are warranted. Obstfeld (2024) draws some apt and encouraging parallels from the darker days of the Cold War:

> Historically, new global challenges and opportunities have led to new forms of international cooperation, even in times of stress. During the Cold War, for example, US–Soviet collaboration led to development of the oral polio vaccine and, a much more difficult task, to the eradication of naturally occurring smallpox worldwide by 1978 (Hotez 2014).
>
> This experience carries at least two important lessons for today. First, universally perceived challenges can prompt productive collaboration between competing superpowers. Second, existing multilateral institutions that are widely viewed as legitimate and more politically neutral are instrumental for channeling superpower competition into positive-sum outcomes that can also attract broad-based international support.

11

AUSTRALIA AND JAPAN AND THE GLOBAL RESPONSE TO CLIMATE CHANGE*

Good things and catastrophes, 1890–1957

Today is ANZAC Day in Australia, a national holiday remembering the horrors of war and the sacrifice of Australians in wars of the past. It commemorates the landing of troops at Gallipoli in Turkey on 25 April 2015, in the first large-scale Australian and New Zealand engagement in World War I. My late father-in-law, great-grandfather of our grandchildren, landed, was wounded and evacuated as the early sun lit up the beach on that first morning.

There is a painting in the Australian War Memorial of the Japanese naval ship HIJMS *Ibuki*, protecting the ships carrying the Australians across the Indian Ocean to that fateful encounter. Australia and Japan had made important contributions to each other's early modern story in the quarter-century before the first ANZAC Day. In 1890, only a couple of decades after the Meiji Restoration began Japan's journey to leadership in global development, Fujishiro Kanematsu moved to Sydney to join the dynamic young Kansai textile industry to the world's main source of woollen textile raw materials. He established an early prototype of the Soga Shosha that came to be crucially important in linking Japanese

---

*   This chapter was originally a presentation to the Tokyo Forum hosted by the Australia–Japan Research Centre and the Japan Research Institute in April 2024.

development to the global resources that it needed for success.

Over the next quarter-century Australia and Japan did many good things together. We also both made mistakes that contributed to the catastrophe of the 1930s and 1940s. We learnt from what we did right and also from what we did wrong in the sixty-seven years between the establishment of the first Sogo Shosha office in Australia, through World Wars I and II, to the establishment of new foundations for partnership in 1957.

Japan–Australia as a model for cooperation

In the sixty-seven years since then, the knowledge from experience has allowed us to do something great, and new in the world. We proved that a big country with exceptional deficiency in natural resources for modern economic development can securely, reliably and economically attain and sustain the highest achievements of modern economic development. It can do this through peaceful, secure commercial trade with a country that has an abundance of resources and deficiency of local demand to use them. We proved that such a relationship can underpin high standards of living in the resource exporting as well as the resource importing country. We proved that this can enhance each country's trade relations with others and therefore regional and global development. We developed a model of trade and development that is now required on an even larger scale to meet the great challenges facing the global community today.

We have demonstrated since 1957 that two societies with very different political, social and economic histories can build the trust, the interpersonal relations and understanding, the institutions and the mutually compatible policies that allow each to rely fundamentally on the other's strengths for national economic prosperity and security. Together we have developed approaches to international exchange that have supported a long period of successful Asia-Pacific development. Together we have developed approaches to international cooperation that can overcome what sometimes seem to be insurmountable obstacles to global security and prosperity, in an era of vulnerability to human-induced climate change and of potentially destructive competition between political systems.

The new era of friendship, understanding and cooperation began with the Australia–Japan Commerce Agreement of 1957. The two countries moved beyond the destructive legacy of a recent war to a new trade relationship that was greatly to expand what was possible in economic development in both countries. In the agreement, Australia was one of the first countries to remove postwar discrimination and extend most favoured nation treatment to trade with Japan. Japan reduced tariffs on products important to Australia, most importantly wool. Crucially, Australia and Japan reduced barriers to trade with each other without introducing any discrimination against any other country.

Of central importance to the new relationship was the growth of knowledge and trust between Australians and Japanese involved in the trade and investment. The Australia–Japan Business Cooperation Committee (AJBCC) had its first meeting in 1964 and ever since has played a large role in building feelings of mutual respect among individuals involved in trade and investment. Leaders of politics and thought in both countries participated in discussions. The sixtieth annual meeting of the group last year was its largest ever.

Close intergovernmental relations supported stable, outward-looking policy that underpinned trade expansion. Japan became Australia's largest destination of exports. Australia became by far the main source of the immense quantities of metallic minerals required for Japanese outperformance of the Japan Economic Planning Agency's plan to double output in a decade in the 1960s and to keep on growing much more rapidly than other developed countries until the late 1980s.

The new approach to international economic cooperation overcame what had been seen as weaknesses of poor natural resource endowments in Japan, and small scale and isolation in Australia.

The new ways were manifested first in large-scale intercontinental iron ore trade. Australia overcame inhibitions dating back to prewar tensions to remove bans on iron exports. Businesses from the two countries established a new way of building major new projects dependent on international trade: project financing underpinned by long-term sales contracts. The Japanese trading companies played major roles in bringing together arrangements that were to open vast new frontiers of growth for both economies.

How the model gave Japan fossil carbon energy security

The bilateral relationship entered new territory when the oil crises of the 1970s increased costs and anxiety about security in energy trade. Confidence in the bilateral relationship supported reduction in energy intensity in the Japanese economy. The energy-intensive aluminium industry, once the largest among the world's market economies, moved offshore. In its place, new smelters in New South Wales, Queensland and Victoria took advantage of low-cost coal-based electricity in New South Wales, Victoria and Queensland. A new uranium trade emerged from long introspection about the safety risks in both countries. The technologically complex new LNG trade was built on long-term contracts and minority investments from Mitsubishi and Mitsui, Japanese government loans, and an agreement from the Western Australian government to take a substantial amount of output for domestic use at prices well above international levels. When those take-or-pay contracts threatened the bankruptcy of the WA state government in 1983, the Commonwealth stepped in with fiscal support to avoid default.

The development of the new coalfields in Queensland and associated aluminium smelting involved heavy state government investments in rail, port and electricity infrastructure, in support of commitments by the Japanese trading companies. Large-scale investment in electricity infrastructure and innovations in electricity pricing by state-owned businesses in New South Wales and Victoria underpinned investment in aluminium smelting.

A major restructuring of Japanese energy use transformed energy trade. Japan's overwhelming reliance on imports of petroleum from the Middle East gave way to diversified energy supply, with Australia in the largest role. Japan now imports nearly 90 per cent of its energy, with Australia supplying more than twice as much as second-placed Saudi Arabia. Australia delivers around two thirds of Japan's coal (metallurgical and thermal), around 40 per cent of its gas, and around a third of its uranium.

The author of Japan's plan to double GDP in a decade in the 1960s, Saburo Okita, then president of the Japan Economic Planning Agency, had seen secure resource supply and a strong relationship with Australia as underpinning Japanese development. Over many years, he built a close and productive working friendship with the Australian official mainly responsible for the 1957 agreement, then secretary of the Australian Department of Trade John Crawford. By the mid-1960s Okita and Crawford were in private roles that gave them even larger opportunities to strengthen Japan–Australia relations: Okita as president of the Japan Center for Economic Research; and Crawford as professor of economics and later vice-chancellor and chancellor of the Australian National University. Okita's Japan Center for Economic Research supported by Professor Kiyoshi Kojima and other economists at Hitotsubashi University became the Japanese end of productive Japanese–Australian work and thought on future bilateral, regional and global economic cooperation. Crawford's Australia–Japan Research Centre supported by Professor Peter Drysdale and other economists became the Australian end. They established the Pacific Trade and Development Conference series, which remains important today for developing and sharing ideas about regional economic relations. They brought in leaders of thought about economic cooperation from Southeast Asia, including Dr Hadi Soesastro and colleagues at the Centre for Strategic and International Studies in Jakarta. They brought in leaders of thought about international economic relations from the United States, including Professor Hugh Patrick at Yale and later Columbia. They brought leading thinkers from Korea, seeking to emulate Japan's successful development as a resource-poor country requiring deep and secure integration with complementary economies. They brought in China after the decisions on economic reform and opening to international trade in the late 1970s, in ways that allowed full participation from Hong Kong and Taiwan.

Trust, knowledge and open regionalism

Okita was made foreign minister by Prime Minister Masayoshi Ohira in 1978. This was the only ever use of a provision in the postwar Japanese constitution for ministers to be appointed from outside the Diet. He immediately accompanied the prime minister on a visit to Canberra to discuss regional cooperation with Australian prime minister Malcolm Fraser. I recall, as clearly as if it were today, our discussion with Okita and Crawford of how the two countries would support the establishment of an institution to expand Asia-Pacific economic cooperation.

The Pacific Community Seminar in Canberra in 1979, at which it was my honour to be assistant chairman to Sir John Crawford, led to the formation of the Pacific Economic Cooperation Council, with participation from leaders of business and thought. This contributed eventually to Asia-Pacific Economic Cooperation (APEC) from its first meeting hosted by the Hawke Australian government in Canberra in November 1989.

There was recognition from the Australia–Japan experience that trust between people involved in the relationship was an essential accompaniment to removal of formal barriers to trade and to deepening trade and investment ties. Trust was built on experience of respectful interaction, and on knowledge about each other. Respect, knowledge and trust reduced uncertainty, lowered transaction costs and increased trade and investment.

Southeast Asian participation reinforced support for informal rather than institutional integration. It reinforced commitment to non-discrimination in the deepening of regional integration. 'Open regionalism' became the guiding concept: deepening trade and investment ties without discrimination against outsiders. Economic integration should be built around support for the multilateral trading system embodied in the GATT (later the World Trade Organization). Economic ties would be richer among regional partners because trust and knowledge of opportunity were greater, and not because trade or investment with third parties was restricted by tariffs or regulation.

Concerted unilateral liberalisation of trade and investment became the modus operandi of open regionalism. Unilateral, because decisions to lower policy barriers to trade and investment would be taken separately by sovereign governments. Concerted, because there was a shared goal of removing barriers to trade, and because the sharing of knowledge and understanding of what others were doing provided confidence that the gains from liberalisation at home would be enhanced by the expansion of regional markets by liberalisation in important trading partners.

Concerted unilateral liberalisation to advance open regionalism underpinned trade liberalisation throughout the Western Pacific through the 1990s until the East Asian financial crisis in 1998. Unilateral liberalisation was supplemented by negotiated measures in the Uruguay Round under GATT auspices for some of the hardest knots of protection, including agriculture in Japan and Korea. Negotiated liberalisation was important again around China's entry into the WTO.

Japan–Australia cooperation contributed substantially to the emergence of China as a major participant in international exchange. China in the early years of opening to the international economy, through the 1980s and early 1990s, even more than Japan and Korea, had initially been reluctant to rely heavily on international markets for resources that were essential for development. Its own energy and metallic mineral resources were larger relative to its economic size than those of Japan or Korea. But as in Japan and Korea, it became clear that reliance on domestic resources would seriously truncate opportunities for development.

The Japan–Australia trading relationship was important as a model, but important more directly as well. As Australia's ambassador to China in November 1985, I was given an honoured place at the opening of China's first steel mill using modern international technology and approaches: the Baoshan steel mill near Shanghai. My place came from the decision to use some high-quality Australian ore. With me was a senior executive of a Japanese trading company which had contributed to understanding of the value of Australian ore in high performance of modern steelmaking technology.

Saburo Okita, back in private life, was appointed as the Japanese chair of a commission to advise on long-term Sino–Japanese relations. On his visits to Beijing, he would call on me in the Australian embassy to discuss the possibilities.

Australia and Japan remained steady in maintaining open people-to-people relations with China through the ups and downs of political and economic change in China. Australia with support from Japan and APEC contributed much to acceptance of China as a member of the World Trade Organization in 2002 – immediately following an APEC leaders' meeting in Shanghai. China became by far the main export market for both of us. The contribution this made to each of our prosperity contributed positively to our trading relationship with each other.

I have discussed at length the history of Australia–Japan cooperation over the past sixty-seven years, because it holds a torch for successful global development in the difficult years ahead.

Applying historical lessons to climate

There are two immense contemporary challenges. One is stopping human-induced climate change before it destabilises global economic development and the international political order. The other is restoring open multilateral trade and investment as the foundation for global development. Our own prosperity and security depend on the international community meeting these challenges.

Australia and Japan and all other countries have agreed to keep temperature increases to 1.5°C above pre-industrial levels. That requires net-zero emissions in the world as a whole by 2050. Developed countries have accepted that some developing countries will take longer. Some European countries have formally committed to net zero by 2045. Most developed countries, including Australia and Japan, have committed to net zero by 2050. That for the time being is the solemn commitment that we have made to each other and to all other countries.

Honouring that commitment means immense change over the next quarter-century in technologies applied to most economic activities, to economic structure in all our countries, and to comparative advantage in international trade.

The Paris and Glasgow agreements at which Australia, Japan and all other countries committed themselves to the 1.5°C objective owe much to the approach to international agreements developed for APEC in the 1990s. After failure of formal negotiations on emissions reduction targets for each country in the Copenhagen Conference of the Parties to the UNFCCC in 2009, concerted unilateral mitigation became the modus operandi of the annual meetings under UN auspices. That was the beginnings of substantive progress in international cooperation on mitigation of climate change.

The countries in Northeast Asia and most in Europe had strong comparative disadvantage in energy and carbon and hydrocarbon inputs into economic activity in the fossil carbon economy. They became the world's largest importers of coal, oil and gas. Comparative disadvantage was greatest of all in Japan and Korea.

Australia's immense coal and gas resources and small domestic demand gave it strong comparative advantage in fossil carbon. It became the world's largest exporter of coal and LNG taken together. Geographic proximity and the high quality of the relationship made Australia by far the main supplier of fossil carbon to Japan.

The zero-carbon economy is in some ways similar and in some ways

different. It is similar because the densely populated, highly industrialised economies of Northeast Asia and Europe have strong comparative disadvantage in producing zero-carbon energy and other industrial
inputs.

It is similar, because Australia has immense natural resources for
solar and wind power generation, and the space to deploy them. It has
space and skills for sustainable production and harvesting of biomass
for zero-emissions transport fuels and industrial inputs. Its advantages
relative to the rest of the world are even greater than in the fossil carbon
world economy.

Australia can be the reliable, secure and economically competitive
source of a high proportion of the energy and carbon-connected industrial inputs in the zero-carbon world. There are fewer alternative sources
for these imports into Japan, so we can expect Australia's role to be even
greater than in the fossil carbon trade.

Japan will have great difficulty in achieving net-zero emissions without high levels of imports of renewable energy and goods embodying
renewable energy. One-third of Japan's fossil carbon fuels and industrial inputs are used to generate electricity. The other two-thirds are
used directly in vehicles, buildings, industry and agriculture. Roughly
15 to 20 per cent of all fossil fuels are used for non-energy purposes, as a
source of carbon for creating plastics and other chemical manufactures,
and reducing iron oxide into iron metal.

Today Japan uses around 955 TWh of electricity. With full decarbonisation of industry and transport through electrification, Japan's economy
would require around 2.1 PWh, or about 2.2 times as much as it presently
uses. This demand must be satisfied by zero-carbon electricity supply.
Today, nuclear and renewables together produce around 268 TWh, or
around 12 per cent of what may be required in the future. Another 88 per
cent remains.

Japan has poor endowments of energy and minerals but is rich in
human and financial capital and quality institutions. This produced its

current trade pattern, and its relationship with Australia. Japan's poor endowments of renewable energy and biomass resources and its human capital and effective institutions will shape its future trade pattern. It will have strong comparative disadvantage in all products and processes that use energy and carbon intensively and which must be supplied with zero emissions in future. It will continue to have strong comparative advantage in the products of complex industrial processes, especially where they utilise capital intensively. Resisting the realities of comparative advantage stalls development, nationally and globally, and will stall climate mitigation.

Japan's renewable resources are among the world's most expensive, and Australia's are among the cheapest. The IEA and IRENA put Japan's solar levelised cost of electricity at between 2.5 and 4.5 times Australia's, at up to US$172/MWh. They estimate costs for Japanese onshore wind at between three and four times Australia's, at up to US$140/MWh. The IEA finds that Japan will be by far the most expensive producer of green steel, with average costs approaching double those of China and 150 per cent of the United States. Japan's Renewable Energy Institute has stated that 'the best approach is to produce crude steel in Australia'.

Japan will use offshore wind, which is generally around 50 to 100 per cent more expensive than onshore wind. In Japan, the IEA estimates costs of US$200/MWh.

Nuclear power may be the cheapest option for clean electricity today, with the IEA estimating a cost of US$87/MWh. This is several times the cost of renewable power at better Australian sites. Utilisation of nuclear is hampered by the difficulty of accelerating rollout; the current pace of expansion would see nuclear shrink to supply only 7 per cent of electricity by 2050. Great acceleration will increase costs, placing pressure on scarce skills and engineering capacity.

Japan's geography makes large-scale imports of renewable energy by cable expensive, risky and unlikely. Importing hydrogen in molecular form or through ammonia or other compounds as carriers is not a low-cost solution. IRENA expects costs to fall by 2050 but at US$100–200/MWh to remain several times costs in Australia.

One big difference between the fossil carbon and the zero-emissions world is that zero-carbon energy is more difficult and expensive to transport between continents than coal, gas and oil. The latter costs little or no more delivered into Japan than in centres of Australian demand away from the regions where the coal and gas are mined. If renewable electricity were transported to Japan by submarine cable, as hydrogen or such hydrogen carriers as ammonia, it would be several times as expensive as in Australia. Japan will need to import some expensive energy for electricity through cables, or as hydrogen or ammonia, or as uranium oxide to power nuclear generators. This is necessary to light and heat homes and offices and to fill car batteries. Perhaps a third of Japan's imports will be supplied through these means at great expense to supplement meagre domestic renewable energy resources. This will be expensive, but unavoidable. But Japan will not import energy in these forms as inputs into industries that supply markets subject to international competition. To remain globally competitive in any industry requiring inputs made from renewable energy or biomass – and this is most manufacturing industry – Japan will need to import inputs embodying the resources that it cannot economically supply for itself. Japan will need to import immense quantities of green iron, green aluminium and other metals produced without carbon emissions; green transport fuels; and green processed materials for the plastics and other chemical industries. Australia is the natural supplier of the green iron made from Australian iron ore and renewable hydrogen; the green aluminium from Australian aluminium ores and renewable electricity; the polysilicon from Australian quartz or sand; bio-carbon and renewable electricity; and the green transport fuels from Australian hydrogen and biomass. Imports from Australia of zero-carbon goods would keep Japanese production globally competitive, for cars, machinery, electronic goods and plastic products using iron, aluminium and silicon metal and biogas or bio-oil.

Let us presume that Japan accelerates output of zero-carbon electricity to an extent that currently seems unlikely. Let us presume that Japan successfully doubles the pace of solar installation, quadruples that of wind, and increases new nuclear builds by an order of magnitude from levels of recent years, and continues at the new high rate until the middle of the century. Let us take leave of geography, economic and social constraints and presume that expansion of none of these activities is constrained in any way. That would still leave a 'gap' of more than half a petawatt hour of power required to decarbonise the domestic economy. Importing iron metal embodying Australian renewable energy in place of smelting iron in Japan would avoid about half of the 'gap' remaining.

For Australia to do well economically in these new circumstances, it will rely on imports from Japan and other countries for the many products in which it lacks comparative advantage.

Australia and Japan can provide a model for the rest of the world in the zero-carbon economy, as we have in the fossil-carbon economy of the past. The role of respect, knowledge and trust among people involved in trade and investment relations between our countries will be as important as ever. There will be a large need for innovation in technologies, business models and policies. We will need to work together to ensure that the innovations are secured in time and knowledge of them spread promptly to all that need to understand them.

Using our model through contemporary stress

We will each need new domestic policies to correct the external costs of carbon emissions and the external benefits of innovation in decarbonisation. Lessons from experience in Japan–Australia relations suggest that Japan and Australia should encourage discussion internally and with each other of the merits of alternative policies for reaching shared objectives.

These next decades of transition to net zero will be full of rapid change and stress. There will be times when we doubt each other's will to meet our solemn commitments on decarbonisation to each other and to the rest of the international community. It is important that we give each other no cause to doubt the other's will.

As with the iron ore and coal and gas trades, success in trade and investment between Australia and Japan can demonstrate to our neighbours and the rest of the world that the most different of economies can support each other in achieving common prosperity.

I conclude by returning attention to one other lesson of the past sixty-seven years. The world faces a special challenge in decarbonising economic activity at a time of intense competition between political systems. China has by far the world's main capacity for manufacturing equipment to decarbonise energy, transport and industry. This partly reflects its manufacturing capacities and skills. It partly reflects its early realisation that the zero-carbon industries would be valuable through the global climate and energy transition. The availability of Chinese solar panels, wind turbines, batteries, electric vehicles and other products increases the chances of the world successfully avoiding catastrophic climate change.

It is, however, inevitable that geopolitical tension, especially between China and our mutual ally the United States, will lead to great pressures for discrimination in international trade. There may be some circumstance in which restriction on international trade and investment is warranted on geosecurity grounds. It is important that claims of such circumstances are examined analytically, and the costs of trade and investment restriction considered alongside any geostrategic benefit. To allow the current tensions to lead to indiscriminate restriction of international trade and investment would guarantee failure for all our political systems.

Open, non-discriminatory trade is even more important now than it was when Japan and Australia moved away from the wartime legacy of trade restriction sixty-seven years ago.

12

AUSTRALIA'S IMPOSSIBLE TASK: RESTORING PROSPERITY BY BUILDING THE SUPERPOWER*

with Rod Sims

(Ross Garnaut)

When I spoke to the National Press Club in June 2008 and again in March 2011 about Australia doing its fair share in the global fight against climate change, my case was defensive. Short-term costs would avoid much larger long-term damage. The message that Rod and I share in this chapter is different. Australia's circumstances are different, and the effects of early action to reduce greenhouse gases are different.

One big thing has changed for the better since we were talking together about climate change in the decade before last. Yes, there are the same defensive reasons for stopping human-induced climate change. But now it is clear, as it wasn't clear then, that Australia's advantages in the emerging zero-carbon world economy are so large that they define the most credible path to restoration of growth in Australian living standards.

The change in our economic circumstances and the big change in economic opportunity in the zero-carbon economy mean that the best policy solutions change. In designing policies to secure our own decarbonisation, we now have to give a large place to Australia's opportunity to

---

*   This chapter is taken from Rod Sims' and my presentation to the National Press Club, Canberra, 14 February 2024.

be the renewable energy Superpower of the zero-carbon world economy. The emissions trading scheme (ETS) recommended in 2008 and 2011 was best when the main concern was doing our fair share in the global effort at the lowest possible cost. It would be good now. The carbon solution levy (CSL) that we propose today is better suited to take advantage of the immense benefits for Australian living standards from building the Superpower.

The global transition to net zero is Australia's opportunity. We can use it to raise productivity and living standards after a decade of stagnation. Other countries do not share our natural endowments of wind and solar energy resources, and land to deploy them, as well as land to grow biomass sustainably as an alternative to petroleum and coal for chemical manufactures. In the zero-carbon economy, Australia is the economically natural location to produce a substantial proportion of the products currently made with large carbon emissions in Northeast Asia and Europe.

Our advantages are more than our land, sun and wind. As a developed country with sound public finances, we have a lower cost of capital than any developing countries except some Middle East oil exporters. This matters, as renewable energy and zero-carbon industrial production are much more capital-intensive than the industries and technologies they replace. The heritage of infrastructure, skills and industrial culture from mining, forestry and agriculture helps. Prudent concern for security of supply will see Europe looking to balance Middle East and African supplies with imports from Australia. In Northeast Asia, Australia has large locational advantages.

Our Superpower story is increasingly recognised in Northeast Asia and Europe. In an article in the *Australian Financial Review* in January 2024, Angela McDonald-Smith reported from the German Ministry of Education and Research: 'Australia wants to be a renewable energy superpower. So, this is a perfect match because Germany is a superpower in the offtake of energy.' Or, as Michael Liebreich wrote in *Bloomberg NEF*: 'The prohibitive cost of long-distance imports means that energy-intensive industries will inevitably migrate to regions with cheap clean energy. It is inconceivable for any country to import iron ore from Australia or Brazil, hydrogen from Australia, the Gulf, Canada or Africa, and make steel at a globally competitive cost'.

These perspectives have been confirmed in conversations in recent months with major business leaders in Japan and China.

Last year, a team from the Oxford School of Engineering Science published in *Nature Communications* the results of an elaborate modelling exercise defining the cost of producing iron and steel in different locations in a zero-carbon world. Australia emerges as by far the world's largest producer of iron metal and steel, more than twice as large as any other country.

Making good use of our zero-carbon opportunity makes it possible for Northeast Asia and Europe – over two-fifths of the world's emissions – to get to net zero. Reuben Finighan at the Superpower Institute is working through the detail. Here is a taste of what will come from this work.

In 2023 China installed enough new renewable energy to supply twice the power from all sources used in Australia's National Electricity Market (NEM). To supply all the renewable electricity China needs for zero net emissions now – converting all the coal, oil and gas where electricity can be used in its place – would take 100 times the amount of power produced and used in the NEM today. That figure will continue to grow as China's economy grows. Its renewable resources are poorer than Australia's and concentrated in the north (much on the latitude of Hobart, where winter days are short), and in the west (far from where industry is concentrated along the coast and in the south). Even if China were willing to pay around twice Australia's expected costs in 2050, it would not be able to satisfy anything like its full requirements for wind and solar power from its own resources. There would be a gap of over 6000 TWh. The cheapest way to source that immense amount of energy is by importing goods that embody renewable energy. Turning the iron ore China currently imports from Australia into metal before it is shipped would fill over a quarter of the gap. Making that iron metal in Australia would require ten times the power now used in Australia's NEM.

The constraints on domestic supply of renewable energy are as severe in Europe as in China, or more so. They are greater still in the rest of Northeast Asia. Japan needs an additional 1848 TWh of renewable energy to decarbonise existing power and industrial and other uses of fossil carbon. The equivalent in Korea is 1170 TWh, and in Germany 991 TWh. These numbers do not include any contribution from products that require biomass as well as green hydrogen and electricity: sustainable aviation and shipping fuels, silicon, petrochemical feedstocks and nitrogenous fertilisers.

Our main message is that export of zero-carbon goods can underpin a long period of high investment, rising productivity, full employment and rising incomes in Australia.

Which are the Superpower industries?

Green hydrogen and hydrogen carriers like ammonia will be important, and there are likely to be exports of renewable electricity through undersea cables. But exports of goods embodying these and other zero-carbon inputs are the main story.

The processing of minerals will be the most important, with iron a long way in front. Aluminium is big. Processing critical minerals, including silicon, lithium, nickel, copper, cobalt, is part of the Superpower story. The South Australian government's plans for the Upper Spencer Gulf lead the way, starting with green copper and green iron.

Australia has advantages in immense new industries requiring inputs of biomass as well as zero-carbon electricity and hydrogen.

Australia would use a tenth of global production of solar panels, wind turbines, batteries, electricity transmission cables and towers and hydrogen electrolysers and pipelines. For manufacturing inputs into these industries, unlike other manufacturing activities, we would suffer no disadvantage from having a small domestic market. We may have a comparative advantage in producing some inputs in which there are cost advantages in local metal or bio-carbon supplies and low-cost energy and capital, and which do not use labour intensively.

How are we going?
Our exceptional resources, legacy institutions from before 2013 (the Renewable Energy Target or RET, ARENA and the CEFC) and action by both Coalition and Labor state governments kept the future alive through the Commonwealth's climate wars.

Remarkably, after the period of Commonwealth policy disputation and incoherence, Australia has the world's largest solar and wind energy share in electricity. The share in South Australia is twice the share of any substantial country in the rest of the world. A sophisticated Australian wholesale power market is making renewable power available at incomparably low cost for batteries or Superpower industries. Australia leads the world in use of battery power storage. Australia is showing the world how a power grid can operate securely and reliably mainly with solar and wind power. Hats off to AEMO and other regulatory agencies.

In the entrails of the market data, we can see the renewable energy share of power generation expanding rapidly, and the average sales price of that power falling. If coal and gas power prices had remained at the levels of a decade ago, renewables expansion would have forced a large reduction in average power prices. But domestic gas prices exploded upwards in eastern Australia, first with the commencement of exports from Gladstone, and then with the Russian invasion of Ukraine. Coal prices also rose dramatically with the war in Ukraine.

In the NEM as a whole, the wind plus solar share rose from 4 per cent in 2012 to 16 per cent in 2019 and 31 per cent in 2023. Both coal and gas generation contracted, with gas more rapidly from 12 per cent in 2012 to 5 per cent in 2023. The average price of wind power was $94 (2023 constant prices) in 2019 and fell back to $55 in 2023. Solar fell spectacularly from $90 in 2019 to $31 in 2023. Meanwhile the average price of gas power lifted from $63 in 2012 to $156 in 2019 and $172 in 2023.

South Australia is in some ways more interesting, because it leads the way to where Australia is headed. Variable renewable energy provided 75 per cent of generation in 2023 – similar to the 82 per cent expected in the NEM as a whole in 2030.

In South Australia, the wind and solar share rose from 29 per cent in 2012 to 51 per cent in 2019 and 75 per cent in 2023. Gas contracted sharply after 2012 despite the closure of coal power generation, with solar and wind replacing all the coal (20 per cent in 2012) and half the gas. The average price of wind power fell from $86 in 2019 to $49 in 2023. Solar fell from $110 to $10 over these four years.

At low prices for renewable energy in South Australia, there are strong incentives for installing storage to shift availability from daytime when solar is abundant to evening when it is valuable. The cost of solar plus storage for evening use is far below the gas that it replaces. Expansion of battery and other storage will over time lift the low prices when solar output is high, and reduce them at other times – so long as participants in the market are confident that there will be no changes in market rules that reduce the value of arbitrage. The emergence of hydrogen and other industries that can ramp up power use when it is cheap will place a floor under the low prices.

Our international commitment to reduce emissions by 43 per cent on 2005 levels by 2030 is the minimum required as a developed country to establish our credibility in the global climate effort. The demands of the emerging Superpower industries will increase total demand and increase the challenge of reducing emissions by 43 per cent. But we do neither the global climate effort nor our own prosperity any good if we meet our commitments in ways that block the emergence of the Superpower by artificially constraining the use of renewable energy in new industries.

The five pillars of national economic success

There are five pillars of national economic success today, as there were in the reform era that gave Australia its two world-beating decades of prosperity. These are also the five pillars of the Superpower.

The first pillar is open trade. That means Australian businesses can use without unnecessary restriction the best and lowest-cost equipment and inputs to production in the world. It also means establishing open access to global markets for our zero-carbon exports. From 2026, the EU Carbon Border Adjustment Mechanism will allow Australian producers to realise a green premium for their products, so long as they can demonstrate a zero-carbon supply chain with genuine additionality, or that all relevant parts of the economy are subject to a carbon charge similar to that in the European Union. Those principles will gradually spread to other importers of zero-carbon goods. We need to strengthen Australia's currently underdeveloped capacity to measure and account for carbon emissions. There are valid offsets to emissions, and we need to ensure that the offsets that we allow have integrity.

The second pillar is strong public finances. This is necessary for Australian producers to have access to a competitive cost of capital and a competitive real exchange rate. In addition, in our small open economy, it is necessary to insulate Australia against international shocks. That requires strong public finances. The budgetary demands of things that only government can do in building the Superpower are large, so we should avoid expenditures on things that governments don't have to do.

The third pillar is securing the support of an informed community, and more specifically ensuring that the human resources are in place. These are necessary for meeting the requirements of rapid structural and technological change.

The fourth pillar is a favourable environment for business investment. Stable policy is important. Only sound policy can be stable. Let's get the policy right in the period ahead and keep it steady from there. Revenue-neutral replacement of conventional accounting profits by cash flow as the base for taxation of business income would increase incentives for investment and innovation. Allowing companies investing in and producing green energy and goods to opt in to cash-flow taxation would accelerate investment and innovation.

The fifth pillar is establishing the right balance between the role of the state and the role of competitive private markets. Only government can supply public goods, including the correction of imperfections in markets. Only government can secure efficient supply of natural monopoly infrastructure services. The things that only government can do are so demanding that the rest should be left to competitive markets.

The electricity wholesale market has had its ups and downs over the last several years. It has had to cope with sudden and large changes in Commonwealth and state policy, including opaque subsidies to keep coal power generators going when the market has called time on them. Currently, the market is delivering negative prices to consumers of energy in regions and at times where variable renewable energy is abundant, and high prices in the early evening when the fading sun doesn't contribute to meeting demand for electricity at the end of a hot day. The current wholesale market is underpinning a storage investment boom and is helping to get Superpower industries started. There is talk in the electricity industry about a capacity market. There is no evidence that a separate capacity market would deliver capacity as efficiently as the current wholesale market is doing. That many countries that are behind us in the energy transition have one is not evidence that we need one. Change has a cost. Change from something that is working well to something problematic has a double cost. Our strong message: don't change the one part of the NEM that is working well.

Markets only work for the community if government corrects any tendency for firms to impose costs on others without paying for them, or to confer benefits on others for which they are not rewarded. Failure to constrain the damage that carbon emissions do to others is a massive market failure. Without a carbon price, we made the correction for electricity in a second-best way, through the RET. That worked surprisingly well. The government is adding the expanded Capacity Investment Scheme (CIS), which will operate with the RET until 2030 and then carry the whole load.

The expanded CIS signals that the Australian government is determined to meet its decarbonisation and renewable energy targets.

There are two systemic risks of the CIS, associated with its claims on the budget and its potential to drift into central planning of renewables investment. The budget risks are mainly in relation to wind and solar, not for underwriting investment in storage. The risks are lower up until 2030, when the green premium provided by the RET augments revenue from energy sales. The budget risks can be ameliorated in two ways. One is to make sure that mechanisms are in place to generate a green premium after the RET ceases in 2030, as a supplement to revenues from the sale of electricity. There will be no green premium without mandatory requirements to use green energy, or some charge on carbon emissions. The second is to make sure that early and rapid development of Superpower industries absorbs power when it is cheap and places a floor under prices.

The second systemic risk arises because governments are now likely to underwrite almost all renewable generation investments. Officials may be drawn into decisions on which projects should be built. In the context of a radically uncertain and rapidly changing energy transition, the most prescient public officials will get many calls wrong. Competitive private markets give better results even if only a small proportion of investors make the right calls, and the right calls are by chance. In a competitive market, the right calls shape the future. Firms guided by wrong calls shrink and become less influential. With central planning, the calls of the captain and their lieutenants shape the future, right or wrong. The intrusion of officials' views on location, technology or timing of investments would place the CIS on a slippery slope to failure.

The government is still thinking through the rules to be applied to the CIS auctions. We suggest that the government consider a generally available CIS scheme, rather than one determined by auction. A formula would determine the levels of payments from and returned to the state. This would reduce the budgetary and avoid the central planning systemic risks.

Government also has to correct for the external benefits that pioneering firms confer on others when they invest in new industries and technologies. At a time of rapid change in zero-carbon energy and industry, there are large external benefits from innovation. The pioneers create knowledge from which business followers and the whole community benefit. ARENA has managed this correction for renewable electricity. We propose a Superpower Industries Innovation Scheme (SIIS), to support early investments in the new industries in a systematic manner.

Government cannot avoid a major role in natural monopoly infrastructure: electricity transmission, and hydrogen transportation and storage. The economic regulation of transmission and distribution in Australia today is deeply problematic. Both need root and branch reform. Hydrogen infrastructure is a clean slate. Developing sound principles for hydrogen infrastructure now can avoid repeating problems that have emerged in transmission. Some states are ahead of others. The Queensland Energy and Jobs Plan provides some capacity for new green industry while decarbonising the old. Incremental change has to proceed in all states, directed mainly at providing for decarbonisation of the established power system. While the incremental improvement is proceeding, we suggest that the Productivity Commission be asked to review electricity transmission and distribution, and hydrogen transport and storage, to meet the requirements of the Superpower.

Finishing the journey to the Superpower
I spoke to Stephen Chu, then President Obama's Secretary for Energy and a Nobel laureate in physics, immediately after the 2010 US midterm elections had shown that the administration's favoured ETS would not pass the Congress. 'How will you reach your targets without the ETS?'

I asked. 'Don't worry, Ross,' Stephen responded. 'We wanted to get there at low cost with an economically efficient mechanism. Now we will get there with less efficient, higher cost instruments. We will keep the costs as low as possible by having a common social cost of carbon guide our regulatory decisions.' He went on to outline for me the many regulatory interventions that were unveiled over the next six years.

The US journey had a large detour through the Trump years and for the time being has landed with the IRA. The first and second pillars, of open trade and strong public finances, would both be fractured by duplication of the US IRA in Australia. The IRA is turbocharging US decarbonisation. Good for the world. But its embodiment of the Trump–Biden support for eyewatering fiscal deficits and protection is making the United States uncompetitive in global markets.

We can probably get to the 82 per cent objective and −43 per cent target by finding second and third and fourth best ways of favouring zero-carbon power generation and industrial production. These are unlikely to get us to the Superpower. Viewed away from the climate wars and the extraordinary history of climate policy, Australia's circumstances call for an explicit payment by firms for the damage that their emissions impose on others.

We suggest consideration of a carbon solutions levy (CSL). This is a levy equivalent to the European carbon price imposed on every tonne of carbon extracted from below the ground or imported into Australia.

This would introduce a green premium to secure access of our zero-carbon goods into international markets. The green premium would reduce the costs of the CIS. And the revenue generated by the CSL would greatly strengthen the budget for the SIIS, natural monopoly infrastructure and other things. The CSL could be integrated into markets for ACCUs and any RET certificates left over from earlier years – companies could purchase and surrender these as an alternative to paying the levy.

Sales to any country with arrangements that generate a comparable green premium from which Australian zero-carbon goods can benefit would receive a rebate for CSL payments. The rebate would apply now to

members of the European Union, the United Kingdom and other countries of Europe. It may apply to the United States if the joint arrangement
with the European Union that is currently under discussions is executed.
We hope that by 2030, our major trading partners in Northeast Asia
would qualify for exemption.

We suggest its introduction in 2030–31, in time to provide the necessary green premium for securing access to green markets and meet the
greater budgetary demands of the CIS at the end of the RET. We note
simply for the discussion that there are advantages in starting earlier. If
introduced over the next year, there is ample rationale for using part of
the funding to reduce the costs of fuel to road users, and to reduce the
cost of electricity – enough to reduce the consumer price index substantially. This would be a circuit breaker in Australia's cost of living crisis.
Inflationary expectations would fall. This would provide an opportunity
for interest rate cuts to be brought forward in time. The risks of rising
unemployment would fall.

We know that the constraints from the climate wars make the implementation of the CSL impossible. But not as impossible politically as
accepting continued stagnation and decline in living standards. It is not
as impossible as passing on to our children and grandchildren lower standards of living than our own parents and grandparents left to us. It is not
as impossible as living with our failure to play our full part in the global
effort to stop the bushfires and cyclones and denudation of our beaches
getting worse. It is not as impossible as being unable to pay for our ageing population, and unable to pay for our submarines.

We expect that the established political parties will rule out this suggestion. That is the way ideas for efficiency-raising reform are discussed
in contemporary Australia. That will not be the end of the matter. If there
is continued community interest and growing support, political leaders
will come back to it.

Conclusions

The Superpower transformation can put us back on a path to higher productivity and living standards after a lost decade. The challenge is as great as any we have faced.

To build the Superpower, Australia will have to invest 5 per cent of incomes or more for several decades. Obviously impossible. Impossible, until you recall that we did more than this for a decade to supply the minerals for Chinese industrial expansion between 2002 and 2012.

We will need continuity of policy over decades. Impossible. Impossible until you recall how the Australian community has enforced consensus from the major political parties for policies that deliver benefits widely in the public interest. Medicare is an example of this. Rising employment with rising incomes, especially in rural and provincial Australia, will enforce consensus.

There is no Superpower without community support in regional Australia for solar farms and wind turbines. Look at Barnaby Joyce and the angry 400 in Canberra last week, and community support seems impossible. Impossible, until you open your ears to the different voices in rural and provincial Australia.

Half a per cent or so of Australia's landmass will power the Superpower. That leaves a lot of room for local people to make choices about what to do with their land. Indigenous Australians own much of the best renewables country. We need not cover the best farmland. We need not cover the land of any people who don't want wind turbines and solar panels on their property.

Drive south from Armidale down the Hunter and wince at the gaping wounds in the earth and the mountains of black rock and dust on rich farmland that nurtured Australia's best merinos, literary art, wine and thoroughbred horses. We can respect Barnaby's friendship with the gas and coal oligarchs, and still wonder at the selective anger at disturbance of this beautiful country.

I have spent a lot of time in the central west of Queensland since seven mayors from the west asked me to help them think through how they could use their sun and wind for permanent jobs. The heartland of the old Australian bush. Where Clancy of the Overflow went droving; the shearers and the teamsters met beneath the Tree of Knowledge and decided to use their new democracy to make a better country; Banjo wrote *Waltzing Matilda*; and the Queensland and Northern Territory Aerial Services built the planes and what is now the world's oldest international airline. Big country with big skies. Where the whole New England electorate could wander lost in the back paddock of an average sheep or cattle station. Where people want jobs so that their children and grandchildren don't all end up in the big smoke in Rockhampton and Brisbane as they have done for two generations. They want renewable power generation if they get sustainable income and local industry from it. They welcome the Queensland government's and Energy Queensland's support for a local renewable energy industrial precinct.

Now, at 11.30 am Brisbane time and 12.30 in Canberra, Premier Steven Miles is preparing to introduce a bill for a law for 75 per cent reductions on 2005 emissions by 2035. That's great for long-term jobs in the Queensland bush.

The Superpower Institute and changing the policy narrative (Rod Sims)

The Superpower Institute (TSI), which I am proud to chair, has been established to change the narrative on the economy and climate change in Australia. Rather than discussion of these issues occurring in isolation, TSI seeks to give climate change and the movement to net-zero emissions in Australia and the world a central role in our economic debate, and to place climate policy in the context of the wider Australian economy.

Australia has active debates on productivity and tax. But no mention is made of climate change, which should be central to both these topics.

The Australian climate debate often appears to solely focus on decarbonising Australia, which we must do, rather than on the larger role

Australia can and must play in reducing world emissions. If we do not focus on the latter we will fail to deliver prosperity for Australians, and we will fail the world's climate goals.

Today Ross and I are outlining the policies Australia needs to follow to achieve prosperity for Australia and for Australia making its maximum contribution to reducing world emissions. These policies integrate economic and environmental policy.

Some of these policies will seem controversial to some and may be rejected immediately.

But this is the beginning of the debate, not the end. TSI will undertake continuing research to show what is possible and what is needed for Australia's success. Too often in Australia ideas are put forward, immediately ruled out, and dropped. This will not happen here. The role of TSI is to ensure this. We will keep 'tilling the soil' so that these policy ideas can take hold and grow and feed into the policy discourse.

Tariff reduction was once impossible; eventually the debate shifted so that tariff reductions occurred. The Tariff Board, then the Industry Commission, provided the facts and the logic and eventually gained support for policy that has benefitted Australia enormously.

While on a much smaller scale, TSI seeks to play its role so that Australia can realise the Superpower opportunity.

Let's be clear on perhaps the most controversial part of the TSI policy package, the Carbon Solution Levy.

We can deal with climate change through a market mechanism, or by numerous specific interventions that are meant to achieve the same goal but at a higher cost.

So today we are putting a market mechanism to deal with climate change back on Australia's agenda via the CSL proposal. And contrary to the rhetoric of the past, all Australians can clearly be winners, except fossil fuel producers who need to pay for the damage their products cause our climate, our prosperity and our security.

We also have a debate about tax reform. Pricing carbon must be central to this and can finance the inevitable compensation costs of true tax reform.

When we have analysed carefully the effects of alternative paths to dealing with climate change and to tax reform, and the community has talked through the information, what is possible will change.

Australia can have more employment and higher incomes in the relatively short term, and be much richer in the longer term, by moving early and decisively in building and expanding the zero emissions Superpower export economy.

Indeed, if Australia seizes the opportunity, it can repeat the experience of the China resources boom which peaked around ten years ago. But this time the opportunity can be sustained, rather than boom and bust, and we can manage it better for broadly based development.

This logic and the data are clear to those who have made the effort to absorb them. TSI's task is to make the logic and facts known to all Australians seeking to understand the forces that will shape Australia's economic future. We expect that that will change what is possible.

THE ECONOMIC POLICY ORCHESTRA*

with David Vines

You mean to say that the theory or science of political economy is a commanding view of the vast combination of agents and operations engaged in producing, for the use of man, the whole of the things which he enjoys and consumes ...

You would further proceed to ask me, I have no doubt, whether the innumerable operations which take place in subservience to that end, may not take place in more ways than one; in short, in a worse way, or a better way? Whether it is not of importance that they should take place in the best way? And whether the difference between the best way and the worst way is not likely to be very great. And to all these questions I should answer in the affirmative.

From 'Whether Political Economy Is Useful: A Dialogue'
by James Mill (1836) quoted by Trevor Swan (1960)

---

* This chapter was originally the keynote address to the 2023 Australian Economic Society's Conference of Economists in Brisbane.

Individual players, the orchestra and the conductor

Economic policymakers are like the instrumental players in a symphony orchestra. Each player needs to play their own tune properly, while the players need to play together effectively. They need to be well led; they need a conductor. The conductor needs a good score – the integrated set of ideas that produce the desired effect. In this chapter we describe what it means to bring together an economic policymaking orchestra. We then contrast two eras in which there was a notable coordination of the components of macroeconomic policymaking, to good effect – postwar reconstruction, and the Hawke/Keating reform era – with two periods in which it did not: the 1970s and early 1980s to March 1983, and the last decade or so. We consider what the coordination of monetary and fiscal policy needs to look like in the twenty-first century.

For most Australians, the economy has performed badly over the past decade. Total factor productivity growth has slumped and real output per person stagnated. Real wages are lower at the end of the decade than at the beginning and have fallen more over recent years than in any earlier period for which comparable data are available. There are no developments in the economy or in economic policymaking that provide any indication of how this position might be reversed.

The last decade has also been hard for most of the developed world, in the aftermath of the global financial crisis, through the pandemic recession, and most recently in the war in Ukraine. There has been a marked deceleration of productivity growth more or less everywhere (Goldin et al. 2022). But the growth in Australian real output per person, and in real disposable income per person, has been among the lowest in all the developed world. Continuing the twenty-first-century approaches to economic policymaking in Australia would entrench this underperformance.

There is, however, growing awareness in Australia that things need to change. The treasurer has released an Intergenerational Report that draws attention to Australian underperformance over the past decade and to large future problems and invites a discussion of far-reaching economic reform (Australian Government 2023a). The Australian government's white paper on jobs and opportunities commits the government to making employment in good jobs available for all Australians 'without too much search' (Australian Government 2023b). Disquiet about policymaking at the Reserve Bank of Australia led to the treasurer commissioning a report on the RBA which was published on 20 April 2023 (de Brouwer et al. 2023). We have argued elsewhere that its findings do not address the RBA's problems (Garnaut and Vines 2023, and Chapter 8 of this volume). And in our view, the problems with economic policymaking in Australia go well beyond Martin Place.

There is a striking contrast between what is happening now and what happened in the two great periods of economic policy success in Australia. The orchestral nature of economic policymaking was widely understood in postwar reconstruction, and in the reform era of the late twentieth century. Our hope is that this might happen again.

At the conclusion of this chapter we briefly discuss the possible identity and location of the conductor, and the relationship between the conductor and the definition of what needs to be played – the musical score. Of course, like any economic model, the metaphor of the conductor is incomplete. But our central message is that good economic outcomes in Australia depend on better coordination of economic policymaking in many areas, and that this will only happen if there is an effective conductor, and a coherent and sound musical score.

What 'bringing the orchestra together' actually means

The Australian economic policymaking orchestra has a large number of players responsible for many instruments of policy.[1] We mainly focus on just two components of macroeconomic policy,[2] namely:

1. monetary policy, including macroprudential policy
2. fiscal policy at an aggregate level.

These policies directly determine levels of unemployment and inflation and the overall levels of debt in the economy. Other policies are discussed briefly towards the end.

Macroeconomic policy involves keeping demand for goods and services growing steadily at the same rate as the growth of supply capacity – thereby maintaining full employment of resources without causing inflation. It also involves doing this in ways that maintain public and foreign debt at levels that achieve a reasonable distribution of potential for consumption across years and generations.

During the era of postwar reconstruction, reaching from World War II until the early 1970s, fiscal policy was the main means by which the overall level of spending in the economy was managed. The exchange rates between national currencies were fixed by international agreement, but adjustable, so that the exchange rate could be used as a macroeconomic policymaking instrument.[3] During that time, wage-setting in Australia was highly regulated across the economy and decisions about wage levels were also part of the macroeconomic policymaking process. There was a clear understanding that all fiscal policy, exchange rate policy and wage-setting should be conducted with an eye to what the other policies were doing. Additional policies were deployed in an overall framework of cooperation – indeed an orchestra – in which all three of these economic policy instruments were understood to provide an essential bedrock on top of which all other aspects of economic policymaking would be erected. Later, economic policymaking was similarly coordinated during the Hawke/Keating period of economic reform in the 1980s and early 1990s.

But things have changed since then.

Since the high tide of influence of Austro-Hungarian views of how the economy works (discussed in Chapter 3) from the early 1980s in the United States and United Kingdom, and during the early twenty-first century in Australia, it has become common to think that each of the parts of economic policymaking should be conducted separately by its own policymaking institution, with its own purpose. Each of the players has been given a virtuoso part to play in a solo performance in a separate room. And each player has been judged on how well it plays its own tune. The RBA and monetary policy have been explicitly identified as operating beyond policy coordination.

Thus the RBA runs monetary policy, with the objective of controlling output and inflation through the use of variations in interest rates. Monetary policy varies interest rates to secure lower inflation or higher employment with limited regard for whether another instrument might achieve the desired outcome more effectively and at lower cost. Treasury ensures that public debt does not grow to an extent that challenges long-term economic stability and intergenerational equity. APRA stops banks lending irresponsibly and makes sure that housing bubbles do not create a financial crisis. Other agencies run policies that have effects on labour supply, output prices, wages, and the allocation of resources with little thought for what the macroeconomic consequences of these policies might be.

This diffuse framework of economic policymaking has been poorly coordinated. That is a large part of the reason for the bad outcomes which we described at the beginning of our paper.

It has not always been so. The need for cooperation among policymakers in macroeconomic management of the economy was recognised in Australia in the early 1930s, long before it was understood anywhere else in the world. Reviewing the origins of this early understanding helps us to see how policy coordination was developed during postwar reconstruction in the 1950s and 1960s, and the policy reform era in the 1980s and 1990s.

Putting the orchestra together: learning from Australia's historical experience

Early Australian ideas about macroeconomic coordination

The early Australian insights into cooperation among policymakers in macroeconomic management go back to the early 1930s. These were brought into the public sphere by Lyndhurst Giblin in his inaugural lecture as Ritchie Professor of Economics at Melbourne University in 1930 (see Giblin 1930; Coleman et al. 2011). The price of wool, overwhelmingly Australia's largest export, had halved in six months, and Australia had a massive current account deficit. Giblin explained that the reduction in revenue received by farmers for their exports would reduce their spending on goods and services from the cities. There would be a downward 'multiplier' process, leading to a loss of jobs and to unemployment in the cities. This was long before Keynes' *General Theory* (1936) and a year before Richard Kahn's article on the multiplier (Kahn 1931).

Sir Otto Niemeyer was invited to Australia from the Bank of England in 1930 to advise on policy responses to the Great Depression. He recommended that the Arbitration Commission cut money wages to deal with unemployment. Giblin doubted the wisdom of this advice, wanting to avoid the effects of deflation. Instead, he recommended suspending the gold standard and devaluing the Australian pound, thus increasing the number of Australian pounds which farmers would receive for their exports. Since the prices of Australia's exports had roughly halved, Giblin and his colleague at the University of Melbourne, Douglas Copland, suggested that this devaluation should be large enough to double the income of farmers in Australian pounds. They calculated that this approach would reestablish the purchasing power of farmers over products from the cities and so eliminate the negative multiplier effects on unemployment. They coupled their advice with a cautious stance on fiscal policy, because of the difficulty of servicing Australian debt in London. They were aware that their proposed devaluation would be inflationary, and so advocated moderating the currency depreciation and combining it with smaller wages cuts, calculated to make the overall package neither inflationary nor deflationary (Copland 1934).

Giblin and Copland believed that their policy would spread the pain from the collapse of export prices fairly through the community. Farmers and people in the cities would both pay more for imports, because of the currency devaluation, but unemployment would be avoided. This was the Giblin approach to policy: first understand the international context and then develop a coordinated policy response, which in this case involved a mixture of currency depreciation and wage cuts.

The Giblin advice was to underpin the Premiers' Plan of June 1931. As it happened, Keynes undermined the implementation of that plan by opposing a further devaluation of the Australian pound in an article in the Melbourne *Herald* (Keynes 1932).[4] The Australian pound had already been depreciated by 30 per cent against sterling in 1930, but not by enough to implement Giblin's plan. It seems that Keynes thought it more important to preserve the integrity of the imperial financial system than for Australians to avoid massive unemployment. He came subsequently to admire what the Australians had done, inviting Copland to give the prestigious Marshall Lectures in Cambridge in 1933 (Copland 1934). The Australian ideas, expanded by Keynesian insights, provided a framework for policy development into the Department of Post-War Reconstruction (DPWR) established by the Curtin government in 1942 with H.C. ('Nugget') Coombs as secretary and John Crawford his director of research. Coombs and Crawford brought a young Trevor Swan into the department as chief economist. All three were to play influential roles in the long period of full employment and steady economic growth under the Menzies governments that followed through the 1950s and 1960s.

Internal balance and external balance in the 1950s and 1960s
The ideas which emerged in the early 1930s were important in the decade which followed and on through and beyond World War II. See Cornish (2002) and Macintyre (2015). The ideas were systematised brilliantly

by Swan in two seminal articles in the early-to-mid 1950s.[5] They were prepared early during his period at the ANU as the first professor of economics in the Research School of Social Sciences, but not published until later (Swan 1960, 1963). Swan prefaces his first article with a quotation from a paper by James Mill in 1836 about the need for policy coordination, part of which we have reproduced above. In the second article, Swan showed in one single diagram how to achieve full employment, price stability and external balance at the same time. The 'Swan diagram' is now taught to undergraduate students of economics in many countries.

The Swan diagram is familiar to most Australian economists.[6] An increase in real expenditure increases aggregate demand so that the real exchange rate (influenced either by the nominal exchange rate or the money wage) does not need to be as low for full employment to be achieved. That is why the internal balance line slopes downwards. Conversely, a depreciation of the real exchange rate causes the trade balance to improve so that external balance is only maintained if at the same time real expenditure is increased. That is why the external balance line slopes up. Internal balance and external balance are both achieved where the two lines cross.[7]

The need for policy coordination is clear. Swan describes a more complete allocation of policy responsibilities than Giblin and Copland. They had underplayed the role of fiscal policy. Indeed, Swan identifies many institutional possibilities as to how policy cooperation might be organised, to adjust real expenditure and competitiveness so as to achieve internal and external balance at the same time.

The setup analysed by Swan does indeed resemble an orchestra, and it clearly needs a conductor. A book of readings on the Australian economy, published in the early 1960s (Arndt and Corden 1963) and widely used in university teaching at the time, provided a clear sense that many policies needed to be thought about in cooperation with fiscal, exchange rate and wages policy.[8]

Saving enough for real incomes to grow in the 1950s and 1960s

Having solved the problem of internal and external balance, Swan argued that one can then 'turn to study the process of economic growth' (Swan 1956). The existence of high postwar immigration, which we have described above, would, said Swan, lead to a need for business investment, and the provision of housing, schools, roads, hospitals and other forms of infrastructure to equip the migrants. That would lead to a need for higher saving if the required investment was not to lead to excess demand or spill over into imports and create balance of payments difficulties. In short, said Swan, how well off the country could become would depend crucially on how rapidly its technology advanced and on whether it saved enough for this technical advance to be accompanied by the necessary investment and accumulation of capital.

Australia's economists are also familiar with the Swan–Solow model of economic growth – even if they make use of Solow's simple diagram to explain the model, rather than the more complicated diagram which Swan produced in his article. What became fundamental in Australia was the assistance the model provided to thinking about how to deal with the high levels of immigration in the couple of decades after the war. Swan used his model to show that how well Australia would perform with high immigration would depend on whether the country ran a fiscal policy which was tight enough to ensure that savings were sufficient to equip the growing labour force. There was less consideration of capital inflow then than before the Great Depression or after the globalisation of finance from the 1980s. Swan was keenly aware that extra immigrants would lead to demand for goods which could be only provided by imports. Australian manufacturing was still highly underdeveloped and the domestic market for such manufactured goods was small. Technical progress could loosen the constraints, but in manufacturing only with increased scale. Swan examined these questions in some detail in his Presidential Address to Section G of the ANZAAS conference in Dunedin in 1957.[9] Concluding his lecture, he said that, 'there may be a case for a policy of high saving and low migration; there is nothing to be said for a policy of low saving and high migration'. These arguments – about the interconnection between immigration and fiscal policy – were widely understood by Australia's economists in the 1950s.

The economy performed better over the quarter-century after the war than ever since Federation. Inflation spiked for a year or so of the first Menzies' government to 25 per cent, when the government baulked at the economists' suggestion of currency appreciation. But tighter budgets (including restricting expenditure from a substantial part of increased rural incomes) contributed to the rapid fall of inflation to around 2 per cent. It mostly stayed there, with occasional sharp increases to around 5 per cent dissipating quickly with fiscal and wage moderation. Average real growth exceeded 4 per cent – well above the interwar years but with high immigration and population growth, generating low per capita income growth by developed country standards at that time. The economy mostly lived comfortably within its external constraint, with a tendency to external deficits in the early 1960s being corrected by moderate fiscal and monetary contraction, and a temporary lift of unemployment above 2 per cent creating nearly fatal political problems for the Menzies government.

Recognition that output and incomes growth was lagging other developed countries focused attention on impediments to long-term economic growth. Stronger growth in the 1960s followed the emergence of large-scale minerals exports to serve vigorous export expansion, underpinned by the Australia–Japan Commerce Agreement of 1957 (see Chapter 11).

Instability and underperformance 1971–83
The Whitlam government's policies from the time of its election in December 1972 contained modernising elements. These were overwhelmed by ill-judged responses to macroeconomic shocks that came from the international economy – some arising from mistakes by economists operating within the postwar tradition and failing to recognise that

the global economy had moved into a new course; and some from the government's ambitions for social change unconstrained by economic policy discipline.

Exchange rate appreciation in response to external inflation was implemented for the first time. Racial discrimination was removed from immigration policy, although the effect of non-European immigration was small when total levels of immigration were greatly reduced as unemployment increased from 1974. There was a large reduction in tariffs against all goods – soon negated by quantitative restrictions on imports for the most highly protected industries as unemployment rose from 1974 (see Rattigan 1986, Anderson and Garnaut 1986).

The first year of the Whitlam government in 1973 experienced high terms of trade and inflation from abroad. Conveniently for a government committed to major expansion of public expenditure and increases in real incomes within programs to broaden access to services across the community and more equitable income distribution, this seemed to provide a favourable environment for accommodation of greatly increased real expenditure. Substantial exchange rate appreciation and a 25 per cent across-the-board tariff cut in 1973 were supported by old and new advisers for their contributions to raising real expenditure without inflation. The government used established regulatory mechanisms to raise all nominal wages more rapidly than previously, with accelerated increases in female and minimum wages in pursuit of equity. Regulatory mechanisms were used to raise wages in states which had previously lagged behind to the levels of the states with the highest levels. Increases in nominal wages and the tariff cuts and exchange rate appreciation markedly increased domestic relative to international costs.

The new, higher levels of domestic expenditure and wages would have been consistent with full employment, moderate inflation and a reasonable amount of debt if the favourable international conditions had continued. But a global recession following the first oil crisis of 1973 sent the terms of trade lower. Unemployment rose to over 4 per cent –

exceeding anything through the long postwar expansion. Public expenditure increased massively – with commitments to the Whitlam government's programs being strengthened by apparent compatibility with the need to counteract growing unemployment. The exchange rate and tariff decisions were partially reversed.

The large increases in average real wages and compression of wage differentials left serious labour market imbalances. High inflation persisted. Unemployment increased and remained high. The labour market imbalances, inflation and unemployment proved to be impervious to the Fraser government's commitment to 'fight inflation first' with new monetarist macroeconomic policies that focused on controlling demand by constraining growth in the stock of money. The Fraser government extended the Whitlam government's modernisation of immigration and foreign policy, with steps to facilitate productive relations with countries in Asia. But it was deeply resistant to major reform of economic policy.

Increasing awareness of the extent and consequences of the deterioration in Australia's economic performance relative to other developed countries generated discussion of new approaches to policy. The Tariff Board led by Alf Rattigan continued its public education on the benefits of trade liberalisation.[10] Private discussion of more far-reaching trade liberalisation became more vigorous, centred on the universities but with concerted support from parts of the print media and a small number of mining businesses and some representatives of the farm sector. The Campbell Committee review of the financial system recommended far-reaching liberalisation of the financial and foreign exchange markets (Australian Government 1981). Sensitivity to Southeast Asian criticism of Australian protection as well as awareness of general underperformance led to the establishment of the Crawford Study Group on Structural Adjustment, with future prime minister Bob Hawke as a member (Crawford et al. 1979). This encouraged the search for coordination of monetary, fiscal (including taxation) and wages policy to define superior macroeconomic outcomes that might be politically feasible.

Discussion of the opportunities and possible approaches to Asia-Pacific Economic Cooperation were encouraged (see Drysdale 1969, 1978, Garnaut 1980, Kasper 1980, and Crawford 1981).

The later Fraser years were characterised by increasing realisation of Australian economic underperformance and considerable discussion of possible elements of reform. It was also characterised by the absence of substantial action to improve Australian economic performance. Protection was increased for the most highly protected industries (Anderson and Garnaut 1986). The Campbell Report recommendations were mostly ignored. There was no official interest in coordination of the arms of macroeconomic policy to reduce unemployment and inflation and raise growth in productivity and incomes. Government floated across the top of an economy experiencing serious difficulties, without recognising either the need or the opportunity for major change.

Another global recession hit the economy in the early 1980s. Unemployment and inflation were both above 10 per cent when the Hawke government took office in March 1983.

The reform era 1983–2001

The Australian challenge in 1983 had two dimensions. One was macroeconomic. The responses to international shocks in the 1970s had led to real average and relative wages that were inconsistent with low levels of unemployment. The second was low underlying productivity growth. Rent-seeking behaviour was blocking the utilisation of new opportunities from sustained economic growth in East Asia.

Hawke came to office committed to reforms which would reduce unemployment and inflation and lift productivity growth. The Fraser government's 'fight inflation first' was replaced by 'fight inflation and unemployment at the same time'. Hawke recognised that community support for far-reaching structural change required confidence that jobs would be available for people displaced from old employment, and in the fruits of disruptive change being distributed equitably. That required explanation of policy to the community. The Hawke and Keating governments shared this orientation with the wartime Labor governments led by Curtin and Chifley. The reform era also shared with postwar reconstruction a respect for the application of knowledge to the policymaking process, confidence in a professional public service, and recognition of the importance of policy coordination across many spheres.

The reform agenda turned out to be stunningly wide in scope, covering fiscal, monetary, wage and prudential macroeconomic institutions and policies; trade liberalisation, taxation, education and training, immigration, science and research policies affecting productivity growth; and taxation, social security, health and education policies securing equitable distribution while supporting macroeconomic stability and economic growth. Social policies were brought to account in macroeconomic policy through discussions on wages within the Accord with the trade union movement.

Reform momentum was broken by deep recession in 1991–92, caused by misjudgement of monetary policy in changed circumstances created by financial deregulation. Broken but not blocked: the last and largest step in removing protection was announced by Prime Minister Hawke in the depth of recession in 1991 (Hawke 1991).

The locus of the orchestra's conductor changed over time. Initially, the conductor's role was taken by a politically strong prime minister leading an effective and unusually able cabinet and its committees. The prime minister and his office and department, making intensive use of the professional capacities of the wider public service, was at the centre in the early years, working closely with the treasurer, his office and department. The Economic Policy Advisory Council (EPAC) and its secretariat were important in analysis and public education in the mid-1980s. Later, a cabinet committee on long-term economic growth was served by a successor secretariat. As with postwar reconstruction, the maturation of the new approaches to policy saw the locus of the conductor move towards the treasurer and the Treasury department, with support, oversight and occasional major strategic intervention from the prime minister.

The reform era, like the time of postwar reconstruction, demonstrates the importance of getting the macroeconomy right at the beginning. Confidence in sustainably rising employment is especially important.

This is partly a question of sequencing: do things in the right order. But it is more a question of policy coordination. Make sure that monetary, fiscal and labour-market policies together maintain an appropriate real exchange rate, while ensuring that policies are in place to secure equitable distribution of income, and enhance public knowledge and support for productivity-raising structural change.

Making use of Swan's ideas in the Hawke/Keating era

Central to the changes in Australia in the 1980s and 1990s were the reduction of tariffs, the abolition of the import quotas, the removal of other assistance to industry, and the liberalisation of Australian capital markets (Garnaut 1994). The sequencing of the policy reforms was important. The removal of protection had to be accompanied by depreciation of the currency, to improve the competitive positions of export and import-competing industries. Wage restraint was essential, to prevent the currency depreciation leading to inflation. And the government's budgetary position needed to be strong enough to allow money to be spent on social programs within the Accord, and to support the lower exchange rate. The reduction in protection was gradual, extending from 1983 to 1996 within policy decisions up to March 1991.

More equitable distribution of living standards was secured through taxation reform and expansion of social, medical and educational services, as well as reduction in unemployment, rather than increases in real wages. Much of the increase in productivity over the period was allocated to such improvement of services, especially during the period of Labor government to 1996. Wage restraint supported expansion of employment. Confidence in equitable distribution of the benefits of growth was important in underpinning political support for rapid structural change.

Stronger productivity growth came from trade liberalisation, and Asia-Pacific and global diplomacy on market access, together with domestic and international financial liberalisation, taxation reform, new incentives for expenditure on research and development, and large expansion of vocational, secondary and tertiary education. Privatisation and corporatisation of public business enterprises became important late in this period.

As time progressed, lower protection increased competitive pressures across the whole economy – specifically on firms which had been sheltered from foreign competition, and generally throughout the economic system. The pressure from reduced protection helped to build a constituency for broader reforms. That led, in turn, to the adoption of institutional and regulatory reforms promoting more efficient delivery of infrastructure services (including, for example, in electricity and communications) and to greater flexibility in Australia's previously rigid and highly centralised labour market arrangements.

Policy coordination was important during the reform era. It has fallen away since then.

Coordinating monetary and fiscal policy in Australia in the twenty-first century

Inflation targeting, implemented in Australia from the early 1990s, seems at first sight to have removed the target of full employment as an objective of macroeconomic policymaking. At the same time, greater capital mobility and the floating of the exchange rate seem to have removed external balance as a policy objective. Full employment received some renewed attention from Treasurer Frydenberg and the RBA in the policy response to the pandemic recession. The focus was extended by the Albanese government's White Paper on Jobs and Skills (Australian Government 2023b). It continues to have equal status with stability of the currency in the law that governs the RBA. And, as we will see, external balance also remains an important target, but needs to be reinterpreted as a longer-term concern about achieving the right amount of public and external debt.

Now, let's look at the meaning of internal balance, external balance and policy coordination in the twenty-first century.

Internal balance

The concept of internal balance has not changed fundamentally since the years of postwar reconstruction,[11] although it is now discussed in different terms. Growth in demand for economic output has to be strong enough to utilise fully the productive capacity of the economy, and therefore to achieve full employment. But if it grows beyond the limits of production capacity, inflation will rise and accelerate, or external borrowing will increase.

We are comfortable with the contemporary conventional wisdom: there is full employment when the rates of unemployment and underemployment are the lowest that they can be while inflation remains moderate and stable. This is the non-accelerating inflation rate of unemployment, or NAIRU. The NAIRU is the lowest sustainable rate of unemployment at a point in time.

The NAIRU is an observable reality. It has come to be seen by some as the output of an economic model based on historical data. This is a mistake. The NAIRU changes over time with the performance of the economy and policy change in taxation, social security and the labour market. We should seek to understand its determinants, and to make it as low as possible (see Chapter 6).

The Reserve Bank's reliance on a model calibrated with historical data has led to serious errors over the past decade.[12] Observation of reality suggests that during the one and a half years from the second quarter of 2022 in which unemployment was around 3.5 per cent, the NAIRU was no higher than that.[13]

There has been an important change in institutional arrangements and the influence of government affecting wages and working conditions over the past three decade. The Arbitration Commission (now the Fair Work Commission) no longer sets wages and conditions for a high proportion of the population, as it did in postwar reconstruction and to a lesser degree in the late-twentieth-century reform era. Neither do trade unions exercise powerful influence over wages and conditions for a high proportion of the work force, as they did in the late twentieth century. Policy now influences wages in less direct ways.

Real labour incomes can be expected to grow in the labour market with productivity if there is full employment, and not necessarily otherwise. A period of wage stagnation or decline in the absence of other sources of rising living standards generates democratic political pressures for interventions to raise wages. These pressures have been influential over the past decade of economic stagnation. The pressures were joined inappropriately by the Reserve Bank governor during the years of a weak labour market preceding the pandemic, with exhortations for workers to bargain harder for higher wages. Changes in monetary policy to secure increases in wages in the labour market through full employment would have been more appropriate.

We see no case for assertion of low inflation's priority over full employment on economic efficiency or income distribution grounds.

External balance

In the modern world of floating exchange rates and highly mobile capital, 'external balance' no longer means a particular level of the current account of the balance of payments. Rather, the term now denotes a pattern of international borrowing, lending and debt servicing that is sustainable without financial crisis and desirable from the perspective of the inter-temporal distribution of income. Public sector balance sheets become an essential element in any assessments of whether external balance has been achieved. The experience of the East Asian (1997–98) and global (2007–08) financial crises demonstrates that under pressure the problems of private sector entities are transmitted to the public sector, so that private sector balance sheets also matter.

Policy coordination

When the exchange rate is floating, changes in the exchange rate must now be secured indirectly. The Mundell–Fleming model (Fleming 1962; Mundell 1962) analyses the coordination of fiscal and monetary policy to vary the exchange rate when there is both a floating currency and mobile capital. A fiscal contraction (say) with no change in the inflation target causes the central bank to lower the interest rate, leading to exchange rate depreciation. This stimulates aggregate demand and inflation in a way which counteracts the negative effects of the fiscal contraction on domestic activity. By contrast, a tightening of monetary policy causes an appreciation of the exchange rate. That reduces aggregate demand and inflation in a way which augments the contractionary effects of the tightening of monetary policy.[14]

Monetary policymakers can bring about movements in *both* the interest rate and the exchange to insulate a country from both domestic and foreign shocks. Rudiger Dornbusch (1976) showed that a country's monetary policymakers can raise interest rates relative to the rest of the world and cause only moderate movements in the exchange rate even with highly mobile capital.[15]

In a world of floating exchange rates, fiscal policy has a different role. In the example given, fiscal contraction, and the resulting depreciation of the exchange rate, lead to an improvement in the trade balance and reduction in external debt. Monetary expansion prevents an increase in unemployment.

In these conditions, a fiscal surplus is helpful if there is a boom in raw-material exports or an increase in international relative to domestic prices, to avoid having to tighten monetary policy, appreciate the exchange rate and crowd out other tradable industries (Corden and Neary 1982). Similarly, but in reverse, fiscal consolidation to constrain public debt requires easier monetary policy and so causes exchange rate depreciation.

We still have two targets, internal balance and external balance, as we did in the Swan diagram. And we still have two policies, fiscal and monetary. But now, the coordination of fiscal policy and monetary policy in the pursuit of internal and external balance needs to take into account the effects of fiscal and interest rate settings on the exchange rate.

Applying these ideas in Australia in the twenty-first century

The failure to absorb and apply the insights from twentieth-century Australian economics in the twenty-first century has severely damaged both economic policymaking and economic performance.

Over recent decades, the policy authorities have tended to see control of aggregate demand as determining internal balance, while the floating exchange rate secures external balance. Both fiscal and monetary policy affect aggregate demand, so, it is said, monetary and fiscal policy should generally be tighter together or looser together – or at least not pull in opposite directions.

That approach ignores how fiscal and monetary policy settings jointly determine the exchange rate, with large implications for internal and external balance.

It is still helpful to look at the underlying realities through a Swan diagram lens. If there is unemployment, there are two paths to increasing employment. One is to increase domestic spending. Part of any such increase is spent on domestic goods and services that have no foreign competitors. As a result, employment increases directly, and in addition indirectly when the supplier spends the increased income.

A second path is to lower the cost of goods and services produced in the country, relative to those produced overseas. This makes the economy more internationally competitive. A more competitive economy supplies a higher proportion of domestic demand from local sources. It also exports a wider range and more of its own produce. More jobs in import-competing and export industries allow full employment to be achieved with fewer jobs from increased domestic demand.

It matters a great deal whether the increase in employment comes from monetary or fiscal expansion. Fiscal expansion increases demand but – given the way monetary policy now operates – also tends to increase interest rates and so to appreciate the exchange rate and reduce competitiveness. It increases the trade deficit and external debt.

Monetary expansion lowers interest rates and so tends to depreciate the exchange rate and improve competitiveness. It reduces the trade deficit and foreign debt.

Once we recognise that the combination of fiscal and monetary policy affects the exchange rate, the effects can then by analysed within the Swan diagram.

How would recognition of the difference between fiscal and monetary expansion have played out through the twenty-first century so far?

Australia experienced the China resources boom from about 2002 to 2012, broken temporarily by the global financial crisis in 2007–08. The world's most populous country grew more strongly for longer than any large country ever had. China's pattern of growth and its relative resource endowments were highly complementary to Australia's relative economic strengths. Demand for Australian exports and especially minerals grew strongly, lifting the terms of trade and investment in the mining industries to unprecedented heights.

A crucial question was whether these were temporary or permanent improvements in the terms of trade. If temporary, most of the increase in purchasing power should have been saved, and major structural change from appreciation of the real exchange rate avoided. Prudence suggested working as if they may be temporary, as such commodity booms had been in the past. However, Australia was imprudent, applying most of the increase in public revenues to business and personal income tax cuts and, to a lesser extent, to higher public expenditure. Monetary tightening offset domestic inflationary impacts, and the nominal and real exchange rates rose to extreme levels. The large, sustained expansion of service and manufactured exports since the beginning of the reform era in 1983 went into reverse (Garnaut 2013). A substantial part of Australian tradable goods and services production capacity closed permanently. The public finances were not as strong against future challenges as they could have been.

The global financial crisis temporarily broke the China resources boom. Timely fiscal and monetary expansion in Australia and China restored growth quickly (Garnaut with Llewellyn-Smith 2009). Australia with the Republic of Korea were the only developed countries to avoid recession and much higher unemployment. But in Australia, more than in other developed countries, the GFC's aftermath brought income stagnation. Prior to the pandemic recession of 2020, budget policy was directed at the achievement of a budget surplus – unsuccessfully, as low output growth and persistent unemployment reduced government revenues and increased expenditures. Monetary policy was directed at low inflation and inflation on average fell below the target range. Unemployment was stuck well above the NAIRU. Underemployment rose. In our view, less restrictive monetary policy alongside the fiscal policies more or less as actually pursued from 2013, accompanied by tighter macroprudential policy, would have moved us closer to both full employment and the right amount of debt.

The pandemic recession saw unemployment rise suddenly above 7 per cent with expectations that it would go much higher. This induced a comprehensive loosening of both fiscal and monetary policy. In response, unemployment fell far more rapidly than anticipated by the Australian authorities to levels unknown for half a century.

Tradable goods prices on international markets increased strongly as global economic activity was restored through 2021 and 2022. The increase was exacerbated by higher food, energy and chemical manufactures prices following the Russian invasion of Ukraine in February 2022. Australia tightened monetary policy from May 2022 – several months later than other English-speaking developed countries but not later than Japan or the European Union. By June 2023 it had implemented the largest increase in policy interest rates over a comparably short period since the introduction of inflation targeting more than three decades earlier.

Fiscal policy remained fairly steady, so that high economic activity, lower unemployment, and higher terms of trade were reflected in a rapid return to budget surplus. Fiscal and monetary policy were both taking pressure from domestic demand, the latter much more actively. The Australian dollar exchange rate fell against the US dollar, but on average rose against other countries. Growth in economic activity decelerated with the monetary tightening, but unemployment remained at the lower levels of mid-2022 through mid-2023. Nominal wage growth remained well below the rate of increase in consumer prices, causing the largest two-year fall in real wages ever observed in Australia. This, in turn, caused per capita consumption to fall.

By mid-2023, it was clear that the global surges in tradable goods prices and especially energy prices had been temporary. Inflation was moderating all over the world – although less rapidly than the authorities desired in many countries. Questions remained about the United States, with its extraordinary and increasing budget deficit. China, overwhelmingly Australia's largest trading partner, was facing deflation. The response in most developed countries including Australia was to cease the monetary tightening, at least for the time being.

Was this the right combination of fiscal and monetary policy in response to the post-pandemic inflation? Applying the Swan diagram insights, we think not. The imported inflation was of moderate dimensions and could have been countered with a moderate earlier tightening of monetary policy. An initial tightening at the same time and to the same extent as that seen in the United States would have been appropriate, leading initially to a moderate appreciation of the exchange rate against a trade-weighted average of currencies. Fiscal policy could have been moderately looser than actually occurred, to avoid the additional monetary tightening increasing unemployment. If looser fiscal policy had compensated consumers more completely for the rise in energy prices, this would have reduced the amount of monetary tightening and exchange rate appreciation required to insulate the domestic economy from the increase in international prices. The deterioration in competitiveness from exchange rate appreciation, and the loosening of fiscal policy, would have led to a moderately smaller reduction in public and external debt – but well within acceptable bounds in the economic circumstances as they have transpired. The incremental monetary tightening and exchange rate appreciation could have been withdrawn as global prices fell from early 2023. With better cooperation in the conduct of macroeconomic policy, macroprudential constraints would have been more restrictive during the pandemic, and would have been eased from early 2023 to avoid excessive downward pressure on housing prices and capital expenditure. The historically extreme reductions in real wages and risk of a substantial and unnecessary increase in unemployment would have been removed.

The wider dimensions of policy coordination in Australia in the twenty-first century

The ideas about open international exchange that framed the Australian reforms and success of the late twentieth century are being challenged in the twenty-first century. Disappointment about economic performance has undermined the use of open markets in the whole world: the protectionism of the Trump administration in the United States and its continuation under President Biden; the United Kingdom's withdrawal from the European Union; and more generally diminished support for the institutions of open multilateral trade. The deterioration in the political relationship between China and Western democratic market economies, especially the United States, has increased transactions costs and risks of international exchange and led to explicit withdrawal from trade in a range of goods and services. And there has been growing support for economic ideas that have elevated alternatives to market exchange as instruments for raising productivity. Some of the latter change has built on established verities in economic thought, and some has thrown out the analytically sound baby along with the bathwater that never served the public interest.

The US government worries that China will gain an advantage relative to the United States. So as Guzman and Stiglitz (2024) say, 'if the old rules tie the US hands, too bad for the rules.'[16] This creates worries about an onrush of protectionism worldwide. What will the new rules look like? And who should design them?

For Australia, this new world creates many new challenges for the policymaking orchestra. How to design Australia's own economic development policies so that they do not – as in the past – degenerate into inefficient rent-seeking? What kind of fiscal and monetary policies should accompany any new development policies? What other policies need to be brought into play alongside fiscal and monetary policy to achieve development goals? What role might the Productivity Commission play in facilitating the changes which such policies might require? What role should Australia play on the international stage in writing the new trade rules? If the United States is in the process of ripping up the postwar trading rules, what can middle-level powers like Australia do to help preserve the best of them, and to make the best of opportunities in a world without them?

The overarching challenge is to conserve the proven wisdom from the past, while taking account of new circumstances requiring policy adjustment. Australian economic policy has been thrust into a brave new world before the ideas on how it works, and on how policy works within it, have been settled. We will need the innovative analysis of which Australian economists have been capable in the past, to build on the wisdom of experience. The economic policy score to be played by the orchestra requires contributions from even more players, coordinated by a conductor with their head around the whole symphony.

Trade policy affecting productivity

Trade policy is intimately connected with productivity growth. Providing open access to imports from their most competitive sources allows reallocation of resources from less to more productive activities. It reduces costs and supports expansion of the most productive industries. It allows greater specialisation in the most economically valuable economic activities. It increases competition in internationally tradable goods and services. It increases knowledge of and access to the world's best technologies and management systems.

Continued high protection was the main cause of Australia's relatively low productivity growth relative to other developed countries during post-war reconstruction. Its removal was the main cause of the superior Australian productivity growth of the 1990s. Increased use of anti-dumping and other protectionist interventions in Australia and disruption of the rules-based multilateral trading system everywhere have contributed to the deterioration in productivity growth in Australia and other developed countries in the twenty-first century. Open international trade remains centrally important to rising incomes, and in particular for seizing the opportunities presented to Australia in the global net-zero transition.

The transition to net zero

The global transition to net-zero carbon dioxide emissions to reduce damage from human-induced climate change has immense implications. Australia is the world's largest exporter of coal and LNG taken together, and these comprise two of the country's three most valuable export products. If the international community meets its agreed climate objectives, coal and gas exports will decline to insignificance at a national level over the next few decades. Australia has a strong comparative advantage in many of the essential inputs into zero-carbon production, and zero-carbon industries could contribute the investment and exports required to maintain full employment with rising incomes into the 2050s (see Garnaut 2019, 2021, 2022). Investment in such industries in which Australia has comparative advantage could contribute for several decades a share of GDP as large as that occupied by investment in mining during the China resources boom of 2002 to 2012 (see Garnaut 2022).

A successful Australian response to the climate-change challenge would involve massive structural change. What kind of fiscal policy and

carbon-pricing support will be needed for economically efficient investments to secure the necessary change?[17] What level of the real exchange
rate will be necessary for the new exports to prosper and to contribute
to full employment with the right amount of debt as the old fossil energy
exports recede into history?[18]

Competition policy

The orchestra of economic policy needs an instrument that comes into
play when greater competition is both possible and the best means to
an important end. The ACCC is a regulatory and not a policy agency.
However, it understands better than other parts of government what can
work, what is best left alone, and how to make things work. It can assist
the conductor in the choice of instruments and the timing of when to call
them into play (see Chapter 9). The Treasury's new Competition Task-
force and review panel will help meet this challenge.

Labour market policies

Many policies affect the amount and quality of labour supply and the
standards of living of wage earners. For Australia, immigration policy is
centrally important. Immigration as a proportion of the labour force has
been much higher in the recovery from the pandemic recession than ever
before. It has raised housing prices and rentals and therefore increased
the inclination of the RBA to raise interest rates. The scale, structure and
composition of post-pandemic immigration place downward pressure
on real wages. That is likely to generate pressures for increases in regulated minimum wages. Beyond some point, accession to these pressures
may raise the unemployment rate corresponding to full employment (the
NAIRU) and lower the participation rate.

Full employment at the NAIRU is a powerful support for productivity
growth (see Chapters 2 and 6). It shifts focus from productivity-reducing
emphasis on job creation to raising productivity and incomes. It leads to
sustainable increases in wages in line with productivity growth and takes

pressure from regulatory measures to raise wages. It lowers the NAIRU itself and raises the participation rate when full employment has been reached (Chapter 7). It increases political support for productivity-raising reform requiring structural change.

Enhancement of labour skills can contribute substantially to productivity growth and labour force participation. The early work of the recently established Jobs and Skills Australia is promising.

Microeconomic detail of fiscal policy

Taxation structures and rates and the composition of public expenditure profoundly affect capital expenditure (and therefore labour productivity growth) and total factor productivity growth. They have a large effect on the distribution of income. With the profit share of income and the increased share of mineral and other rents in total profits rising to historic highs in recent years (Chapters 8 and 9), efficient rent taxation becomes critical to ensuring that higher productivity raises living standards. The Henry Review took up the issues more than a decade ago but was overwhelmed by the dysfunctional political economy leading into the Dog Days (Henry 2010). Carbon pricing with payments to low- and middle-income households can reconcile incentives for movement to zero-carbon production and consumption with equity in income distribution, while securing more efficient allocation of resources. Personal income tax structures and their relationship to social security have large effects on disposable incomes net of tax and social security, and therefore on pressures to modify wages for reasons of fairness, as well as on incentives for labour force participation.

Health, education and social security are important dimensions of the standard of living. Within the Accord of the reform era, improvements were explicitly accepted by the trade union movements as alternatives to wage increases. This helped to avoid increases in institutionally determined wage increases. They could be brought to account in macroeconomic and growth strategies again.

Defence and security

Defence and security expenditures, while foundational for the state and the democratic polity, have negative effects on productivity growth. When unemployment is the dominant concern, expenditure on defence raises demand for labour like any other public expenditure. But at full employment, it becomes a drag on growth in productivity and incomes in a country that lacks comparative advantage in the production of defence materials. Demands for higher current defence expenditures are sometimes justified by an assertion that they contribute to economic growth. That is a false assertion. Defence expenditures can only be justified by their contributions to defence. Potentially even more costly for long-term economic growth are calls for restrictions on trade with strategic competitors – obviously China in the current discussion – on grounds that open trade will expand the competitor's economy and future defence capacity. US National Security Director Jake Sullivan has argued for excluding trade with China and some other countries in goods and services that are important for national security. Well and good. But the costs are high without corresponding defence benefit when trade restriction is extended beyond the 'small yard, high fence' surrounding commodities the open trading of which really does damage national security interests (Sullivan 2023). The boundaries of the fences need to be assessed rigorously, with realistic calculation of genuine defence benefits and economic costs.

The important coordinating role of the Productivity Commission

Australia is fortunate to have an institution with the human resources and traditions that allow it to play a leading role in discussion and assessment of the many influences on productivity growth. It began as the Tariff Board and became the Industries Assistance Commission, the Industries Commission and now the Productivity Commission.

Variations in the effectiveness of Productivity Commission advice over time illustrate the importance of coordinating productivity-raising reforms with macroeconomic policy. The Productivity Commission's public education on the effects of protection provided important support for the Whitlam government's 25 per cent tariff cut in 1973. Regrettably, the macroeconomic soil was not fertile at the time, and the tariff cut was overwhelmed by political reaction to the rise in unemployment in the recession of the mid-1970s. Whitlam did not retreat on the cut itself but imposed quantitative restrictions on imports of goods receiving the highest levels of tariff protection. A new prime minister, Malcolm Fraser, increased restrictive and costly quantitative restrictions on imports in subsequent years (Anderson and Garnaut 1986).

Hawke laid the ground for trade liberalisation carefully from the time of his election in 1983, with speeches explaining the advantages of reducing and then removing Australian protection. The benefits included the improvement in competitiveness of potential Australian export industries, which would be able to take advantage of growing markets in East Asia. The publications of the Productivity Commission were important in providing authoritative evidence of the gains from opening up the economy, which allowed economically literate journalists to explain the case to a wider public (Garnaut 1994, 2001). The Commission responded with more far-reaching recommendations on trade liberalisation when it saw where the prime minister was leading the public discussion. However, its failure to recognise the increased opportunity for productivity-raising trade liberalisation with the fall in the floating exchange rate after 1986 and the Hawke government's public education on reform at that time caused it to be excessively cautious in the late 1980s. Its recommendation on across-the-board reduction of tariffs to a maximum of 10 per cent in 1988 were immediately accepted by the government. But the Hawke government took the opportunity to go much further following advice offered by an official report on trade opportunities in Northeast Asia in November 1989 (Garnaut 1989). The reduction of the maximum tariff to a maximum of 5 per cent and removal of all quantitative restrictions was announced by the prime minister in March 1991, with the changes to be phased in over the next five years (Hawke 1991). The announcement was made in the depths of a deep recession at a time of high unemployment. However, the phasing in of the decision meant that structural change would occur in the favourable macroeconomic circumstances of recovery from recession.

If macroeconomic policies are the brass of the orchestra, and productivity the percussion, then the Productivity Commission is the big bass drum. But it needs the conductor if the orchestra is to play in tune.

How Australia's economic policy orchestra can be conducted to play in tune to the best score

Australia after the pandemic recession faces a historic choice: reset to utilise new opportunity; or continue the policies that have delivered a decade of underperformance.

History and now

Australia has faced such choices before. In the 1920s, in the 1970s into the first few years of the 1980s, and over the past decade, the polity implicitly chose continued underperformance by failing to face up to large problems. In the 1930s, when the problems were greatest of all, creative Australians went a long way to understanding what needed to be done, and made some progress, but the nation stumbled at barriers that turned out to be too high.

Twice Australia took up arms against a sea of troubles, and by opposing, overcame them. On those two occasions, Australia entered long periods of rising living standards. Neither reform era was perfect. Good, but could have done even better.

The Albanese government came to office in 2022 aware of many of the problems and opportunities. It has made a start on dealing with some of them. It is constrained in dealing with others by its promises at the last election not to change policy much in several important areas where change is needed. Time, public discussion and education and new election mandates can ease those constraints. Time in office will give the government the chance to reset.

The previous government's fiscal and monetary policies during the pandemic provided a glimpse of near full employment and its advantages.

The general objectives are now clear enough. The government's White Paper on Jobs and Opportunities defines full employment and says that it is a central objective. This sits alongside objectives of rising incomes and living standards over time, moderate inflation, and an amount of debt that avoids the risks of future generations having lower standards of living than we enjoy today. Clarity on these general objectives follows the underperformance of the past decade and then the much lower unemployment and higher participation rates achieved in recovery from the pandemic recession.

The score, the conductor and the performance

We have relied heavily in this article on Keynes' metaphor of the conductor of the orchestra. As we noted in the first section of this chapter, the underlying reality is more complex and nuanced than the metaphor. Real economic policy in a democracy emerges from the interaction of ideas, political leadership and administrative process.

Real economic policy begins with the score. This is the written music which forms the basis of policy action, the statement of what needs to be done to solve the economic problems of the day. The outcomes depend on how well, on the day, the conductor manages to help the orchestra play the score.

In complex reality, the score – the statement of what needs to be done – must come from extensive discussion of ideas leading to decisions and announcements by the political leadership. In a democratic parliamentary setting, the written music is the product of interaction of the national policy discussion, detailed bureaucratic advice and political judgement. An active civil society is important in identifying the problems. An innovative economics profession, independent of vested interests and of commitment to erroneous conventional wisdom can identify problems and the best economic policy solutions. There is value in some parts of the system of advice to government having degrees of independence from direction by the political leadership. But eventually political leadership both defines the objectives and a way towards a preferred set of solutions. This leadership must explain to the polity the reasons why new policies are needed and contribute to community understanding of the problem and the proposed solutions. The prime minister and ministers are final arbiters on the score.

The *conductor* coordinates policymaking and implementation in different parts of government. The conductor requires support from officials to work through the details that link statements of what needs to be done with an understanding of what operational programs will be required. The relevant officials are placed in many parts of government. Good political leadership coordinates them effectively.

For the *performance* the players need to play their instruments well, in tune and in concert, following the score. In some cases, the political leadership can delegate management of particular activities to players away from the main orchestral performance. It is desirable for the administration of many areas of settled policy to be undertaken in this way, to ensure that the rules are applied impartially to all participants in economic processes. Examples are the roles of the Australian Taxation Office and the ACCC. This is separate from the roles of independent entities in policy discussion and advice. But the political leadership does not and cannot delegate responsibility for outcomes. The granting of independence is to assist the achievement of desired objectives. If the delegation does not achieve the desired outcomes, the government is held responsible for failure in the electorate.

It is desirable for much of the work on ideas – i.e. on the score – to be undertaken independently of political government. This allows innovation in thought, free criticism of proposals and contributions from competitive debate to sorting the good from the bad. A vibrant system of non-government entities – universities, independent centres of thought, and public interest journalism – has an important role in developing ideas for sound policy, for consideration and decision by the prime minister and ministers. Such independent advice can also emerge from government institutions operating under clear rules about independence.

Once the score is set for the time being and adjusted from time to time, the conductor can sit in one of several places within the machinery of government to make sure that the various policy instruments are playing in tune. What is crucial is that it is a place from which the conductor can be seen by all the players, and that the conductor has the authority to keep the orchestra playing in tune. Linking political leadership to coordination of policy at a public service level is crucial to success.

Advice coming through the coordinating centre to the prime minister and cabinet, and political direction of policy development and implementation, can be assisted by policymaking coming together in a subcommittee of cabinet. This could be an established subcommittee for economic management – like the Expenditure Review Committee. Or the focus on today's objectives may argue for a new Cabinet Committee on Full Employment and Economic Growth. This would integrate perspectives from the prime minister's department (including its responsibilities for the Net Zero Authority), the Treasury (including through its responsibilities for the RBA, the Productivity Commission and the ACCC), the Department of Employment and Workplace Relations (including its responsibility for Jobs and Skills Australia), the Department of Climate Change, Energy, the Environment and Water (including its responsibilities for the various energy regulatory agencies) and the Department of Industry, Science and Resources (including its responsibilities for the National Reconstruction Fund). Either way, within the current allocation of cabinet responsibilities, success depends on effective cooperation between the prime minister and the treasurer.

The institutional framework for more productive policymaking must build on what is already in place or under construction. Current practice suggests that it is a role best shared by the prime minister and treasurer and their departments.

Implementation

Governments in the two reform eras relied heavily on a professional public service. Those capacities declined through the first two decades of this century, and especially over the past decade from 2013, with arbitrary cuts to personnel numbers in the policy departments and outsourcing of policy development and advice to commercial consultancies. The current government is committed to rebuilding these capacities.

Coordination of macroeconomic policy is centrally important. Much can be contributed by the macroeconomic research institution proposed in Recommendation 3 of the RBA Review, with transparent interaction with related university-based and other external institutions, and a role in public discussion. Within this framework for sharing ideas and information with Treasury and the public, and with the government defining objectives of full employment and moderate inflation, the RBA could take independent decisions on interest rates and other monetary policy parameters. Independence would be subject to the constraints defined in the 1959 law governing the RBA. It would also have the wider coordination responsibilities discussed below.

The RBA's independent role in monetary policy has a unique history and rationale. It has been said that complete independence is necessary because political government is unlikely to take decisions to tighten monetary policy when they are required in the public interest, because higher interest rates attract political costs that leaders dependent on democratic elections are not prepared to accept. Much the same could be said of many areas of policy. Can we rely on democratically elected governments to raise taxation when this is required for good economic outcomes? Or to place a tax on carbon emissions at an economically justified rate to avoid catastrophic costs of climate change? Or to avoid political favouritism in allocation of public expenditures? Or to reduce protection that favours some interests while damaging the national interest? Or to impose taxation on economic rents that is in the public interest but imposes costs on powerful interests?

In an important final statement as governor of the RBA, Philip Lowe commented that there is as strong a rationale for making decisions on some macroeconomic aspects of fiscal policy independent of government, as there is for independent monetary policy (Lowe 2023). It is an empirical reality that governments cannot delegate responsibility for the consequences of monetary policy decisions simply by delegating responsibility for making the decisions. Democratic governments lose support with poor economic outcomes, whether those outcomes are the immediate consequence of decisions taken by them or delegated to others. That is the reality of political responsibility. It is also the correct allocation of responsibility in a democracy.

The right degree and form of delegation to a central bank of decisions on monetary policy is an economic policy decision, to be guided by assessments of what is likely to generate the best economic outcomes. There is no rule of nature or of experience favouring absolute independence. A degree of independence in setting interest rates can lead to better results under some conditions. Our companion essay in this volume (Chapter 7) expresses the view that the statutory scope for and limits on RBA independence established as law in 1959 get the balance right.

Making everything fit together

We began by invoking Trevor Swan's recollection from James Mill that there are many ways of ordering economic relationships, which have very different effects on society. The better outcomes are greatly superior to the worst for the welfare of most citizens. After a decade of underperformance, this is a time when democratic market polities and societies are under pressure to demonstrate that they can serve the interests of most people. Now is the time to put effort into defining the better policies, and to putting them into effect, drawing on old Australian wisdom and experience.

LOOKING FORWARD: BUILDING THE SUPERPOWER AND RESTORING PROSPERITY

Parliaments and prime ministers do not choose the challenges that absorb their greatest efforts, nor the issues to which history will attach the greatest weight. It was the opportunity and fate of the forty-seventh parliament and thirty-first prime minister to deal with the legacy of the COVID-19 pandemic. But the context is always shaped by the march of historical forces and events. Global inflation accompanied the recovery from recession, when massive fiscal and monetary expansion throughout the developed world was combined with extreme disruption of supply chains from the pandemic. That inflation was exacerbated by the energy price explosion and new supply disruptions from the Russian invasion of Ukraine.

The energy price shock coincided as closely with the arrival of the Albanese Labor government in 2022 as the Wall Street Great Crash did with that of the Scullin Labor government in 1929. There was a public interest case for Australia, as a major global exporter of gas and coal, to insulate its domestic standard of living from the Russian war price. Forcefully prosecuting that case would have required the government to disappoint large corporate interests that are accustomed to disappointment being experienced by smaller people. It is easy to understand why the government chose mostly to let big sleeping dogs lie. Even the shaving of profits with gentle price caps on coal and gas that were immaterial in their effect on record profits caused loud barking. Australians lived with the consequences for their standard of living. The government is living with the electoral consequences of the choice.

A start has been made on important elements of Australia's reset over the past two years. But we are a long way yet from the policy decisions that give us reasonable prospects for a long period of full employment with rising incomes. Chapter 2 ran through what needed to be done early in the life of the Albanese government. We chose not to do many of them in this parliament. Don't do them through another parliament, and Australia has chosen post-pandemic Dog Days. That is a restless and unhappy place for a democratic polity.

What we must do to secure prosperity for Australians in the future contains one element that seems impossible. That's carbon pricing. Break down the challenges that we face into their parts, and face honestly the consequences of avoiding them, and removing the impossible barrier becomes the easier way forward. Dismantling the barrier to carbon pricing eases budget, productivity, incomes growth and income distribution sorrows. That makes other productivity-raising reform possible.

This final chapter outlines the essential elements of the reset for prosperity that must be understood and put in place through the forty-eight parliament. The government after the next election will have to manage a general economic and political environment at least as difficult as that confronting the Albanese government in its first term. As to Claudius in *Hamlet*, sorrows will come not as single spies but in battalions. Which and whose battalions? The starting point is a grumpy electorate in which ordinary citizens have lower real wages and consumption than a decade before – for the first time in the statistical record. We have had a decade of historically low productivity growth and no prospects for change without doing some hard things.

It is wonderful for everything that our budget has recovered to a surplus far more quickly than anticipated by analysts and commentators during the pandemic recession (including by me in my book *Reset*).

Achieving the surplus required discipline in retaining a far higher proportion of unexpectedly high revenues than Australia had seen for a long
time. Chapter 2 showed that all the trends are unfavourable to future
fiscal strength. In July 2024 we can add to the sorrows the considerable
chance that Donald Trump will be restored as president of the United
States. He is committed to higher protection, tax cuts that will set record
highs for budget deficits, a trade war with Australia's largest trading
partner with a risk of worse, and comprehensive withdrawal from international cooperation and domestic action to reduce climate-changing
emissions of greenhouse gases. Global financial crisis is not out of the
question. A Kamala Harris victory would be better for Australia on climate change, and on risks of financial crisis, but not fundamentally so on
other interests. Australia's own commitments to open multilateral trade
and strong public finances are more important than ever. Both are challenged by new protectionist and inward-looking sentiment encouraged
by developments in the United States.

Building the Superpower is crucial to the reset. The Commonwealth and some state governments have backed the concept with well-
conceived policy frameworks. The Commonwealth's Future Made in
Australia National Interest Framework established sound principles for
allocating public resources to building the Superpower. But there are big
policy gaps to be filled.

There is strong general support across the Australian community
for renewable energy, for contributing to global efforts to defeat climate
change, and for building the Superpower. But doubts from unanswered
questions hold back commitments to the public and private investment
and the full suite of policies necessary to make it work. The answers will
only come convincingly to many in the community when there are successful examples of the new industries working on Australian ground.

The two most important elements of future prosperity are achieving
full employment and building the Superpower. The foundations for general restoration of strong economic performance are: free trade; strong

public finances; establishing a favourable business environment for private investment; securing community support and the necessary human capital for large change; and getting the balance right between state intervention and market exchange.

Strong action, including on carbon pricing, in the new parliament can defeat the battalions of sorrows. Introducing a carbon price to stop companies and people damaging others by freely emitting greenhouse gases is important to every pillar supporting the Superpower and restoring prosperity. We cannot deal with our budget, trade, productivity and income growth and distribution problems if we put off forever something that we haven't wanted to talk about for over a decade. We will have to put a price on carbon, or else live with the sorrows that come from continued income stagnation.

The Albanese government's first term

The Albanese Labor government was elected on a promise mostly to avoid large changes to the policies inherited from the Coalition government. This has been called the 'small target' approach. It has largely honoured that promise.

The Labor government has taken important steps towards the reset in two crucial areas: reestablishing full employment as an objective; and joining the international effort on climate change and establishing a framework for building the Superpower. So the reset has begun. But most of the barriers and certainly the hardest of them have been left for future parliaments and governments.

Fiscal and monetary policy in the pandemic pushed us closer to full employment than we had been for many decades. Josh Frydenberg was the first treasurer in a long time to speak about full employment as we moved in its direction in late 2021 and early 2022. Treasurer Jim Chalmers kept a discussion of full employment going. The Albanese government has moved strongly on the policy foundations of the climate and energy transition, but has not yet put up much in the way of permanent structures.

The barriers to reestablishing full employment are mainly of thought: resistance in the minds of the guardians of ideas about money and finance. By contrast, although barriers in thought have played some role on climate change and building the Superpower, the most effective resistance has been in the political economy – from interests that did very well from the unconstrained use of fossil carbon.

Beyond full employment and the Superpower, there is a need for reform of immigration. There was a huge increase in immigration levels relative to the established population from early in the twenty-first century. This was accompanied by an increase in the proportion of migrants who lack skills that have high value in Australia and have no path to Australian citizenship. This radical change in migration policy was established under the Howard government and continued through to the pandemic. These developments held back productivity and income growth through the Dog Days. Policy changes during the pandemic, including removing limits on hours of work by residents on student visas, exacerbated the problem once international movements of people were restored. Immigration then rose to unprecedented levels, again with a high proportion of unskilled temporary migrants. This pushed up prices of housing and other goods and services required by new arrivals. The former senior public servant and economist Martin Parkinson was commissioned to undertake a review of immigration (Parkinson 2023). His thorough and sound report in December 2023 advised that the system was so badly broken that it required a ten-year rebuild. That rebuild has commenced. The government's acceptance of the Parkinson recommendation that wage levels be used to determine the value of skills, as suggested in my book *Reset*, was a welcome development. Increased mobility of employee-sponsored skilled migrants reduced scope for exploitation. Overall, the Albanese government moved on skills later and on numbers less than would have been desirable for rising productivity and living standards. For the time being, policy leaves immigration with an appropriately increased focus on skills, but with numbers proportionately even higher than in the Dog Days. In short, there has been a partial reset.

There has been a modest partial reset on personal taxation. The change to the stage 3 tax cuts was in the direction of reducing effective marginal tax rates. It made those tax cuts more equitable. But there has been no movement on structural change to taxation and social security. Structural reform of personal income taxation in the past has involved net losses of revenue in the short term. In *Reset*, I suggested that fiscal expansion in recovery from recession created a favourable setting for structural reform. That opportunity was lost by the time of the change of government. Another opportunity could be created by allocating multiple years of anticipated 'bracket creep' to funding of reforms announced now for implementation several years in the future. This was the approach adopted with the stage 3 tax cuts, where treasurer Scott Morrison announced changes in tax schedules in 2018 that would apply from 2024.

One of the great benefits of full employment is that it widens access to labour incomes, raises wages through market exchange, and raises wages of lower income workers more than others (Krugman 2024, Autor 2023). Carefully calibrated taxation and social security reforms of the kind discussed in Chapter 6 can enhance equity. They interact with lower unemployment to increase labour force participation. That is good for growth in economic output and fiscal strength. In the absence of full employment and equitable personal taxation and social security, the Albanese government has sought equity through regulatory intervention in wage outcomes. Taxation and social security reform and full employment would deliver more favourable outcomes for equity, productivity and incomes growth.

The rise in the rent share of national income in the twenty-first century seems to mark an historic turning point in global development. Chapters 8 and 9 discuss the extraordinary Australian part of that story. Mining profits approached and in the final quarter of 2022 exceeded profits from all other Australian businesses. The increase in rents has large implications for Australian living standards. The contrast between

Australia and the only other developed country in which mineral rents play a comparably large role in the economy, Norway, is a depressing reflection on the relative capacities of the two democracies to serve the interests of their citizens.

There are a couple of success stories on management of rents in the public interest. A good start has been made on the competition policy issues discussed in Chapters 8 and 9. The increase in coal royalties in Queensland after the Russian invasion of Ukraine has supported payments to households for energy to offset higher prices from the Russian war, investment in infrastructure that is valuable for the energy transition, expansion of some health services, and a reduction in Queensland debt.

The Henry Tax Review showed that a general movement to higher taxation of rents would strengthen the budget and support other measures to raise Australian productivity and standards of living (Henry 2010). While implementation of mineral rent taxation as suggested by Henry would have greatly strengthened the Australian economy and lifted the trajectory of Australian living standards over the past decade, I have not included it in the essential next steps. I give higher priority to economically rational carbon pricing, which incidentally would reduce rents in coal and gas mining to some extent.

Chapters 8 and 9 discussed how a change in the base of corporate income tax from standard accounting income to cash flow could shift the tax burden towards economic rent and away from firms that are investing in new and innovative activities. That would be helpful to productivity and incomes growth and to equitable distribution of income. There has been no substantial progress yet on corporate tax reform. The productivity-raising changes suggested in Chapter 8 would reduce total Commonwealth revenue in the early years but recoup the loss over time. As with personal income taxation and social security, there would have been advantages in introducing reform as part of the anti-recessionary fiscal policy through 2020 and 2021, when the stimulatory effects of higher investment and lower taxation would have been helpful to recovery. That opportunity had passed by the time of the change of government. Corporate tax reform around movement to a cash-flow base could be prepared now and introduced as a stimulus measure in some future downturn.

The Albanese government's approach has been generally cautious and incremental, leaving much of the heavy lifting to future parliaments. The weakness with small changes is that they only make small contributions to dealing with problems. The problems are large, and urgent. Concerns about the standard of living dominate expressions of opinion about public policy. The economic facts tell a vivid story. After half a dozen years of stagnation of living standards and real wages through the Dog Days, and reasonable maintenance of incomes through the pandemic through massive payments from government, there were unprecedented falls in its aftermath. Real hourly wages in Australia were 4.8 per cent lower in mid-2024 than in the last quarter of 2019, just before the pandemic. This fall was much bigger than the average in developed countries, and bigger than in all but a few countries (OECD 2024). This is remarkable through a period in which terms of trade and national income were lifted in Australia and lowered in other developed countries by the large increases in coal and gas prices from the Russian war.

Prime Minister Albanese said from the early days of the government that his aim was not immediately to do all the things that needed to be done. His aim was to establish a multi-term Labor government that would make necessary reforms over several parliaments. The Albanese government so far has delivered the beginnings of a reset to restore Australian prosperity within that gradual approach. The moment of truth is approaching with another election and a new parliament. Of course, there is no certainty that there will be a second Albanese government. And there is no certainty that a second Albanese government would be supported by an ALP majority in the House of Representatives.

Testing times for democratic governments

Several decades of stagnation of real wages and living standards of ordinary people from about 1980 in the United States, followed by the global financial crisis, set the scene for a collapse of confidence in government in the 2010s. There was rebellion against established economic and international policies manifested in the election of Donald Trump as president in 2016. In the United Kingdom, a long period of stagnant wages and living standards of the general run of citizens led to the series of chaotic conservative governments that presided over Brexit, falls in incomes from Brexit, and then the pandemic recession and Russian war spike in energy prices. That led to a historic collapse in electoral support for the Conservative Party in the July 2024 general election. Governments and leaders in Canada and New Zealand rode high in opinion polls into, through and in early recovery from pandemic recession. Their support collapsed with rising interest rates, falling output per person and rising unemployment from 2022. The New Zealand Labour government suffered decisive defeat in October 2023. The opinion polls suggest that the Canadian Liberal government faces a defeat of historic proportions in elections due by mid-2025. Support fell away from what had been the strongest governments in Europe, in Germany and France, as recovery from pandemic recession left living standards lower than a few years before.

None of this recent experience of other developed countries would surprise observers of Australian economic and electoral history. All but one of the five Australian recessions since 1949 have been followed by a change of government between Coalition and Labor. All changes occurred immediately following the recession, except that Paul Keating's devastating attack on John Hewson's Fightback! program delayed the change from 1993 to 1996. The exception, the recession of 1960–61 followed by Menzies' defeat of Calwell in 1961, proves the rule. The 1960–61 recession was only a handful of years after the split with the Democratic Labour Party greatly raised the electoral bar for the ALP. Despite the split, Menzies' long ascendency was nearly broken in 1961:

the Coalition's one-seat majority was delivered by James Killen winning Moreton with a 50.1 per cent two party–preferred vote, following 60.3 per cent in 1958.

Output per person grew at historically low rates throughout the developed world over the past decade. It grew less rapidly in Australia than in other developed countries from 2013 until the pandemic (Garnaut 2021). It held up reasonably well relative to other developed countries through the pandemic but declined more than the average in recovery from the recession.

Each national political story has its own dynamics. There are local factors that may cause the Albanese government to buck the global tendency. The Albanese government may be returned with a majority in the House of Representatives at the election due by May 2025.

Maybe.

Or the Labor Party may win more seats than the Coalition, but have to seek support from the crossbenches on votes of confidence and money. Or the Coalition may win more seats than Labor but need crossbench support to form a government. A Coalition government relying on crossbench support would need to make major adjustments to its climate and energy policy.

A Labor or Coalition government supported by some combination of others in the House of Representatives will have undivided responsibility for completion of Australia's reset for prosperity and building the Superpower. Full responsibility, and an opportunity to exercise it well. As prime minister, Julia Gillard demonstrated that governments dependent on support from minor parties and independents can be effective on policy. Her government's electoral defeat in 2013 was driven by leadership instability, not by the electorate favouring Coalition over Labor climate policies.

The fourth possibility, majority Coalition government, would seem to require major change in policy and political culture to regain support from former Coalition voters for whom climate, gender and integrity were of major importance in 2022.

The Coalition once saw itself as a broad church with conservative and liberal elements. The state Coalition governments in New South Wales, South Australia and Tasmania in the late 2010s all had climate change and energy transition policies at least as strong and effective as the average of their counterparts in the Labor states.

In any case, preservation of a stable climate, and of the society, economy and polity that depend on it, is a conservative issue. The early global leaders of action to stop climate change were leaders of British and German conservative governments. Malcolm Turnbull in the Commonwealth; Gladys Berejiklian, Dominic Perrottet and Matt Kean in New South Wales; and Steven Marshall in South Australia were all conservatives who wanted effective action to protect the Australian economy and society against damage from climate change. There are now few conservatives by the old definitions in Coalition ranks in the federal parliament. But genuine conservatism – the desire to preserve continuity in what is good in our civilisation across the generations – remains important through our community and is unlikely to be denied political representation forever.

In 2021 in Glasgow, the last Commonwealth Coalition government committed itself to net-zero emissions by 2050. The Coalition in Opposition has not resiled from that commitment. Its embrace of government-owned nuclear power generators is presented as a path to net zero by 2050. And while the Coalition expresses reservations about renewable power generation, it does not oppose the building of new industries that use solar and wind power.

The use of the market – carbon pricing – to achieve net-zero emissions by 2050 would once have been a Liberal approach. The alternative, in action since 2014, has been multifarious arbitrary government interventions in business investment decisions.

Nor is there anything conservative or liberal about opposing full employment. Robert Menzies in Opposition in 1949 had expressed doubts about some Labor policies to achieve full employment. But as David Vines and I record in Chapter 13, on winning office Prime Minister

Menzies promptly asked the main author of the Curtin government's White Paper on Full Employment, H.C. Coombs, to stay on in a high official role. Full employment underpinned Menzies' unequalled electoral success. More recently, progress towards full employment in recovery from the pandemic recession was an achievement in which Coalition treasurer Josh Frydenberg justifiably takes pride (Frydenberg 2024).

Full employment with moderate inflation and the right amount of debt

One big idea and two concepts need to be understood if we are to place full employment at the centre of a reset for sustained Australian prosperity. The big idea is embodied in the Australian Swan diagram discussed in Chapter 13. Full employment can be established for a while by increasing government spending, or by causing private citizens to spend more by cutting taxes or reducing interest rates. But that will not be sustainable over time unless the right balance is found between expenditure and competitiveness. That balance allows full employment to be achieved with moderate inflation and the right amount of debt.

In the highly regulated postwar Australian economy from 1945 until 1983, competitiveness could be secured directly through the interaction of wages and exchange rate policy. After the floating of the Australian dollar in 1983, the level of the exchange rate could be moved by the interaction of fiscal and monetary policy. Labour market reform made wages less amenable to direct intervention by government, although the Fair Work Commission retained a role in setting minimum wages. So it became essential to establish the right balance between fiscal policy and monetary policy, and to ensure that wage regulation is managed consistently with the objectives of fiscal and monetary policy. Coordinating policy in these and other connected areas requires the right musical score (good economics), a conductor, and an orchestra with competent players on sound instruments.

Competitiveness can be increased by tightening fiscal policy without changing monetary policy, or by lowering interest rates without changing fiscal policy. The challenge is to keep demand for labour matched with its supply and so maintain moderate inflation with full employment, while avoiding too much debt or so great a budget and external payments surplus that domestic living standards are kept unnecessarily low.

The Swan idea was influential in the long period of postwar full employment with rising living standards from 1945 until the early 1970s. With adaptation to the floating currency, it played a role in the reform era from 1983 until the end of the century. It has largely been lost in the twenty-first century so far. Under inflation targeting, there has been a tendency to see expenditure alone as the focus of macroeconomic policy, with the exchange rate presumed to vary automatically to balance external payments and indebtedness, and wages to adjust automatically with unemployment to secure full employment. A single policy instrument, interest rates, has been varied to achieve one objective: holding inflation to a target (in Australia a range of 2–3 per cent).

It has been assumed that competitiveness, employment and indebtedness look after themselves if monetary policy is keeping inflation on target. If inflation rises above the target range, interest rates are increased. This reduces economic activity and increases unemployment. Higher unemployment reduces pressures for higher wages and so reduces inflation in goods and services. Inflation eventually falls to the target range. Unemployment rises until the non-accelerating inflation rate of unemployment (NAIRU) is reached. Unemployment is as low as it can be without pressures from the labour market leading to accelerating inflation and raising it above the target range. If inflation falls below the band, interest rates are reduced. This increases economic activity and reduces unemployment, raises wages in the marketplace and increases goods and services inflation. This continues until inflation rises to the target band.

New Zealand was the first country to introduce inflation targeting. The target range was 0–2 per cent. Keeping inflation within this range was the sole objective of an independent central bank: there was no full employment mandate alongside price stability. All OECD countries followed New Zealand, with varying degrees of rigidity. Australia and some others kept full employment alongside an inflation objective. New Zealand, pioneer and exemplar of inflation targeting, had three recessions through Australia's three decades of continued growth without recession, including two that were very deep and extraordinarily costly. It is now in its second recession since the pandemic – the fifth NZ recession that Australia hasn't had in three and a bit decades. New Zealand added an employment mandate to the Reserve Bank's objective in 2018 and has moved to greater flexibility.

Australian inflation targeting was introduced informally in 1993 and formally in 1996. It was more flexible than New Zealand's, retained at least a legal full employment objective and generated far better economic outcomes. In practice, it tended over the twenty-first century towards the single objective of low inflation. Between 2013 and 2019, raising inflation was not an urgent concern when the rate of price increases was below the target range. On employment, the Reserve Bank of Australia took comfort from a presumption that maintaining inflation at a low and steady rate would eventually bring unemployment back to the lowest rate possible without accelerating inflation – the NAIRU. This approach contributed during the Dog Days to unnecessarily high unemployment and under-employment; the stagnation of output per person and incomes; and persistent budget deficits.

The two concepts that need to be understood are the NAIRU and the 'natural' or 'neutral' rate of interest These are both empirical concepts: their levels at a point of time require observation of the economy at that time. They change over time with economic phenomena, including economic policy.

We know that unemployment has fallen to the NAIRU – the lowest rate that is consistent with stable inflation – when we see wage pressures in the labour market contributing to accelerating inflation. It is an analytic mistake that can lead to mistakes in economic policy to see the NAIRU as an output from a quantitative economic model calibrated by labour market, wage and price experience from the past. In recovery from pandemic recession, there has been a tendency in the Reserve Bank and the commentariat to accept a NAIRU from the models, and to want to raise interest rates to increase unemployment towards the presumed NAIRU. For examples, use of models from historical experience suggesting that the NAIRU is 4.5 per cent has led to calls for interest rates to be raised because unemployment is below that level.

The natural interest rate is the real rate at which private savings equals private investment when the economy is fully employed, inflation is stable and the budget in reasonable balance. The natural rate of interest, too, is an empirical phenomenon. There is a tradition in neoclassical economics to presume that it is substantially positive. That introduces a presumption that if real interest rates are not substantially positive, the difference is an aberration that will be corrected. If policy rates are near or below zero in real terms, they will eventually have to rise to substantially positive levels. Having an unrealistically high natural rate in a central banker's model or mind leads to a bias towards setting official rates uneconomically high.

Chapter 9 discusses reasons for large falls in the natural rate of interest in the twenty-first century. Short-term rates set by central banks for policy reasons vary from time to time but are ultimately anchored to the long-term natural rate. Many commentators on and participants in financial markets have seen real interest rates near zero over the past decade as reflecting short-term policy and other conditions that will go away. That has introduced a bias towards interest rates that are too high for full employment, unless government runs larger budget deficits than it would otherwise judge to be wise.

One complication affects interpretation of the natural rate of interest in today's world. The world's governments are running budget deficits in excess of anything previously known outside the major global wars and deep global recessions. The United States leads the way. There is a chance that public deficits will become so large that they absorb the whole of the surplus global private savings at contemporary interest rates and significantly raise international real interest rates. As presidential candidate, Donald Trump announced policies that may lead the world into such a space. All countries must take account of this upward pressure on international interest rates in setting their own monetary policies. However, the tendency for private savings to exceed private investment even at zero real interest rates is so strong in the mid-2020s that even a second Trump presidency may not make capital scarce and expensive in the world as a whole. Obviously it will not put upward pressure on global interest rates if it precipitates financial crisis, deep recession and large declines in private investment.

The pandemic recession and the response from the Morrison government and the Lowe Reserve Bank put aside all earlier preconceptions of monetary policy. This experience, followed by changes in personnel and decision-making structures in the RBA after the review of its charter and operations, have allowed these issues to be examined with fresh eyes. Full employment remains a statutory objective of the central bank after the review, and the government's white paper and public discussion have restored this mandate as a real objective.

The financial year 2024–25 is critical for testing how far the Australian mindset has changed from the settings that contributed to the stagnation of incomes and unnecessarily high unemployment and underemployment – and incidentally, inflation below the target – through the Dog Days. In July 2024 there is talk of possible increases in Australian interest rates to accelerate the decline in inflation. Inflation fell from more than 7 per cent in late 2022 to about 4 per cent early in 2024. Money wage increases early in 2024 ran slightly ahead of inflation, as regulated real wages through the Fair Work Commission and public sector wage increases for health, care and some other workers caught up a small part of earlier decline. That contributed to a pause in the decline in inflation. None of this reflected wage pressures from the labour market, which would signify that unemployment was as low as the NAIRU.

Other countries are beginning or preparing to cut interest rates in mid-2024 in response to rising unemployment and declining output per person. The prices of exports and import-competing goods and services have been falling and Australia's largest trading partner, China, is experiencing deflation. Expectations of higher Australian relative to international interest rates increased the value of the Australian dollar against the average of our trading partners. That has been another source of downward pressure on the prices in Australia of internationally traded goods.

Prices of non-traded goods in Australia, disproportionately services, have not come down so quickly. Wages are a major component of prices for non-traded goods and services. Stickiness of non-traded prices is to be expected as the large reductions in real wages did not result from any structural change requiring such a fall.

Inflation tending down but only slowly would only be a problem requiring higher interest rates in response if there were signs of accelerating increases in market-determined wages, or increases in inflationary expectations. In July 2024, there were no such signs. Australia is in danger of getting itself back into the position it was in through the Dog Days, of devaluing the full employment objective in practice and running tighter monetary policy against the rest of the world when its economy is not growing more strongly.

The OECD issued its own caution in mid-2024:

Real wages are now growing year-on-year in most OECD countries, in the context of declining inflation. They are, however, still below their 2019 level in many countries. As real wages are recovering some of the lost ground, profits are beginning to buffer some of the increase in labour costs. In many countries, there is room for profits to absorb further wage increases, especially as there are no signs of a price-wage spiral. (OECD 2024)

It is often remarked that Australian interest rates are below US ones as if this must be a mistake, without taking into account the stronger US economy, the extraordinary differences in fiscal settings, and different rules and practices for bank lending.

So we have made some ground but remain, for the moment, in no man's land in the battle between Dog Days and Reset perspectives on full employment. The battle may be resolved decisively in favour of full employment through 2024–25, through one of two mechanisms. One will operate if the RBA holds out too long on lowering interest rates – or even raises them above the levels of July 2024. Higher unemployment, loss of economic output, larger budget deficits and further declines in real wages will follow. As Keynes observed in 1925, persisting with a wrong policy will certainly achieve the lower inflation desired, whatever the unnecessary human and economic cost. The human sacrifice to the sun god will have been made, and the sun will have risen in the morning and moved across the sky. But I suspect that there has been too much discussion of the causal mechanisms this time for the old stories to remain credible. The more likely outcome is discrediting of the Dog Days approaches to full employment and monetary policy.

The other mechanism will come into play if timely adjustment of policy sees inflation easing back over a couple of years sustainably into the target range, without significant increases in unemployment from mid-2024 levels or further reductions in Australians' real incomes. The unsatisfactory monetary policy of the Dog Days will then go the way of the Aztec sun gods. After Cortez's capture of Mexico and the murder of the Aztec emperor, the ritual human sacrifice ceased. The sun still came up in the morning and moved across the sky through the day. The people no longer believed the old stories.

The Superpower's contribution to Australian prosperity

The economic rationale for the Superpower is now well known to some Australians. Australia had large economic advantages from relatively rich resources of coal and gas – relative, that is, to other economic capacities and other countries. That made us the world's biggest exporter of coal and gas taken together, and before the internationalisation of eastern Australian gas and coal markets in the twenty-first century, a significant exporter of processed metals (Sandiford 2022).

Our natural resource endowments relative to the rest of the world give us even greater advantages in the zero-carbon world. They are led by solar and wind resources and land to put them on without displacing other high-value activities, and low-cost opportunities to grow and sustainably harvest biomass. The biomass is a source of renewable carbon and hydrocarbon to replace petroleum and coal in the chemical industries of the future, and for permanently sequestering carbon in soils and plants.

The governments of all significant economies are now committed to net-zero carbon emissions at some time between 2045 (Germany and some other European countries) and 2070 (India). Australia belatedly joined all other developed democracies in commitment to net zero by 2050 in Glasgow in 2021. The Paris Agreement in 2015, to which all United Nations members are parties, requires net zero for the world as a whole by 2050. Some countries would have great difficulty reaching net zero from their own natural resources. They could only do so at high cost to their communities' standards of living. They are in a different place to Australia, where abundance of relevant domestic resources allows us to achieve net zero with higher living standards than would have prevailed if the fossil carbon economy had continued undisturbed by climate change. The densely populated industrial economies of Europe (including the United Kingdom and others outside the European Union) and Northeast Asia (Japan, Korea, the People's Republic of China and Taiwan) would face exceptionally high costs in taking a self-sufficient approach to net zero. These economies account for over 40 per cent of global emissions. Southeast Asia (first of all, Indonesia) and South Asia (first of all, India) have contributed most of the growth in global emissions over the past decade and will join Europe and Northeast Asia as regions that have difficulty in achieving net zero from their own resources as industrialisation proceeds and incomes rise over the next several decades.

Europe and Northeast Asia are highly dependent on imports of petroleum and coal in the old fossil carbon economy. Their development and high living standards have depended on reliable supplies of immense quantities from abroad. Achieving energy and raw material security from imports to support industrial development and rising living standards required innovation in technology, economic institutions and international relations.

The cost of moving fossil carbon between countries and across oceans is relatively low. That has meant that there is no large economic advantage in processing goods requiring coal or petroleum in the countries in which the carbon or hydrocarbon is produced. Most large exporters of fossil carbon (including Saudi Arabia, Qatar, the United Arab Emirates, the United States, Indonesia and Russia, but not including Australia, except for gas in Western Australia) have created some local industrial advantage by domestic reservation, differential taxation or other means, but that has left immense volumes of intercontinental trade in coal, oil and gas.

Renewable electricity can be moved across oceans through submarine cables, or converted into green hydrogen or ammonia and other hydrogen derivatives for international trade. It can be used as an energy source or industrial input in countries which have high demand for, but low endowments of, renewable energy. But the international transport is expensive, more than doubling the cost in the importing country. So the economics argue for renewable energy and hydrogen mainly to be converted into zero-carbon goods for export from the countries in which they are produced.

The new trading relationships require technological, economic and international political innovation, just like the old trade in fossil carbon. We have learnt a great deal from the old trade that is relevant to the new. We learnt by the middle of last century that the imperialism that had accompanied much international trade in resources in the early stages of industrialisation in Europe and Japan was unnecessary and undesirable. Humanity got rid of most of it in the first couple of decades after World War II. Through that period, we learnt that commercial relationships based on knowledge and trust can make secure and mutually beneficial trade work for development in both resource-abundant and resource-exporting countries. We can apply those lessons to the new trade in zero-carbon goods.

The densely populated industrial countries with weak endowments of renewable energy have demand for energy of two kinds. One is for what we can call 'domestic' or 'non-tradable' energy. This is the energy that must be directly consumed in the country of final use, to light and heat buildings, provide essential services and run vehicles for transport. In the zero-carbon economy, this will mostly be energy used in electrical form, with electricity generated locally. There will be some use of green hydrocarbon fuels in specialised transport and other activities. The other kind of demand is for 'tradable' energy, embodied in goods such as metals and chemical manufactures. At present, Northeast Asia and Europe account for a large majority of world production of emissions-intensive forms of these goods, supported by imports of fossil carbon.

Europe and Northeast Asia will need to generate a large amount of electricity domestically to meet their demands for non-tradable energy. They will give highest priority to meeting these requirements by using their limited local resources. Where it is extremely expensive to meet even these limited proportions of energy demand from their own renewable resource, they will have to import electricity by cable, or as hydrogen or its derivatives, or use nuclear energy. They will import hydrogen in ammonia or other derivatives or generate nuclear power no matter what the cost. They have no choice. The cost of power for domestic use will be several times that in Australia.

Nuclear will play an important role in supplying non-tradable electricity to these countries. That will increase Australian export opportunities for uranium. Australia has among the world's largest resources of high-grade uranium oxide. It is a major exporter of uranium. Uranium enrichment is highly energy-intensive. Uranium enrichment can contribute to Australian development and global decarbonisation if it passes other tests. It is a Superpower industry.

For tradable energy, the economics will not support use of nuclear energy or import of power by cable or of hydrogen and its derivatives. That would render downstream manufacturing industries uncompetitive in global markets. Using iron and aluminium processed from expensive green electricity and hydrogen at home would handicap the competitiveness in international markets of cars and other metal manufactures made in Germany and Japan and Korea. Economic realities will drive them to import zero-carbon metals to reduce the requirements for electricity at home.

The Superpower Institute is working through the capacities for domestic supply of zero-carbon energy in Europe and Northeast Asia (Finighan 2024; Burfurd 2024). Japan, Korea and Taiwan, and Singapore in Southeast Asia stand out for their incapacity to supply even their requirements for non-tradable energy from domestic sources at costs comparable to imports of hydrogen and its derivatives, or of nuclear power generation. They will be large markets for imported ammonia (as a hydrogen carrier) in addition to zero-carbon goods. For most of Europe and China, more of the non-tradable energy requirements will come from domestic sources, with imports mainly of zero-carbon goods.

Australia is not the only potentially competitive supplier of zero-carbon goods. Its competitors will be mainly developing countries with rich endowments of renewable energy and low domestic demand. These include the Middle East, Central Asia and North and Southwest Africa. Australia has an advantage of political stability and reliable institutions to support international trade and investment. Only the Middle East has comparable or lower costs of capital. Australia has richer combinations of solar and wind energy resources and biomass than any of the competitors. It has similar access to cost-competitive Chinese capital goods unless Australian departure from open trade gives others an advantage. None of the competitors has comparable endowments of minerals requiring energy-intensive processing. And none of the competitors has anything like the potential scale of Australian production.

Note that the major competitors do not include some regions with substantial endowments of renewable energy resources but large domestic demand. These include North America, Brazil and South Africa. The United States may secure some export sales of zero-carbon products through high levels of subsidy in the early stages of the transition. But its renewable energy will be directed mainly to home markets.

The Superpower will be built on five general pillars: fiscal strength; free trade; favourable private investment environment; human resources and community support for change; and the right balance between the roles of the state and the market.

A strong fiscal position is necessary to support a competitive cost of capital and real exchange rate. This is challenged by the fiscal demands of defence spending, care for an aging population and underinvestment over a long period in many public services, and reluctance to raise total taxation above levels that are low by the standards of democratic developed countries. We need new sources of taxation that do not reduce productive investment or reduce general living standards.

Free trade is necessary to support a competitive real exchange rate, strong productivity growth and access to the world's most competitive capital goods and services for production of renewable energy and zero-carbon goods. It is also necessary for access on competitive terms to the markets of the European and Northeast Asian and later Southeast and South Asian countries that have strong comparative disadvantage in producing renewable energy.

A favourable environment for private business investment builds on financial stability from strong public finances and on open international trade. It would be assisted by corporate tax reform. Above all, it requires stable rules, operated through clear policies and laws with a minimum of official discretion. Only soundly based policy can be stable. Soundly based policy will be built around correcting market imperfections from negative carbon externalities and positive innovation externalities. Soundly based policy will have government doing well the things that only government can do, and leaving to market exchange all activities in which competition among private firms is possible.

The Australian business environment over the past decade has been characterised by myriad interventions by government in the energy and energy-using sectors of the economy, and by extraordinary instability in policy and law. The shift from carbon pricing to 'direct action' in 2014 made that inevitable. That has increased the supply price of capital and increased the cost and reduced reliability of energy. It is inconsistent with restoration of growth in productivity and incomes in the economy in general, and in globally competitive production of energy and zero-carbon goods.

The fourth pillar – securing the human resources and community support for the new economy – depends on building a shared understanding of the shape of the successful future economy. Young Australians can only commit their careers to the new economic activities if they have confidence that opportunities for employment will be available for them. Australian governments will only commit to the policy reform, and the public investment in provision of services that only government can provide well, if there is broad community support for structural change. Governments have critical roles in public education and in building support for productive structural change in the economy. Australian and international investors will only commit to building the new economy if there is sound and stable policy based on broad community support for the directions of change. Governments and businesses in the economies which must provide markets for the zero-carbon exports from the Australian Superpower industries must have confidence in security of

Australian supply of goods that are important to their own economic security. This can only be based on observation of the durability of commitments from Australian communities, governments and business.

We are in the early stages of building broadly based understanding of the Superpower opportunity. There is considerable recent progress. With the election of the Albanese government, all Australian governments at Commonwealth, state and territory levels are committed to some version of the Superpower economic future. The government's commitments to 82 per cent renewables and reducing emissions by 43 per cent by 2030, its participation in international sectoral agreements and its support for decarbonisation in developing countries took us into the company of the developed world after several years of hanging out with Russia and Saudi Arabia.

The deep divisions on climate and energy policy over the past one and a half decades will remain until the benefits of building the Superpower take tangible form in regional Australia. The sceptics take comfort in a slump of investment in renewables, to substantially lower rates than at the Morrison end of the Coalition government. They take comfort from reasonable doubts about whether the emissions reduction and renewable energy objectives will be met. Slow rollout of renewables and the 'wind drought' in southern Australia in the June quarter of 2024 (AEMO 2024) raised doubts about whether a mainly renewables electricity system would ever be able to provide reliable electricity supply through the winter months. The higher coal and gas electricity generation and higher emissions through this period provided additional fuel for doubt. The sceptics take comfort from household electricity bills rising despite a government statement before the election, based on unwarranted faith in economic forecasting, that they would fall. They are encouraged by high wholesale prices of electricity being converted into expectations of green hydrogen costs that are too high for some proposed Superpower industries to be globally competitive. The retreat by Andrew Forrest's Fortescue Future Industries from its hydrogen export targets and statements by former Commonwealth chief scientist Alan Finkel that he had been wrong to speak of great prospects for hydrogen exports encourage sceptical comment about the Superpower. Producers of gas-based alternatives to zero-emissions goods advertise their merits as having lower emissions than established coal-based alternatives, and lower costs than genuinely green goods. Debates about alternative zero-emissions technologies become passionate differences of belief rather than being resolved by dispassionate market competition and exchange.

In the febrile contemporary Australian political discussion of energy, each of these hill-scale encouragements to doubts about the zero-carbon economy becomes a mountain. Each of them has paths for crossing, but the ways ahead become hidden behind the mountains.

The healthy rate of investment in renewable energy through the years of the Morrison Coalition government was driven by the tailwinds from the Renewable Energy Target (RET) that had been introduced by Howard, strengthened by Rudd and weakened but still left with considerable power by Abbott.

The RET provided revenue from renewable energy sales above that available to sales of power made with high emissions from gas or coal – it provided a "green premium". Investment in renewables withered as the end of the RET in 2030 drew closer and took away expectations of a green premium for renewable energy. Two state governments came to subsidise coal generation in competition with renewables. Far from renewable power generation receiving a premium, coal power receives much higher prices in the market than solar or wind and are also now supported by subsidies. In 2023, the government realised that the renewables investment slump was so severe that the renewables objective and emissions target were receding out of reach.

The government announced in November 2023 that it would extend the Capacity Investment Scheme (CIS) for underwriting investment in storage to renewables generation. The CIS had worked for storage, where the market dynamics were quite different from those for renewable energy generation. The extension of the CIS was a bold intervention, with costs and risks. It would lift investment above the low levels to which it had fallen in a world looking ahead to the absence of carbon pricing or a RET. But it would dampen, perhaps freeze, renewable generation investment outside the CIS. Investors' concern about the value of sales of renewable energy beyond the RET was exacerbated by government statements that there would be reform of the post-2030 electricity market, without saying anything about the shape of the new arrangements. Now, the announced volume of new generation to be underwritten and the processes of the CIS, the low investment outside the CIS, and increasing demand for power mean that renewables generation will fall far short of 82 per cent without major new policy.

That looks like good reason for doubt. But there is time to recover to 82 per cent by 2030. There are enough well-developed renewables generation projects for an announcement by mid-2025 on suitable post-2030 market design to lift the rate of investment by enough to reach the renewables objective. The suitable design would have two main elements. One would remove uncertainty about preservation of the main features of the current electricity market. The other would establish reliably a green premium for renewable power after the RET ends in 2030. Data on the falls in electricity prices from solar and wind and the rises from gas are presented in Appendix 14.1.

Yes, the wind drought of 2024 does highlight a special challenge to providing reliable electricity supply through the winter months. The inevitable challenge in the months of low sunshine is exacerbated by the effects of climate change. The climate models advise that warming may lead to some movement south of the westerly winds that brought rain and energy to southern Australia through the winter months. Lower wind power is not a surprise, although the extent of the fall in 2024 is unexpectedly large. Warming and drying have reduced stream flows into dams. That led to low water levels in Tasmanian dams, leading to the island state becoming a large net purchaser of power from, rather than a supplier to, Victoria. The solution to the winter wind drought lies in clever use of multiple opportunities provided by the natural development of the electricity system in the years ahead.[1]

Pending emergence of the mechanisms that will eventually provide reliability through the most challenging winters, reliability is secured through thermal peaking generators fuelled by gas, with some green hydrogen as storage for industrial uses expands and reduces the cost of hydrogen.

Wind and solar power prices have fallen spectacularly over the past decade, including in the past few years. The increase in average electricity prices and much more has been contributed by higher coal and gas prices. The higher gas and coal power generation and emissions in the June quarter of 2024 will recede if steps are taken to put Australia back on track for 82 per cent renewables by 2030.

Hydrogen costs in Australia really would be uneconomically high if electrolysers had to draw power from the grid at mid-2024 average prices. The average prices are a mixture of very low and often negative prices when renewables are abundant and set the price, and very high prices when gas is needed and sets the price. Hydrogen for the Superpower industries will utilise the low prices, storing some hydrogen for use by industrial plants at other times. Or it will be produced in locations with especially rich combinations of wind and solar, perhaps with some battery storage, generating electricity prices well below those in the regional grids centred on the major cities.

Far from being a setback for the Superpower narrative, Forrest's and Finkel's retreats from hydrogen exports mark their return to the Superpower base camp after a wander in the wilderness. Australia's opportunity arises precisely because it is difficult and expensive to export hydrogen. Coal is easily shipped abroad at low cost and used to smelt Australian mineral ores in other countries. The high cost of moving renewable energy and hydrogen across the seas means that the processing of Australian raw materials is most economically undertaken in Australia in the zero-carbon world.

The argument that gas-based metals processing is lower in emissions than coal has been used to smuggle in developments under the Superpower umbrella in Western Australia and parts of the Commonwealth government. That is at best a detour from the main trajectory. The task of reducing emissions to hold temperature increases to 1.5°C is so demanding that there is no time for detours. Emissions from industry can only fall enough to meet global climate objectives if we start early and move rapidly on technologies with zero net emissions. Strategies that leave high levels of metals processing and chemical manufactures using coal and gas in 2050 are premised on failure to deal with the climate problem. Producing hydrogen from gas in Australia and exporting it or manufacturing iron metal or fertilisers for export from it helps importing economies achieve zero net emissions. But it pushes achievement of our international obligations – and compliance with our own law on emissions reduction – out of reach. The solution is to have examples of genuinely zero-carbon projects operating soon with commercial success. That is possible with support for innovation at levels justified by the benefits the first movers confer on others, and with green premiums equal to the social cost of carbon. That and movement to green premiums reflecting the social cost of carbon everywhere will do the rest.

Disputes about which zero- and low-carbon technologies do and do not warrant government support are inevitable for as long as direct action by government rather than an economically rational price on carbon drives the climate and energy transition. The solution is to put a price on carbon.

Pillars for success: correcting the balance between market and state

Get policy right in the forty-eighth parliament, and Australians lift markedly and perhaps decisively humanity's chances of dealing with the climate challenge. We now have a government and parliament wanting timely transition to net zero. We have a government and parliament wanting to build Australia as the renewable energy Superpower of the zero-carbon world economy. For the time being, we have favourable international settings for using our opportunity. The government of Australia has embraced the Superpower narrative, taken some big steps towards supporting its emergence, and articulated sound principles for guiding further policy development.

But Australians in business and the community wanting to make large efforts to turn opportunity into reality find themselves in a tangle of policy uncertainty and contradiction. The sceptics can find more encouragement in the daily facts than those who are invested in building the new economy.

The source of the problem is the abolition of carbon pricing in 2014. Since then, the Commonwealth government has worked within constraints that rule out success. We can make a start towards net zero and the Superpower without moving the constraints, but we can't get far. This is a problem for any government of Australia, and not only for the current Labor government. We will not rise sustainably out of post-pandemic Dog Days until we get energy policy right and make strong headway on building the Superpower.

Striking the right balance between state intervention and market exchange is always essential for successful economic development, in all places. The market generally delivers goods and services more cost-effectively than the state where there is genuine competition among suppliers and purchasers of goods and services. The difference is especially large and important at a time of structural change and uncertainty. State decisions inevitably tend towards continuation on established paths and slow response to new opportunities. Australia will not make use of more than a small fraction of the Superpower opportunities available to it without immense contributions from an innovative, competitive private business sector. So we have to design energy and related markets that provide the widest possible scope for competition among enterprises within clear rules understood in advance of investment decisions by all market participants.

The state has to do well the things that only the state can do. Because government capacity is a finite resource, it is much more likely that it will do the essential things well if it doesn't try to do the things that markets do well.

The state must define the boundaries between the services that it delivers and those to be delivered by the market. In the electricity sector, government must take responsibility for design of the market rules and compliance with them. It must provide the natural monopoly services of electricity transmission and hydrogen transportation and storage. It must take ultimate responsibility for system security and reliability.

For any markets to work, individual market participants must be blocked by regulation from damaging others through their business decisions, or subject to a tax equal to the costs they impose on others. And they must be rewarded for large benefits that they confer on others. This is essential economics. Its understatement in Productivity Commission and financial media commentary on energy and climate policy discussion over the past decade reveals the debasement of Australian political culture that gave us the Dog Days. It has been politically incorrect to tell the truth out loud.

Transmission of electricity and transportation and storage of hydrogen are natural monopoly services, best provided by the state. The three southeastern mainland states privatised most electricity transmission some time ago. The state remains responsible at least for infrastructure planning and making sure that plans are implemented – for ensuring that adequate transmission investment is made at the right time and in the right places. It also regulates prices. The other states have retained responsibility for transmission. Only Queensland and South Australia are near a path to delivering effective outcomes. Costs of delivering transmission services have increased much more rapidly than in other countries or at other times since privatisation and corporatisation. We need a large expansion of the network, and fundamental change in its geographic location and role. The existing arrangements have become a bottleneck for investment in generation, decarbonisation, reliability and reduction in costs to users. In Chapter 12, Rod Sims and I proposed that the Productivity Commission undertake a root-and-branch review of transmission. The review should consider the merits of the high-voltage backbone connecting the new Superpower renewable energy and industrial regions (the Sungrid sketched in Appendix 1.2 of *The Superpower Transformation*). This would link the Southwest WA, Pilbara and Northern Territory systems to the eastern grid. A large state-controlled transmission system would provide connections to private generators and users close to the planned grid. Private investors would meet the incremental cost of connecting generation and loads. Some Superpower investors would make use of the large grid. Some would provide for their own requirements or as consortia of firms operating independently.

Australia separates transmission from local distribution of power. There are large opportunities to use the new decentralised technologies – rooftop solar, small batteries and electric vehicles – to decarbonise, increase reliability and reduce costs of power through flexible use of distribution systems. This requires innovation on a scale and at a pace that is beyond the inclination of established operators. The Institute for Energy Economics and Financial Analysis (IEEFA) has suggested that this be the subject of a Productivity Commission review. The suggestion has merit.

Retail electricity services are potentially competitive. In the southeastern states, private ownership dominated by a few suppliers has required the usual competition policy responses. The states which have retained state ownership of integrated electricity businesses have opened the market for customers above specified sizes. This avoids problems of oligopoly in supply to households and small business.

Generation of power is potentially competitive. In the early years after privatisation and corporatisation, generation in the southeastern states was dominated by a few integrated 'gentailers' with access to large coal and in some cases gas-based generators. The growth of renewable generation has increased contestability and actual competition. There is a strong case for the state vacating the generation field. In practice, recent movements have been in the opposite direction. The extended CIS underwriting of renewable generation means that, while the CIS continues, official decisions will shape investment in renewable energy.

The wholesale electricity energy-only market has worked effectively over the past three decades. An elaborate set of hedging instruments has developed for sharing risks of various kinds among market participants. The energy-only market experiences large price fluctuations. In recent years, it has generated negative prices in regions and at times when renewable energy is abundant. When demand is strong and renewable energy supply limited, high prices attract generation from high-cost gas-based peaking generation.

The variability of prices has sometimes been seen as a problem. It is a strength of the system. It has encouraged high levels of investment in storage. This will eventually place a floor under low prices and downward pressure on high prices. The existing energy market is well suited as the clearing house for increasingly complex interaction of many generators, batteries and other forms of storage with rapidly growing and to some extent flexible demand in the Superpower industries.

The Department of Climate Change, Energy, the Environment and Water has advised that market design after 2030 is under review. The first requirement for sound design is certainty from the earliest possible time. There is now great uncertainty about costs to power users and revenues from storage and generation after 2030. Genuinely private investment in the transition and the Superpower transformation awaits the conclusion of the official processes. Uncertainty has high costs. Better that we had settled these questions years ago. Australians will be poorer if the uncertainty continues much longer. It would be wise to announce soon that the government has considered post-2030 market design and confirms that the energy-only market will continue much as it is now. If that is not done and a review of longer duration is to be commissioned, there is a strong case for opening up public discussion through review by the Productivity Commission, alongside the study of electricity transmission and distribution. However it is done, it must be done quickly.

The second crucial element of post-2030 market design is introduction of a green premium for zero-carbon energy. It is obviously necessary for low-cost decarbonisation and expansion of the electricity sector and building the Superpower. The green premium is crucial for securing international market access for the zero-carbon export industries.

One of the Dog Days constraints on policy is that there should be no mandatory demands on private investors. Those constraints must be broken for the green premium to reflect the social cost of carbon, as it must if we are to achieve net zero by 2050 and build the Superpower. The economically efficient way of achieving the premium is carbon pricing. It would be most efficient within an economy-wide system, although it could be introduced initially for the electricity sector and extended to other industries later. Investors now need to know soon that there will be a premium reasonably related to the social cost of carbon after the RET ends in 2030.

What matters for the Superpower industries is the green premiums for which they are eligible in other countries. Pending the emergence of appropriate premiums, the Commonwealth is proposing payments from the budget. That is appropriate. It can get the early movers started. It would be expensive if it continued for long. The Superpower industries will grow rapidly if they have access to premiums corresponding to the social cost of carbon. Over time, payments from the Australian budget will be replaced by market premiums in destination countries.

There are several possible forms of carbon pricing. The system operating in Australia from 2012 to 2014 was economically and environmentally efficient. It would have been linked to the EU Emissions Trading System from 1 July 2014 if it had not been abolished the day before. The Australian carbon price would be equal to the European price – now about $110 per tonne. We would be introducing a European-type Carbon Border Adjustment Mechanism to ensure that Australian producers were not disadvantaged by competition in the domestic market from suppliers who were not subject to similar carbon constraints. The ETS would be contributing around 2 per cent of GDP to public revenues – going a substantial part of the way to answering the daunting budget challenge to restoration of Australian prosperity. As suggested in Chapter 12, part of that increased revenue could support payments to power users to ensure there was no increase in power prices to users until expansion of renewable generation and storage had brought costs down – along the lines but larger than the $300 per household introduced in the 2024 budget. The arrangements would provide automatic access for zero-carbon Australian goods to the high-priced European market. There would be no need to provide for a green premium for sales to Europe from the Australian market. The green premiums in other markets would at first need to be covered, as they are now, from the Australian public revenue.

Rod Sims and I suggested a carbon solutions levy (CSL) in Chapter 12. It is administratively simpler than the ETS. It would initially raise much more revenue. We propose exemption for coal and gas exports to countries in which Australian zero-carbon exports attract a premium comparable to the EU carbon price, even if it is not generated through an ETS. We would hope that if the CSL were to be introduced from 2030, our major trading partners would by that time have introduced green premiums that justify exemption from the CSL for coal and gas exports to those countries. The European Union would be exempt from the beginning. The Northeast Asian economies are moving towards eventual justification of exemption. China now has a country-wide emissions trading system. The carbon price in July 2024 is about A$21 per tonne, having increased by 50 per cent since early in the year. The price is expected to continue rising until it is playing a major role in transformation of Chinese industry. Incidentally, China undertook to the United Nations Framework Convention on Climate Change that its emissions would peak by 2030, but rapid expansion of renewable energy generation, electric vehicles and zero-carbon industrial technologies suggest that the peak may have come in 2023. Japan is working on direct budgetary support for importers of zero-carbon products which could pass through into a premium for zero-carbon exports from Australia. During a visit in April 2024, I was advised that the government is working towards issue of 'green bonds' to pay for the premium. A carbon tax from 2035 would meet the cost of servicing and retiring the bonds. Korea and Taiwan are introducing their own mechanisms for supporting premiums for zero-carbon imports.

One initial criticism of the CSL is that it would cause leakage of Australian exports to competing suppliers of gas and coal. There would be some leakage, alongside substantial transfers from rents to the public revenues, and for metallurgical coal in particular, some increase in export prices. The price increase would introduce an element of green premium for Australian green iron exports. The Superpower Institute has commissioned the Centre of Policy Studies at Victoria University to quantify the extent of leakage, transfers from rent and higher export prices. The results will be available for public discussion early in 2025. The study will also calculate the effect of the levy on Australian public finances, real incomes and real consumption.

Australia's main competitor in regional coal markets is Indonesia. Its main competitors in gas markets are Papua New Guinea, East Timor, Indonesia, Brunei and the Middle East petroleum producers. No informed person would suggest that there could be an economic problem with leakage to the Middle East: Saudi Arabia and the small Gulf states extract revenue from petroleum exports at much higher rates per dollar than Australia would after imposition of the levy. There is a case in the Australian national interest for not seeing expansion of export sales from Papua New Guinea and East Timor as being entirely a waste. But in their national interest and ours, I suggest that we seek to negotiate a four-way Agreement on Climate and Energy with Indonesia, East Timor and Papua New Guinea. We would all impose CSL-type levies at similar rates. This would be a major source of revenue for all of us. Participation of Indonesia removes leakage of coal exports. Indonesia already has an emissions trading scheme, although it generates a carbon price of only a few dollars per tonne. It may choose to remove other imposts on fossil carbon exports at the time of introduction of new carbon-related measures – such as the requirement to make 35 per cent of coal exports available at prices well below international prices for domestic power generation. Participation of the four countries removes the leakage issue for gas. The four neighbours would cooperate in major development programs based on expansion of zero-carbon energy supply and goods production. There is active discussion in Indonesia of archipelago-wide electricity transmission infrastructure, to allow the superior renewable energy resources of the outer islands – Papua, Nusa Tengarra, Sulawesi, Kalimantan, Sumatra – to contribute to decarbonisation and growth of zero-carbon industry everywhere including in the Java heartland. The Indonesian grid would run close to neighbouring Australia, Papua New Guinea, East Timor, East and West Malaysia and the Philippines. It would be the geopolitically practical means of linking Australia and Singapore, as envisaged in the SunCable project in the Northern Territory. The Indonesian national grid could link to the Australian Sungrid discussed in *The Superpower Transformation* in Darwin and the Pilbara.

The alternatives to economy-wide carbon pricing are likely to turn out to be short-lived expedients that lead sooner rather than later to the return of today's incoherence and underperformance.

The state must provide reliability of power supply to the general population. The Commonwealth government can do this without distorting competitive electricity markets by establishing the energy reserve proposed in Appendix 1.1 of *The Superpower Transformation*.

The Superpower industries depend on electricity and hydrogen markets operating efficiently and embodying carbon prices. Otherwise the market design issues relevant to their development are similar to those for electricity. Negative carbon externalities need to be corrected by taxation or alternative carbon pricing mechanisms. Positive externalities from innovation should be rewarded.

Positive innovation externalities are important in the introduction of new industries, technologies and business models for the zero-carbon economy. The general principles set out in the economic development stream of the Future Made in Australia National Interest Framework are well conceived.

Economy-wide carbon pricing at the social cost of carbon is essential to getting the balance right between state intervention and market exchange. Once it is in place with fiscal rewards for innovation, the government can let businesses decide which new industries and technologies warrant investment. Once the carbon pricing is known to be coming into place reasonably soon, there is no further need for government underwriting of investment in power generation. The CIS will have done its job.

There is no need to include a climate trigger in assessment of a project of any kind: if it emits carbon, it will pay for the climate damage it does. Other environmental tests continue to be applied in the usual way. There is no need to be concerned on climate grounds how much gas peaking enters the market. Carbon pricing ensures that the gas peaker plays on an economically level playing field with renewable generation and storage. There is no need for government to take a view on climate grounds about the merits of nuclear power generation. It is zero-emissions generation and, like renewable energy, not subject to the carbon price. If it can compete with other forms of generation, it will find a place in private investment decisions on the energy mix. There is no need for government investment in nuclear power generation. Private investors will have the same incentives to invest in nuclear as in other zero-carbon generation technologies.

Other environmental tests continue to be applied in the usual way. There will be no need for the government to take a view on incentives for carbon capture and storage (CCS). If it is effective and emissions are actually reduced, carbon payments will be correspondingly reduced. If CCS is said to be included in a project, and its operations are delayed or incomplete, the relief from carbon payments automatically adjusts.

Genuine sequestration of carbon in plants and soils would be allowed as a credit against carbon pricing obligations. We need comprehensive carbon accounting mechanisms and authoritative systems of measurement to support them. Credits would be confined to demonstrated increases in carbon stocks. Entrants to the system would need to accept reciprocal obligations to pay for objectively measured depletion of land carbon stocks.

The carbon price will allow private investors to get on with the job of expanding renewable energy supply at a rapid pace and decarbonising the economy more generally. If it is announced soon that it would operate from 2030, it would provide incentives for investment in renewables and storage sufficient to achieve the 2030 renewable generation target. It will support the opening of international markets to Superpower goods. It will strengthen the budget. And it will empower Australian and foreign businesses of many kinds to build the Superpower.

An old dog for a hard road

As I conclude this book, I am the age of Joe Biden when he became president of the United States. The laws of biology are as insistent as the laws of physics and economics. This fifth book in the quintet will be my last on the general challenges of Australian economic and climate policy since we entered the Dog Days a decade and a year ago.

I began my consuming work on climate and energy policy on Anzac Day 2007, when I met Anna Bligh and Kevin Rudd in Brisbane and agreed to undertake what became the Garnaut Climate Change Review. In the covering letter to the prime minister and premiers with the final report in September 2008, I invoked an old Australian bush saying: 'An old dog for a hard road.'

What turned out to be the first stage, and not the whole journey, had been a hard road. The second stage was much harder, when I prepared a second review for the Gillard government and the Multi-Party Climate Change Committee. Harder, but more directly productive. That second review led to legislation establishing the Australian Renewable Energy Agency, the Clean Energy Finance Corporation, the Climate Change Authority, the Carbon Farming Initiative and the carbon pricing system that operated successfully from 1 July 2012 to 30 June 2014. All but the last remain. Regrettably, the last is especially important for building the Superpower and restoring Australian prosperity.

I said at the end of that first hard stage on the road in 2008: 'Observation of daily debate and media discussion in Australia and elsewhere suggests that this issue might be too hard for rational policymaking. It is too complex. The special interests are too powerful, numerous and intense. The time frames within which effects become evident are too long, and the time frames within which action must be effected too short (Garnaut 2008).

And so it seemed, as the Abbott government moved away from effective climate action in 2013 and a new president of the United States elected in 2016, Donald Trump, asserted that the scientific atmospheric physics that was taught in all of the world's best universities and developed in all of the best scientific research organisations was a Chinese hoax concocted to give China an advantage in international trade.

But I also noted in the first review that 'there is a saving grace that might make all the difference. This is an issue in which a high proportion of Australians are deeply interested ... There is a much stronger base for reform and change on this than on any other big issue of structural change in recent decades, including trade, tax and public ownership reform' (Garnaut 2008).

That saving grace, and the relentless press of the effects of climate change have indeed made all the difference. The issue may be put aside by one government in one country for a while. But community pressure brings it back. Donald Trump, in his acceptance of the Republican Party's nomination for the 2024 presidential election, expressed strong views that are inconsistent with US participation in the global effort to contain the damage from climate change. He may soon be president of the United

States again. Governments of other countries, including our own, may go through periods of weak action on climate change, or no action at all.

But that will not be the end of the matter. No matter how disruptive the climate change that is already with us, higher greenhouse gas concentrations in the atmosphere will make things worse. It will still be worth pressing to reduce emissions in any way we can, including through changes in policy by future governments. There will be many Australians, and many people elsewhere – most of the people in the world who are informed and care about public policy in the public interest – who will want to do what they can to stop the worst. Here in Australia, it will become clearer over time that without large contributions from new zero-carbon export industries, it is unlikely that our country can lift itself out of the stagnation, insecurity and disappointment of the post-pandemic Dog Days.

Postponement of the achievement of zero net emissions will increase costs of climate change, perhaps to shockingly high levels. As I said in 2008, 'When human society receives a large shock to its established patterns of life, the outcome is unpredictable in detail but generally problematic. Things fall apart.'

Life has become hard for many Australians through the Dog Days, the increasing disruption from climate change, the pandemic recession and the falling real incomes in its aftermath. But things have not yet fallen apart in our country. We have made a start on a reset and on building the Superpower. The challenge now is to move further, faster and more decisively in a new parliament.

Appendix 14.1.

South Australia now has around three-quarters of its power coming from renewable resources – similar to Australia as a whole in 2030 if the 82 per cent renewables objective is achieved. The behaviour of wholesale prices in South Australia now is therefore a source of insights into price formation in the whole of Australia in the medium-term future.

In 2012, with the carbon price in operation for the second half of the year, the average price for wholesale power sold into the SA grid was similar whether it came from coal, gas, wind or solar (Figure 14.1).

By 2019, the last full year before the COVID disruption, there was no coal power generation in South Australia. Prices for gas power were around three times as high after adjusting for inflation in 2019 as in 2012. The huge increase reflected the increase in eastern Australian gas prices following the commencement of massive exports of gas from Gladstone in Queensland. Average wind and solar prices sold into the grid, were higher in 2019, but the increase was much less than for gas power.

In 2023, the first full year after the pandemic, the average price of gas power sold into the grid had increased a bit more. The average price of wind power was dramatically lower than in 2019. The average price of solar had fallen almost to zero. Wholesale prices paid by users were the average of extremely high prices from gas, low prices from wind and almost zero prices from solar.

Prices in the second and third quarters of 2024 were affected by unusually low availability of wind power – a winter 'wind drought' – as well as by Tasmanian hydroelectric production being low because of a rainfall drought. In the first half of 2024, average gas prices remained extremely high. Wind, in the 'drought', was receiving average prices between 2019 and 2023 levels. Solar prices were pulled up a bit by the wind prices, and by the extremely high prices for gas power at times when some gas generation was required during solar hours.

In the early part of the September quarter, gas power prices rose to astronomical levels, with scarcity and high prices for gas, and as the two local gas generators made profitable use of their oligopolistic positions at times when wind and solar power were not available in large quantities. The astronomical price of gas power lifted the price for wind and solar power at times when the wind was blowing and the sun shining but some gas was required in the system.

The general story is that the high average prices of wholesale power in recent times are the result of extraordinary increases in gas power prices. Increased supply of wind and solar have put downward pressure on average prices – but less when weather conditions have reduced their availability.

Figure 14.1

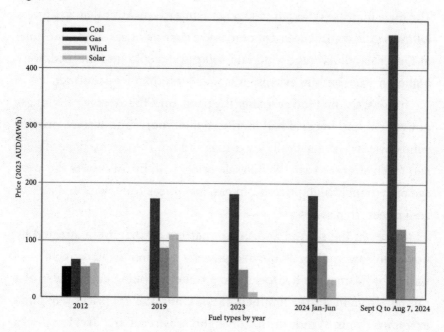

ACKNOWLEDGEMENTS

This book brings together twelve papers and public lectures presented during the first two years of the Albanese Labor government, with an overall assessment in the introductory and concluding chapters of what still needs to be done. It builds on work over many years at the University of Melbourne, where I am an emeritus professor in the Faculty of Business and Economics, and the Australian National University, where I am an emeritus professor in the Economics Department of the Crawford School. My thanks to Paul Kofman, Abigail Payne and Beth Webster at Melbourne and Ligang Song at the Australian National University for continuing institutional support.

This book is the fifth in a quintet over the past eleven years on the challenge of contemporary Australian economic policy and development in an era of adjustment to the realities of global climate change, and diminished respect for the public interest in Australia and other industrialised democracies. The main lines of analysis and narrative continue through the five books. I have acknowledged in earlier books the intellectual debts I owe to many scholars and practitioners of public policy. For this volume, I would like to thank especially David Vines at Oxford University, Yiping Huang and Justin Lin Yifu at Peking University, Peter Dawkins and Craig Emerson at Victoria University, Jeff Borland, Abigail Payne and Guay Lim at the University of Melbourne, and Ligang Song, Shiro Armstrong, Peter Drysdale, Hal Hill and the late Peter McCawley at the Australian National University.

Thanks to my hosts for the public lectures and speeches presented as chapters in this book: Prime Minister Anthony Albanese and Treasurer Jim Chalmers for the after-dinner speech at the Jobs and Skills Summit

(Chapter 2); the Gruen family and the Faculty of Economics at the ANU for the Gruen Lecture (Chapter 3); Frank Bongiorno and Manning Clark House for the Manning Clark Lecture (Chapter 4); Simon Corden, Nicholas Gruen, Paul Kofman, Phillip McCalman and the Department of Economics and Faculty of Commerce and Economics at the University of Melbourne for the Corden Lecture (Chapter 5); Peter Dawkins, Abigail Payne, Craig Emerson and the Melbourne Economic Forum and the *Australian Economic Review* for Chapter 7; Catherine Cashmore, Tim Helm and Prosper Australia (formerly the Henry George Society) for the Henry George Oration (Chapter 8); Gina Cass-Gottlieb, the Australian Competition and Consumer Commission and the Law Council of Australia for the Bannerman Lecture (Chapter 9); David Vines and the *Oxford Review of Economic Policy*, and also Yiping Huang and *China & World Economy*, which published an earlier article of mine on a similar topic in 2022, for Chapter 10; Shiro Armstrong, the Australia-Japan Research Centre and the Japan Research Institute for Chapter 11; Laura Tingle and the National Press Club for Chapter 12; and Bob Gregory and the Australian Economic Society for Chapter 13.

For this book, my debt is greatest to my colleagues at The Superpower Institute, especially Alison Hill, Baethan Mullen, Rod Sims, Ingrid Burfurd, Reuben Finighan, and Susannah Powell. The Superpower Institute now has momentum in its presumptuous task of integrating understanding of the contribution that the new zero-carbon industries can make to full employment and rising incomes for an expanding Australian population into the national economic policy discussion. I look forward to working with others at The Superpower Institute to deepen understanding of this extraordinary Australian opportunity in the years ahead.

I am again greatly indebted to Chris Feik and Kirstie Innes-Will at Black Inc. for excellent editorial work, on structure and presentation. The high professional quality of the support has been very important to this, as to earlier books in the quintet. As always, it has been a pleasure to work with Black Inc. and Chris and Kirstie. The collaboration between Black Inc. and La Trobe University Press has been productive and valuable.

Ross Garnaut
Melbourne
7 August 2024

REFERENCES

Anderson, Kym, and Ross Garnaut, 1986, *Australian Protectionism: Extent, Causes and Effects*, Sydney: Allen & Unwin.

Arndt, H.W., and W.M. Corden (eds), 1963, *The Australian Economy: A Volume of Readings*, Sydney: F.W. Cheshire.

Australian Bureau of Statistics (ABS), 2022a, 'Consumer Price Index (CPI) March 2022', *Wage Price Index Australia*, Canberra.

——, 2022b, 'Household Income and Wealth Australia: Key Information from the *Survey of Income and Housing 2019–20* Including Distribution of Income and Wealth by Various Household Characteristics', Australian Bureau of Statistics, 28 April, www.abs.gov.au/statistics/economy/finance/household-income-and-wealth-australia/latest-release.

——, 2023a, 'Consumer Price Index (CPI) March 2023', Canberra.

——, 2023b, 'Wage Price Index (WPI) March 2023', Canberra.

Australian Energy Market Operator, 2024, *Quarterly Energy Dynamics, Q2 2024*, AEMO, July 2024.

Australian Government, 1945, *Full Employment in Australia (The White Paper on Employment)*, Canberra: Government of Australia.

——, 1965, *Report of the Committee of Economic Enquiry*, Canberra: Government of Australia.

——, 1981, *Australian Financial System – Final Report of the Committee of Inquiry*, The Treasury, 1 September.

——, 2022, Pre-election Economic and Fiscal Outlook, The Treasury and Department of Finance, 20 April.

——, 2023a, *Intergenerational Report 2023: Australia's Future to 2063*, Canberra: Government of Australia.

——, 2023b, *Working Future: The Australian Government's White Paper on Jobs and Opportunities*, Canberra: Government of Australia.

Bean, Martin, and Peter Dawkins, 2021, *University–Industry Collaboration in Teaching and Learning*, Canberra: Australian Government, Department of Education, Skills and Employment.

Bhagwati, Jagdish, 1964, 'The Pure Theory of International Trade: A Survey', *The Economic Journal* 74(293): 1–84.

Bishop, James, and Emma Greenland, 2021, 'Is the Phillips Curve Still a Curve? Evidence from the Regions', Research discussion paper (no. 2021-09), Reserve Bank of Australia.

Blanchard, Olivier, 2023, *Fiscal Policy Under Low Interest Rates*, Cambridge, Massachusetts: MIT Press.

Blanchard, Olivier and Bernanke, Ben, 2023, 'What Caused the US Pandemic-Era Inflation?', Conference paper, The Fed: Lessons Learned from the Past Three Years, Brookings Institution, Washington DC, 23 May 2023.

Borland, Jeff, 2002, 'Comment on "The Five Economists" Plan: The Original Ideas and Further Development', *Australian Journal of Labour Economics* 5(2): 239–42.

——, 2021, 'Labour Market Snapshot #77: Another Reason Why Australia's Target Rate of Unemployment Should Be Low', Jeff Borland @ University of Melbourne, Blog, 16 March 2021, https://drive.google.com/file/d/1dQiYjKuhjNYKqNC08Kjn9MUzA Ct8e4Vr/view.

——, 2023, 'With Unemployment Steady at 3.5%, Inflation Fears Shouldn't Stop Australia Embracing a Full Employment Target', *The Conversation*, 13 April 2023.

Borland, Jeff, and Steven Kennedy, 1998, 'Dimensions, Structure and History of Australian Unemployment', in *Unemployment and the Australian Labour Market: Proceedings of the Economic Group, Reserve Bank of Australia and Centre for Economic Policy Research Conference*, Canberra: Australian National University.

Bristol, Nellie, 2023, 'Smallpox Eradication: A Model for Global Cooperation', Centre for Strategic and International Studies, Blog, 17 May 2023, www.csis.org/analysis/ smallpox-eradication-model-global-cooperation.

Bullock, Michele, 2023, 'Achieving Full Employment', Speech, AI Group, Reserve Bank of Australia, Newcastle, 20 June.

Burfurd, I., 2024, 'Can Australia be a Renewable Energy Superpower?' *Australian Economic Review*. Forthcoming.

Card, David, and Alan B. Krueger, 1994, 'Minimum Wages and Employment: A Case Study of the Fast-Food Industry in New Jersey and Pennsylvania', *American Economic Review* 84(4): 772–93.

Centre for Policy Development, 2021, *Starting Better: A Guarantee for Young Children and Families*, East Melbourne: Centre for Policy Development.

Coates, Brendan, and Carmela Chivers, 2019, 'Rising Inequality in Australia Isn't About Incomes; It's Almost All About Housing', *The Conversation*, 19 September.

Coleman, William, Selwyn Cornish, and Alf Hagger, 2011, *Giblin's Platoon: The Trials and Triumph of the Economist in Australian Public Life*, Canberra: ANU Press.

Chen, Yuyu, Avraham Ebenstein, Michael Greenstone and Hongbin Li, 2013, 'Evidence on the Impact of Sustained Exposure to Air Pollution on Life Expectancy from China's Huai River Policy', *Proceedings of the National Academy of Sciences* 110(32): 12936–41.

Committee of Inquiry into the Australian Financial System, 1981, *Australian Financial System: Final Report of the Committee of Inquiry*, Canberra: AGPS.

Commonwealth of Australia, 1954, 'The Australian Post-War Economy: A Study in Economic Administration', *The Canadian Journal of Economics and Political Science* 20(4): 421–38.

——, 1965, *Report of the Committee of Economic Enquiry (The Vernon Report)*, Canberra: AGPS.

Copland, Douglas, 1934, *Australia in the World Crisis, 1929–1933*, Cambridge: Cambridge University Press.

Corden, Werner Max, 1967, 'Australian Tariff Policy', *Australian Economic Papers* 6(9): 131–34.

——, 1968a, 'Australian Economic Policy Discussion in the Post-War Period: A Survey', *The American Economic Review* 58 (3, Part 2, Supplement): 88–138.

——, 1968b, *Australian Economic Policy Discussion: A Survey*, Melbourne: Melbourne University Press.

——, 1971, *The Theory of Protection*, Oxford: Oxford University Press.

——, 1974, *Trade Policy and Economic Welfare*, Oxford: Oxford University Press.

——, 1977, *Inflation, Exchange Rates and the World Economy*, Chicago: University of Chicago Press.

——, 2018, *Lucky Boy in the Lucky Country: The Autobiography of Max Corden, Economist*, London: Palgrave Macmillan.

Corden, Max, and Ross Garnaut, 2018, 'The Economic Consequences of Mr Trump', *The Australian Economic Review* 51(3): 411–17.

Corden, W. Max, and J. Peter Neary, 1982, 'Booming Sector and De-industrialisation in a Small Open Economy', *The Economic Journal* 92(368): 825–48.

Cornish, Selwyn, 2002, *Sir Roland Wilson: A Biographical Essay*, Canberra: ANU Press.

Crawford, J.G. (ed., assisted by Greg Seow), 1981, *Pacific Economic Co-operation: Suggestions for Action*, Singapore: Heinemann Asia.

Crawford, J.G., B.S. Inglis, R.J.L. Hawke and N.S. Currie, 1979, *Study Group on Structural Adjustment*, Canberra: AGPS.

Creedy, John, Alan S. Duncan, Mark Harris and Rosanna Scutella, 2002, *Microsimulation Modelling of Taxation and the Labour Market: The Melbourne Institute Tax and Transfer Simulator*, Cheltenham: Edward Elgar Publishing Limited.

Dawkins, Peter, 2002, 'The "Five Economists" Plan: The Original Idea and Further Developments', *Australian Journal of Labour Economics* 5(2): 203–30.

Dawkins, Peter, and Ross Garnaut, 2021, 'Let's Plan for Full Employment', *Australian Financial Review*, 8 December.

Dawkins, Peter, David Johnson, Rosanna Scutella, Gillian Beer and Ann Harding, 1998, 'Towards a Negative Income Tax System for Australia', *Australian Economic Review* 88(1): 83–95.

Dawkins, Peter, Alan Duncan and John Freebairn, 2003, 'Modifying Income Support in the Australian Tax and Transfer System', Paper presented to the Melbourne Institute and *The Australian* joint conference, 'Pursuing Opportunity and Prosperity Conference', Melbourne, 11–12 November.

Dawkins, Peter, John Freebairn, Ross Garnaut, Michael Keating and Chris Richardson, 1998, Letter to the Prime Minister, 28 October. Reprinted in Peter Dawkins, 'A Plan to Cut Unemployment in Australia: An Elaboration on the "Five Economists" Letter to the Prime Minister, 28th October 1998', *Mercer-Melbourne Institute Quarterly Bulletin of Economic Trends* 1(99): 57–9.

Dawkins, Peter, Peter Hurley and Peter Noonan, 2019, *Rethinking and Revitalising Tertiary Education in Australia*, Melbourne: Mitchell Institute.

De Brouwer, Gordon, Renée Fry-McKibbin and Carolyn Wilkins, 2023, *An RBA Fit for the Future*, Canberra: Commonwealth of Australia.

De Loecker, Jan, and Jan Eeckhout, 2018, 'Global Market Power', Working paper (no. 24768), National Bureau of Economic Research.

De Loecker, Jan, Jan Eeckhout and Gabriel Unger, 2020, 'The Rise of Market Power and the Macroeconomic Implications', *The Quarterly Journal of Economics* 135(2): 561–644.

De Long, J. Bradford, 2022, *Slouching Towards Utopia: An Economic History of the Twentieth Century*, London: Basic Books.

Dixon, Janine and Helen Hodgson, 2020, 'Modelling Finds Investing in Childcare and Aged Care Almost Pays for Itself', *The Conversation*, 19 October.

Dixon, Peter B., and Maureen T. Rimmer, 2001, 'A Wage-Tax Policy to Increase Employment', *Australian Economic Review* 34(1): 64–80.

Dornbusch, Rudiger, 1976, 'Expectations and Exchange Rate Dynamics', *The Journal of Political Economy* 84(6): 1161–76.

Drysdale, Peter, 1969, 'Japan, Australia and New Zealand: The Prospects for Western Pacific Integration', *Economic Record* 45(111): 321–42.

——, 1978, 'An Organisation for Pacific Trade, Aid and Development: Regional Arrangements and the Resource Trade', in Lawrence B. Krause and Hugh Patrick (eds), *Mineral Resources in the Pacific Area*, San Francisco: Federal Reserve Bank of San Francisco.

Duggan, S. 2024. Keynote speech, Australian Clean Energy Summit 2024, Department of Climate Change, Energy, the Environment and Water.

Ellis, Luci, 2019, 'Watching the Invisibles', 2019 Freebairn Lecture in Public Policy, University of Melbourne, Reserve Bank of Australia, 12 June, www.rba.gov.au/speeches/2019/pdf/sp-ag-2019-06-12-2.html.

Finighan, Reuben, 2023, 'Stabilising Liberal Societies in a World of Radical Innovation: Committed Actors, Adaptive Rules, and the Origins of Social Order', PhD thesis, London School of Economics.

——, 2024, 'The New Energy Trade: Harnessing Australian Renewables for Global Development', The Superpower Institute, Melbourne. Available at superpowerinstitute.com.au/#work.

Fleming, J. Marcus, 1962, 'Domestic Financial Policies Under Fixed and Floating Exchange Rates', *IMF Staff Papers* 9(3): 369–79.

Frydenburg, Josh, 2024. Personal communication, 3 July.

Garnaut, Ross (ed.), 1980, *ASEAN in a Changing Pacific and World Economy*, Canberra: Australian National University Press.

——, 1989, *Australia and the Northeast Asian Ascendency*, Canberra: AGPS.

——, 1994, 'Australia', in J. Williamson (ed.), *The Political Economy of Economic Reform*, Washington DC: Institute of International Economics.

——, 2001, *Social Democracy in Australia's Asian Future*, Canberra: Asia Pacific Press.

——, 2002, 'Investing in Full Employment', in Ross Garnaut, *Social Democracy in Australia's Asian Future*, Canberra and Singapore: Asia Pacific Press and Institute of Southeast Asian Studies, 183–236.

REFERENCES

——, 2008, *The Garnaut Climate Change Review*, Melbourne: Cambridge University Press.

——, 2011, *The Garnaut Review 2011: Australia in the Global Response to Climate Change*, Melbourne: Cambridge University Press.

——, 2013a, *Dog Days: Australia After the Boom*, Collingwood: Black Inc.

——, 2013b, 'Macro-Economic Implications of the Turning Point', in Yiping Huang and Fang Cai (eds), *Debating the Lewis Turning Point in China*, London: Routledge.

——, 2013c, 'Removing Climate Change as a Barrier to Economic Progress: Twenty-Second Colin Clark Memorial Lecture November 2012', *Economic Analysis and Policy* 43(1): 31–47.

——, 2018, '40 Years of Economic Reform and Development and the Challenge of 50', in Ross Garnaut and L. Song (eds), *China's 40 Years of Reform and Development: 1978–2018*, Canberra: Australian National University Press.

——, 2019, *Superpower: Australia's Low-Carbon Opportunity*, Carlton: La Trobe University Press.

——, 2021, *Reset: Restoring Australia After the Pandemic Recession*, Carlton: La Trobe University Press.

—— (ed.), 2022a, *The Superpower Transformation: Making Australia's Zero-Carbon Future*, Carlton: La Trobe University Press.

——, 2022b, Speech, Jobs and Skills Summit, Parliament House, Canberra, 1 September, https://cpb-ap-se2.wpmucdn.com/blogs.unimelb.edu.au/dist/a/142/files/2022/09/SUMMIT-SPEECH-1-SEPTEMBER-2022.pdf.

——, 2023, 'The Economic Consequences of Mr Trump and Mr Biden', *The Australian Economic Review* 56(4): 417–30.

—— and David Vines, forthcoming, 'The Economic-Policy Orchestra', *Economic Record*.

Garnaut, Ross, and Anthony Clunies-Ross, 1975, 'Risk, Uncertainty and the Taxation of Natural Resource Projects', *The Economic Journal* 85(2): 272–87.

——, 1983, *Taxation of Mineral Rents*, Oxford: Clarendon Press.

Garnaut, Ross, with David Llewellyn-Smith, 2009, *The Great Crash of 2008*, Carlton: Melbourne University Press.

Garnaut, Ross, and David Vines, 2023, 'Monetary Policy Mistakes and Remedies: An Assessment Following the RBA Review', *Australian Economic Review* 56 (3): 273–87.

Garnaut, Ross, and Yiping Huang, 2006, 'Continued Rapid Growth and the Turning Point in China's Development', in Ross Garnaut and Ligang Song (eds), *The Turning Point in China's Economic Development*, Canberra: Asia Pacific Press.

Garnaut, Ross, Craig Emerson, Reuben Finighan and Stephen Anthony, 2020, 'Replacing Corporate Income Tax with a Cash Flow Tax', *The Australian Economic Review* 53(4): 463–81.

Giblin, L.F., 1930, *Australia, 1930: An Inaugural Lecture*, Melbourne: Melbourne University Press.

Goldin, Ian, Pantelis Koutroumpis, François Lafond and Julian Winkler, 2022, 'Why Is Productivity Slowing Down?', Working paper (no. 2022-8), the Oxford Martin Working Paper Series on Technological and Economic Change.

Gregory, R.G., 1976, 'Some Implications of the Growth in the Mineral Sector', *Australian Journal of Agricultural and Resource Economics* 20(2): 71–91.

Gross, Isaac, and Andrew Leigh, 2022, 'Assessing Monetary Policy in the Twenty-First Century', *Economic Record* 98(322): 291–95.

Gruen, David, Adrian Pagan and Christopher Thompson, 1999, 'The Phillips Curve in Australia', Research discussion paper (no. 1999-01_, Reserve Bank of Australia.

Guzman, Martin, and Joseph E. Stiglitz, 2024, 'Post-Neoliberal Globalization: International Trade Rules for Global Prosperity', *Oxford Review of Economic Policy* 40(2): 282–306.

Hamilton, Steven, 2022, 'Let's Talk About Bold Tax Reform Truly Worthy of a New Accord', *Australian Financial Review*, 18 August.

Hawke, Robert J.L., 1991, Industry Policy Statement to the Parliament of Australia, 12 March, Canberra.

Heckscher, E., 1919, 'The Effect of Foreign Trade on the Distribution of Income', *Economisk Tidskrift* 21(4): 497–512.

Henry, Ken, 2010, *Australia's Future Tax System: Report to the Treasurer*, Canberra: Commonwealth of Australia.

Higgins, Timothy, and Bruce Chapman, 2015, *Feasibility and Design of a Tertiary Education Entitlement in Australia: Modelling and Costing a Universal Income Contingent Loan*, Melbourne: Mitchell Institute.

Holden, Richard, 2022, 'Boosting Productivity Means Everything for Wages', *Australian Financial Review*, 16 May.

Hotez, Peter J., 2014, '"Vaccine Diplomacy": Historical Perspectives and Future Direction', *PLOS Neglected Tropical Diseases* 8(6): 1–7.

Hurley, Peter, and Sarah Pilcher, 2020, *Skills for Recovery: The Vocational Education System We Need Post-Covid-19*, Melbourne: Mitchell Institute.

Hutchens, Gareth, 2023, 'Paul Keating Warns Treasurer Not to Remove Government's Power to Override RBA Decisions', *ABC News*, 28 April.

IMF, 2022, 'Wage Dynamics Post-COVID-19 and Wage-Price Spiral Risks', in *World Economic Outlook: Countering the Cost-of-Living Crisis*, Washington DC: International Monetary Fund.

IMF, 2023, 'The Natural Rate of Interest: Drivers and Implications for Policy', in *World Economic Outlook: A Rocky Recovery*, Washington DC: International Monetary Fund.

Ingles, D., and M. Stewart, 2018, 'Australia's Company Tax: Options for Fiscally Sustainable Reform, Updated Post Trump', Working paper (no. 31208), Tax and Transfer Policy Institute, ANU Crawford School of Public Policy.

Irwin, Douglas A., 2017, *Clashing Over Commerce: A History of US Trade Policy*, Chicago: University of Chicago Press.

Jones, Evan, 2015, 'Australian Trade Liberalisation Policy: The Industries Assistance Commission and the Productivity Commission', *The Economic and Labour Relations Review* 27(2): 181–98.

Kahn, R.F., 1931, 'The Relation of Home Investment to Unemployment', *The Economic Journal* 41(162): 173–98.

Kasper, Wolfgang (ed.), 1980, *Australia at the Crossroads: Our Choices to the Year 2000*, Sydney: Harcourt Brace Jovanovich.

Keating, Michael, 2022, 'Many Jobs Summit Ideas for Wages Don't Make Sense – Upskilling Does', *The Conversation*, 25 August.

Keating, Michael, and Simon Lambert, 1998, 'Improving Incentives: Changing the Interface of Tax and Social Security', *Australian Economic Review* 31(3): 281–89.

Keynes, John Maynard, (1925) 1931, 'The Economic Consequences of Mr Churchill', *Essays in Persuasion*, New York: Harcourt Brace.

——, 1930a, *A Treatise on Money*, London: Macmillan.

——, 1930b (1932), 'Economic Possibilities for Our Grandchildren', in John Maynard Keynes, *Essays in Persuasion*, New York: Harcourt Brace.

——, 1932, 'Report of the Australian Experts', *Herald* (Melbourne), 27 June.

——, 1936, *The General Theory of Employment, Interest and Money*, London: Macmillan.

Lewis, W.A., 1954, 'Economic Development with Unlimited Supplies of Labour', *The Manchester School* 22(2): 139–91.

Lin, Justin Yifu, and Yan Wang, 2017, *Going Beyond Aid: Development Cooperation for Structural Transformation*, Cambridge: Cambridge University Press.

Lowe, Philip, 2021, 'The Labour Market and Monetary Policy', speech, Economic Society of Australia, Brisbane, 8 July.

——, 2023, 'Some Closing Remarks', speech, Anika Foundation, Sydney, 7 September.

Macintyre, Stuart, 2015, *Australia's Boldest Experiment: War and Reconstruction in the 1940s*, Sydney: NewSouth Publishing.

Martin, Peter, 2022, 'Why Unemployment Is Set to Stay Below 5% for Years to Come', *The Conversation*, 16 August.

McLean, Ian W., 2013, *Why Australia Prospered: The Shifting Sources of Economic Growth*, Princeton: Princeton University Press.

Meade, J.E., 1951, *The Balance of Payments*, Oxford: Oxford University Press.

Meinshausen, Malte, Zebedee Nicholls, Rebecca Burdon and Jared Lewis, 2022, 'The Diminishing Carbon Budget and Australia's Contribution to Limit Climate Change', in Ross Garnaut (ed.), *The Superpower Transformation: Making Australia's Zero-Carbon Future*, Collingwood: La Trobe University Press.

Michl, Thomas R., and Robert Rowthorn, 2023, 'Optimal Inflation Targeting with Anchoring', Working paper, PERI Political Economy Research Unit.

Mill, James, (1836) 1966, 'Whether Political Economy Is Useful', in Donald Winch (ed.), *Selected Economic Writings*, Edinburgh and London: Oliver and Boyd.

Millmow, Alex, 2005, 'Australian Economics in the Twentieth Century', *Cambridge Journal of Economics* 29(6): 1011–26.

Mumford, Karen A., Antonia Parera-Nicolau and Yolanda Pena-Boquette, 2020, 'Labour Supply and Childcare: Allowing Both Parents to Choose', *Oxford Bulletin of Economics and Statistics* 82(3): 577–602.

Mundell, Robert, 1962, 'The Appropriate Use of Monetary and Fiscal Policy Under Fixed Exchange Rates', *IMF Staff Papers* 9(1): 70–79.

REFERENCES

Murphy, Chris, 2018, 'Modelling Australian Corporate Tax Reforms: Updated for the Recent US Corporate Tax Changes', Working paper (no. 2/2018), Tax and Transfer Policy Institute, ANU Crawford School of Public Policy.

Neumark, David, and William Wascher, 2000, 'Minimum Wages and Employment: A Case Study of the Fast-Food Industry in New Jersey and Pennsylvania: Comment, *American Economic Review* 90(5): 1362–96.

Noonan, Peter, and Sarah Pilcher, 2015, 'Financing Tertiary Education in Australia: The Reform Imperative and Rethinking Student Entitlements', Issues paper, Melbourne: Mitchell Institute.

Noonan, P., A. Blagaich, S. Kift, L. Loble, E. More and M. Pearson, 2019, *Review of the Australian Qualifications Framework: Final Report*, Canberra: Department of Education.

OECD, 2024, *Employment Outlook 2024: The Net-Zero Transition and the Labour Market*, OECD, Paris.

Obstfeld, Maurice, 2024, 'Economic Multilateralism 80 Years after Bretton Woods', Working paper, Peterson Institute for International Economics.

Ohlin, Bertil, 1933, *Interregional and International Trade*, Cambridge: Harvard University Press.

Parkinson, Martin, 2023, *A Migration System for Australia's Future*, Department of Home Affairs, Canberra.

Piketty, Thomas, 2013, *Capital in the Twenty-First Century*, translated by Arthur Goldhammer, Cambridge, Mass.: Harvard University Press.

Productivity Commission, 2018, *Rising Inequality: A Stocktake of the Evidence*, Productivity Commission Research Paper, Canberra: Commonwealth of Australia.

Rattigan, Alf, 1986, *Industry Assistance: The Inside Story*, Carlton: Melbourne University Press.

Ricardo, David, (1817) 1962, *The Principles of Political Economy and Taxation*, London: Dent.

Richardson, Chris, 1999, 'Reducing Unemployment', in *Rebuilding the Safety Net: Proceedings of a Conference, Thursday 29 April 1999, Hotel Sofitel, Melbourne*, Melbourne: Business Council of Australia.

Robertson, D.H., 1936, 'The Future of International Trade,' *The Economic Journal* 46(182): 1–14.

Sandiford, Mike, 2022, 'The Net-Zero Opportunity for Australian Minerals', in Ross Garnaut (ed.), *The Superpower Transformation: Making Australia's Zero-Carbon Future*, Collingwood: La Trobe University Press.

Schmitt, Carl, 1922 (1988), *The Crisis of Parliamentary Democracy*, Translated by Ellen Kennedy, Cambridge, Mass.: MIT Press.

Scutella, Rosanna, 2004, 'Moves to a Basic Income-Flat Tax System in Australia: Implications for the Distribution of Income and Supply of Labour', Working paper (no. 5/04), Melbourne Institute of Applied Economic and Social Research, University of Melbourne, April 2004.

Snape, Richard H., 1977, 'Effects of Mineral Development on the Economy', *Australian Journal of Agricultural and Resource Economics* 21(3): 147–56.

Solow, Robert, 2017, private letter, 17 September, cited with permission from Max Corden.

Song, Ligang, 2022, 'Decarbonising China's Steel Industry', in Ross Garnaut (ed.), *The Superpower Transformation: Making Australia's Zero-Carbon Future*, Collingwood: La Trobe University Press.

Stern, Nicholas, 2007, *The Economics of Climate Change: The Stern Review*, Cambridge: Cambridge University Press.

Stewart, Miranda, 2018, 'Personal Income Tax Cuts and the New Child Care Subsidy: Do They Address High Effective Marginal Tax Rates on Women's Work?', Policy brief, Tax and Transfer Policy Institute, Australian National University.

Stewart, Miranda, and David Plunkett, 2022, 'Childcare Cameos: Effective Marginal Tax Rates, May 2022', Miranda Stewart, Blog, 18 August 2022, https://profmirandastewart.com/wp-content/uploads/2022/08/childcareemtrcameochartsmay2022.pdf.

Stolper, Wolfgang F., and Paul A. Samuelson, 1941, 'Protection and Real Wages', *Review of Economic Studies* 9(1): 58–73.

Sullivan, Jake, 2023, 'Remarks on Renewing American Economic Leadership', Speech, Brookings Institution, Washington DC, 27 April.

Summers, L. 2020, 'Accepting the Reality of Secular Stagnation', *Finance & Development* 57(1): 17–19.

Susskind, Daniel, and David Vines, 2024, 'Global Economic Order and Global Economic Governance', *Oxford Review of Economic Policy* 40(2): 189–219.

Swan, Peter L., 2022–23, *Trevor Winchester Swan*, 2 vols, Cham: Palgrave Macmillan.

Swan, Trevor W., 1956, 'Economic Growth and Capital Accumulation', *Economic Record* 32(2): 334–61.

——, 1960, 'Economic Control in a Dependent Economy', *Economic Record* 36 (73): 51–66.

——, (1955) 1963, 'Longer Run Problems of the Balance of Payments', in H.W. Arndt and W.M. Corden (eds), *The Australian Economy*, Sydney: Cheshire.

Vines, David, n.d., 'Escape from Empire: How Australia Learned to Thrive in a Volatile World Economy', unpublished manuscript, last modified 2024.

Whelan, Karl, 1997, 'Wage Curve vs Phillips Curve: Are There Macroeconomic Implications?', Working paper, Division of Research and Statistics, US Federal Reserve.

Wilkins, Roger, 2017, 'Income Inequality Exists in Australia, but the True Picture May Not Be as Bad as You Thought', *The Conversation*, 20 June.

Wolf, Martin, *Financial Times*, details to come

Wood, Danielle, Owain Emslie and Kate Griffiths, 2021, *Dad Days: How More Gender-Equal Parental Leave Would Improve the Lives of Australian Families*, Carlton: Grattan Institute.

Wood, Danielle, Kate Griffiths and Owain Emslie, 2020, *Cheaper Childcare: A Practical Plan to Boost Female Workforce Participation*, Carlton: Grattan Institute.

ENDNOTES

7 Monetary Policy for Full Employment with Low Inflation

1 See www.rba.gov.au/chart-pack/aus-inflation. html.

2 See www.rba.gov.au/chart-pack/factors-prod-labour-mkt.html.

3 Luci Ellis was at the time the RBA's Assistant Governor, Economic, responsible for the bank's economic analysis and economic research departments, the chief economic adviser to the governor and the board.

4 That is to say, on how much an increase in unemployment will actually cause wage demands to be reduced.

5 It is of course possible that the increases in the regulation of wages currently being contemplated, and a lifting of the JobSeeker allowance, will raise NAIRU.

6 There is a large literature on this question in labour economics, known as the wage-curve versus the wage-Phillips-curve discussion, which was largely triggered by the UK–US economist Danny Blanchflower. Blanchflower and Oswald (1995) argue that workers will attempt to restore their real wage, in the manner which we describe in our text. In an alternative approach, it is assumed that workers only attempt *temporarily* to defend themselves from a fall in their real wage and that the level of the real wage can be successfully pushed down by a sufficiently lengthy period of unemployment. The evidence for the United States is muddy, but closer to the wage-Phillips-curve case. By contrast for Australia we think that the situation is likely to be closer to that captured by the wage-curve version of the story. How the two cases might be distinguished in econometric work was clearly explained in 1997 in a paper by Thomas Whelan (1997).

7 See IMF (2023).

13 The Economic Policy Orchestra

1 A large number of policies affect productivity growth, the distribution of income and the level of investment and therefore future real wages and standards of living. These include the microeconomic detail of fiscal policy (taxation structures and rates and the composition of public expenditure); trade policy; defence and security policy; competition policy; labour-market policy (including immigration, education and training, housing, wages regulation, and social security policy affecting labour supply); industry policy; climate and energy policy; and other policies affecting productivity, including the part played by the Productivity Commission.

2 Until Keynes wrote his *General Theory* there was nothing called 'macroeconomics'. There was just 'economics' as a whole. The distinction which we make between

macroeconomic policy and other economic policies is to an extent arbitrary, but often helpful.

3   This was true for all the advanced countries only until 1971, when the Bretton Woods system collapsed, but remained the case for Australia until the exchange rate was floated in 1983.

4   Sir John Melville, who was one of the Australian economists advising the Australian government at the time, told Ross Garnaut in 1991 that Keynes' article had been decisive. As prime minister and as treasurer, Joseph Lyons had expressed support for the economist's advice in another devaluation before the publication of the article. After its publication, he offered another devaluation.

5   See the account of Trevor Swan's life and work by his son, Peter (Swan 2022–23).

6   Swan put the *instruments* of policy on the axes. Here there is an important contrast with the IS-LM system which is used to present Keynesian economics in nearly all economics courses. In that diagram the *outcomes* – income and the interest rate – are depicted on the axes and are solved for by finding out where the curves cross. Changes in the policy instruments shift the curves – changes in the money supply shift the LM curve and changes in fiscal policy shift the IS curve. In the Swan diagram each of the curves depicts where one of the desired outcomes can be achieved, and where the two curves cross must be the point at which both are achieved. The outcomes on the axes show what values the instruments – fiscal policy and the real exchange rate – must take to bring about that outcome.

7   Nobody else, anywhere in the postwar world, had really understood this properly, even though Keynesian ideas were catching on everywhere at the time. Nobody except perhaps James Meade. It is true that Swan's analysis has much in common with that presented by Meade in his book *The Balance of Payments* (1951), for which Meade won the Nobel Prize. But Meade's book is 300 pages long and has an eighty-page mathematical appendix, and some important ideas are very nearly impenetrable. At the very least, Swan gave Meade to the world. Swan acknowledges his debt to Meade in a handwritten note scribbled at the end of his own copy of the first of his two papers, which can be seen in the National Library in Canberra.

8   This was also true of a slightly later description by Max Corden of postwar Australian economic policy discussions (Corden 1968a, 1968b) and of a much later paper by Alex Millmow (1985).

9   We do not have a text of his talk and depend on notes taken by Heinz Arndt which are in the Swan papers at the National Library of Australia. These notes are included in Peter Swan's edition of his father's papers.

10   The Tariff Board became the Industries Assistance Commission (IAC) in 1974. This change marked a significant shift in Australia's approach to industry policy and assistance, moving towards a more systematic and analytical method of evaluating the effects of tariffs and other forms of assistance. See Rattigan 1986 and Jones 2015.

11   See Chapter 7 for postwar discussion of full employment. The recent Australian White Paper (Australian Government 2023) defines full employment as all Australians being able to secure employment in a secure and reasonably

remunerated job without too much search – and recognises appropriately the amenability of the NAIRU to changing economic conditions.

12 The RBA's economic modelling over at least the past decade has consistently and by large amounts overestimated the rate of increase in wages associated with any given level of unemployment. See Graph 3 in Lowe (2021). Commitment to the output of the models has persisted despite the repeated evidence that they are generating outcomes at odds with reality. See our companion paper (Garnaut and Vines 2023 and Chapter 7, this volume).

13 See Garnaut and Vines (2023 and Chapter 7, this volume).

14 The appreciation of the exchange rate also reduces the price of imported goods and so the consumer price index. This complements the effects of the monetary tightening on inflation within the domestic economy.

15 Of course if exchange rate expectations become extrapolative this can give rise to much bigger exchange rate movements, which may cause the regime to break down. This has not happened in Australia.

16 Guzman and Stiglitz ask us to consider a new potential market for which entry is costly and where future profits are uncertain and depend on information (such as demand for the product) that cannot be known until the market is operative. As they say, no firm has the incentives to be the first that pays the fixed costs of entry. Every firm prefers to free-ride on other firms, and then to benefit from the information they generate, without paying the cost of acquiring this information. This behaviour results in an outcome in which a market that has social value is simply not created. To solve this problem, the state could subsidise or be – through a public company – the first entrant.

17 For a discussion of this question some time ago see Garnaut and Clunies-Ross (1975, 1983).

18 For earlier discussions of this question see Gregory (1976), Snape (1977) and Cordon and Neary (1982).

14 Looking Forward

1 The following seven elements would add up to a solution to winter shortages of renewable electricity in future when Australian electricity generation has been greatly expanded to supply large Superpower industries:

1. Draw power from the large conventional hydroelectric systems in Tasmania and the Snowy Mountains disproportionately in the winter months.

2. Run desalination systems now supporting water supply in all mainland state capitals mainly in summer when solar power is abundant and cheap.

3. Shift shutdowns for employee holidays and maintenance in energy-intensive industries from mainly in summer to mainly in winter.

4. Increase inter-regional trade in power through the Supergrid (Garnaut 2022, appendix 1.2), which will ease short-term squeezes on renewable electricity supply in each region and make tendencies to greater renewable energy surpluses in winter in the north to be made available in the south.

5. Make more intensive use of electrolysers for hydrogen production in summer with inter-seasonal storage in natural salt caverns.
6. Inter-seasonal variation of zero-carbon liquid fuels such as methanol in heritage petroleum storage facilities.
7. Summer bias for exports of ammonia and other hydrogen carriers (which corresponds to seasonal peaks in energy demand in Northeast Asia and Europe).

INDEX